RICHARD SPECK AND THE EIGHT NURSES: DECONSTRUCTING A MASS MURDER

While every precaution has been taken in the preparation of this book, the publisher assumes no responsibility for errors or omissions, or for damages resulting from the use of the information contained herein.

RICHARD SPECK AND THE EIGHT NURSES: DECONSTRUCTING A MASS MURDER

First edition. May 30, 2023.

Copyright © 2023 B D SALERNO.

ISBN: 979-8988478515

Written by B D SALERNO.

Table of Contents

INTRODUCTION 1

PART I 5

CHAPTER ONE 7

CHAPTER TWO 11

CHAPTER THREE 33

CHAPTER FOUR 45

CHAPTER FIVE 49

CHAPTER SIX 57

CHAPTER SEVEN 73

CHAPTER EIGHT 77

NOTES | PART I: THE CRIME 101

Chapter One: "The Long, Hot Summer" 103

Chapter Two: "Nowhere Man" 105

Chapter Three: "Day of Infamy" 107

Chapter Six: "Illogical Logistics" 109

Chapter Eight: "The Nurses" 111

PART TWO 113

CHAPTER NINE 115

CHAPTER TEN 147

CHAPTER ELEVEN 155

CHAPTER TWELVE 165

CHAPTER THIRTEEN 171

CHAPTER FOURTEEN 187

CHAPTER FIFTEEN 209

NOTES | PART II: THE EVIDENCE | Chapter Nine: "Dragnet" 235

Chapter Ten: "Doctor Dad" 237

Chapter Eleven: "The Six Faces of the Panel" 239

Chapter Twelve: "Cry for Me, Argentina" 241

Chapter Thirteen: "Untying the Knots" 243

Chapter Fourteen: "The Evidence" 245

Chapter Fifteen: "The Trial" 247

PART III 249

CHAPTER SIXTEEN 251

CHAPTER SEVENTEEN 261

CHAPTER EIGHTEEN 275

CHAPTER NINETEEN 291

CHAPTER TWENTY 315

CHAPTER TWENTY-ONE 321

CHAPTER TWENTY-TWO 327

CHAPTER TWENTY-THREE 335

EPILOGUE 339

NOTES | PART III: THEORIES | Chapter Seventeen: "Hypocritical Oath" 341

Chapter Eighteen: "Do These Dots Connect?" 343

Chapter Nineteen: "The Aftermath" 345

Chapter Twenty: "Myth-Information" 347

Chapter Twenty-One: "There's Something About Gloria" 349

Chapter Twenty-Two: "Crimes of the Century" 351

Epilogue 353

APPENDIX A 363

APPENDIX B 371

APPENDIX C 373

APPENDIX D 375

This work is dedicated to the memory of the eight nurses:

Mary Ann Jordan

Suzanne Farris

Patricia Ann Matusek

Merlita Gargullo

Valentina Pasion

Nina Jo Schmale

Gloria Jean Davy

Pamela Lee Wilkening

INTRODUCTION

The Broken-Hearted

After emerging from the crime scene carnage, the ashen-faced coroner gasped to a frenzied mob of reporters, "It is the crime of the century!" Just hours before, Corazon Amurao, sole survivor of the massacre, had jumped from her second-floor bedroom window onto a ledge, shouting to the street below, "Help! They are all dead! All my friends are dead!"

News of the murders shot across the country like an electric bolt, shocking everyone in its path. The headlines screamed out:

EIGHT STUDENT NURSES SLAIN!

Chicago, July 14, 1966 - The bodies of eight student nurses of South Chicago Hospital, stripped of their clothing and strangled with nylon stockings, were found in a two-story building at 2319 East 100th Street at 6:25 AM today.... Two of the student nurses were gagged, raped, and sexually molested.... All the bodies were either molested or raped.[1]

It was the most horrible thing I had ever read, and it bothered me for days. All in their early twenties, the eight student nurses were just setting out in life, as I would do in a few short years. In another time, another place, they could have been my role models.

I was about to enter my junior year of high school back then. My own uncertain future was bobbing on the horizon, but I didn't like the scenery. The Cuban missile crisis. The Kennedy assassination. The Vietnam war. Now, the slaughter of eight student nurses. There were no rainbows on that horizon, only the glum forecast of radioactive fallout. It was the Sixties, complete with cold wars, hot bombs, chaos, and carnage.

I found my solace in music. A hit song by Jimmy Ruffin, "What Becomes of the Broken-Hearted," was popular that summer, and played on the radio constantly. Since that time it has been a reminder of the eight student nurses whose senseless deaths broke the hearts of a nation and shattered my rose-colored glasses for good.

Miserable as it was, that day lit the spark that fueled my interest in true crime. I wanted to know why they didn't scream, why they didn't fight back, why they didn't try to escape. And how did one lone attacker do this all on his own, outnumbered nine to one? Even today, in true crime circles, these same questions arise, and there have been no satisfactory answers.

I never forgot the mass murder of the nurses and hoped to someday find answers to those troubling questions. In March 2020, housebound by the pandemic, that day finally came. I ordered hundreds of pages of FOIA reports, gathered every bit of information I could get my hands on, and took the plunge. As far as in-depth investigations go this was my first rodeo. I soon would learn that I had chosen the biggest bucking bronco in the stable. And I had no idea what I was in for.

I'm not an expert at investigating crimes. I'm not a detective, attorney, profiler, pathologist, psychologist, or criminologist. My tools were curiosity, common sense, and critical thinking. These alone brought me to some very shocking and unexpected findings, ones that I felt needed to be shared, even though as a novice, I often found myself a stranger in a strange land.

Aware of my lack of expertise, I researched complex topics as much as possible, cited all relevant references, and refrained from gross speculation without some factual basis for my opinions.

I emerged from my three-year journey with some shocking answers to the questions that have persisted in the wake of this crime. Those answers shed light on old secrets kept in the dark for decades - secrets that have been buried under cover of a false narrative - secrets that may have cost the lives of eight lovely student nurses. Secrets that now beg for disclosure.

One secret will soon become apparent: The mass murder of the eight student nurses did not happen as we were told. And the motivation behind it may be even more nefarious and depraved than anyone could have imagined.

When examined up close, the official story of the mass murder reminded me of the old rhyme of Humpty Dumpty. Once he fell off the wall, his pieces couldn't be put back together again. And once deconstructed, neither could the official story.

PART I

THE CRIME

CHAPTER ONE

THE LONG, HOT SUMMER

Events preceding the mass murder of the nurses had already bled a dark stain on Chicago's crime blotter. Mid-July of 1966 brought a record-breaking heat wave to the city. Temperatures soared while tempers flared. "Sizzling 100 Is Forecast for Today," warned the July 13th headlines of the *Chicago Tribune*.

Eight thousand five hundred miles to the west, another conflagration was in progress, also rife with bloodshed and chaos. The war in Vietnam was approaching peak intensity that summer. Photographs of smiling boys that once graced the pages of my high school yearbook now lined the obituary column under the heading "Killed In Action." University campuses across the country were besieged by anti-war protests and demonstrations.

It was a sweltering summer of unrest for the Windy City as well. During the week of the murders looting and violence had erupted to catastrophic proportions, leaving thirty people dead and dozens of businesses in shambles.

It all began innocently enough. On the predominantly black West Side, children pried open fire hydrants, seeking relief from the sweltering heat. Opening up fire hydrants was nothing new, but this time police shut the hydrants off.

This incident set the stage for racial tensions that escalated quickly out of control. While patrolling the area the next day, two policemen spotted a known offender, William Young, a 26-year-old who was wanted for armed robbery. They chased him down through the neighborhood, tackled him, and placed him under arrest.[2]

During the pursuit, Young shouted out to onlookers that the police were out to kill him. Passions ignited, culminating in three days of riots, looting, fire bombings, and arson. Snipers strafed the city streets with errant gunfire. The unpredictable violence prompted the Chicago Transit Authority to shut down the bus and El lines and block off streets considered too dangerous to traverse. At the corner of Lake and Wood, police and rioters engaged in a shootout, leaving six policemen dead.

On July 14th Mayor Richard J. Daley entreated Governor Otto Kerner to call in 1,500 National Guardsmen to restore order. Two hundred forty-four arrests quickly followed. The West Side riots were also called the "Division Street Riots," "division" an apt term for the hostile relations between police and the black community. Martin Luther King, Jr., declared that it was going to be a long, hot summer. But no one knew the extent of depravity that was about to befall the beleaguered city. And no amount of armed security forces would restore order to the emotional devastation that would soon follow.

While fires raged and gunfire blazed on the troubled West Side another brand of madness was about to strike the quiet residential neighborhood of Jeffery Manor. This predominantly white neighborhood of 7,000 citizens, built during the post-World War II housing boom, lay just west of the Calumet Harbor, where jobs in the steel mills, factories, and shipping industries sustained the local economy.

Jeffery Manor was a peaceful haven for the burgeoning middle class. Property crimes were infrequent and violent crime was unheard of, but the night of July 13, 1966 would change all that.

One of the quieter residential streets of Jeffery Manor was East 100th Street, which ran from Calumet Harbor in the east to S. Van Vlissingen Road, the farthest point west. The western end of the street was a mix of residences, schools, and small businesses—a Tastee Freeze, Aldo's Pizzeria, and the National Maritime Union (NMU), which provided short- and long-term employment for sailors and seafaring workers on board the region's many shipping vessels.

Among the residences were six two-story townhouses. Built only three years earlier in 1963, these townhouses reflected a modern look, with light green wooden facades and screened-in windows. Three of these residences - 2311, 2315, and 2319 - were rented out by South Chicago Community Hospital (SCCH) as dormitory housing for student nurses in training. Eight nurses occupied each townhouse.

The student nurses in 2319 had much to be excited about: Graduation was just around the corner on August 7th. But none would live to receive their diplomas. Mayhem and murder was about to strike the townhouse, claiming eight innocent lives. As the story goes, the monster was 24-year-old Richard Speck, a disaffected loner with a long rap sheet and an affection for drinking, drugs, and knives.

CHAPTER TWO

NOWHERE MAN

Eve of Destruction

At 1:00 AM on December 6, 1941, the seventh of eight children was born to Benjamin Franklin "Frank" Speck and Mary Margaret Carbaugh Speck in the rural farming town of Kirkwood, Illinois. Struggling to support his growing family, Frank gave up farming and took a job as a stoneware packer with the Western Stoneware factory in nearby Monmouth.

Any joy over the arrival of their third son was short-lived. Within thirty-six hours America would be attacked at Pearl Harbor in a shocking event of mass destruction. Twenty-five years later, the child born on the eve of World War II would be convicted of mass murder.

The boy was named Richard. He was the apple of his father's eye, and the feeling was mutual. Richard later adopted both his father's names, Benjamin and Franklin, as his own middle names, alternating between Richard Benjamin Speck and Richard Franklin Speck. The name paid homage to a revered family idol, Benjamin Franklin, eminent American statesman, inventor, and philosopher of the Eighteenth Century.

Barely three months had passed in the life of infant Richard when he contracted pneumonia. He survived, but with permanent ill effects. The disease had temporarily limited the supply of oxygen to his brain, leaving him developmentally challenged. His mental aptitude would not progress beyond that of a twelve-year old.

In middle school his IQ measured 87, below normal, or "dull normal." He often stared blankly into space as if in a trance, his lips parted, his watery blue eyes fixed in the distance. He could be jovial and talkative one moment, but sullen and moody the next.

Young Richard enjoyed the adoration of father Benjamin and mother Margaret. He was closest in age to his youngest sister Carolyn, three years his junior, with whom he forged the strongest bond. His older siblings – Erma, Sara Madeleine, William Howard, Robert Coleman, Shirley, and Martha Jean – were already maturing into adulthood while Richard still played in short pants.

And play he did. A hyperactive and accident prone child, he suffered many catastrophic and permanent injuries. At the age of five, he struck himself in the head with a claw hammer; at ten, he fell headfirst from a tree and lost consciousness for ninety minutes; the following year, he ran into a shop awning, striking his head full force on a steel support rod. Fourteen was an especially dangerous year: he fell off his bike and suffered a head injury. And he hadn't learned his lesson about trees – once again, he climbed a tree, fell on his head, and was knocked unconscious for several minutes.

A Glassy Haze

As a juvenile, Richard couldn't keep his head out of trouble. During the burglary of an auto shop the owner struck him in the head several times with a tire iron. That experience didn't curb his bad behavior; after another fracas with the law, he was dealt several blows to the head by a policeman's baton. It wasn't like Richard to learn from his mistakes.

If ever there was a candidate for the diagnosis of traumatic brain injury, it was Richard Speck, but the diagnosis of TBI did not exist at the time. I am not qualified to make any diagnosis, but my research showed that he suffered from common symptoms of TBI: frequent headaches, dizziness, and memory loss. He experienced both white-outs and blackouts: "I get a glassy haze, like when you look into the sun," and "there was lots of times when I'd black out like that and not remember a thing."[3]

At the age of six, Richard's recurring physical injuries were supplanted by a crippling emotional blow. On December 29, 1947, during Christmas week and just 23 days after Richard's sixth birthday, father Frank died of a heart attack at the early age of 53. Gone was his role model, mentor, and moral compass. The Specks were a strongly faith-based Christian family who abhorred drinking and other indulgences, but the loss of his father propelled Richard in the opposite direction.

Three years later his mother Margaret, perhaps pressured by financial concerns, married Carl Augustus Rudolph Lindberg, a traveling insurance salesman from Dallas with a penchant for everything father Frank had opposed – drinking, quarreling, and domestic violence. Richard and his younger sister Carolyn had remained with family in Illinois for a while following their father's death, but in time Margaret, relocated to Dallas, sent for them.

By the time his mother married and moved to Dallas with her new husband, Carl August Rudolph Lindbergh, the older children had already established their own lives in Illinois. Richard and younger sister Carolyn were left to bear the brunt of Carl's reckless drinking and violent outbursts. The two became very close, with Carolyn his staunch defender and enabler when he got into trouble. His mother Margaret, perhaps feeling guilty over her poor choice for a husband, pampered and spoiled Richard, making excuses for his errant behavior.

The move to Dallas was much for the worse, and marked the beginning of a vicious downward spiral in Richard's life. His stepfather, perhaps jealous of Margaret's blind devotion to the boy, constantly challenged the boy with taunts, insults, and threats. Carl had lost his right leg in an accident and required a crutch or cane to get around. He didn't hesitate to use it during his drunken rages, waving it wildly at Richard while threatening to bash his head in. The verbal and physical abuse goaded Richard into increasingly rebellious behavior.

But there was no relief in sight. Richard's festering emotions were ravaged again, when Robert Coleman Speck, his twenty-four year old brother, died in a traffic accident in 1952 when Richard was just ten years old. Life's dizzying downward spiral was continuing. Richard took to breaking into Carl's liquor cabinet and consuming its contents. He later told police he had begun drinking between the ages of twelve and fourteen. With the exception of some odd days off here and there, he never really stopped.

Now that his despised stepson had begun to challenge his authority, Carl decided he had had enough. He left Margaret and moved to California. It was a blessing for the family, but the emotional damage had already been done. Richard remained in school for a brief time, but then dropped out of Crozier Tech in Dallas at the age of fourteen.

The idle time did not serve him well. Always in search of male approval, he took up with gangs of boys with bad intentions whom he longed to impress. Already a drinker, he added glue-sniffing and pill-popping to his resume. The colorful street drugs of the day - "red birds," "yellow jackets," and "goofballs" – became as much a part of his diet as hamburgers, Cokes, and any beverage with an alcoholic content.

He also picked up the habit of carrying a knife. Joyriding and public drunkenness evolved into petty theft, vandalism, and burglary, and Speck racked up thirty-six investigative arrests as a juvenile in Dallas. He was high school's answer to Marlon Brando in the 1953 movie "The Wild One," minus the motorcycle.

Richard went along with whatever the crowd was up to, mostly vandalism, joyriding, and drunk and disorderly conduct. On one rowdy night they all went out and got tattooed, literally and otherwise. Speck's new body art proudly boasted "Born to Raise Hell," a cheaply inked inscription on the inside of his left forearm.

He later regretted the tattoo, and while incarcerated he tried to burn it off with a cigarette, which left permanent scars. This painful attempt earned him thirty days in solitary for "defacing prison property." The tattoo was a main identifying feature in his capture, and sealed his place in the annals of true crime as a mass-murdering monster.

Speck added several other tattoos to his lean, muscular frame during his wild years on the rough streets of Dallas: a vulgar depiction of a penis bearing the description "Texas Dickie Bird" graced his left shin; an aviator's face bearing goggles and a hat covered his upper left arm, a serpent entwined around an ominous dagger colored his right forearm.

By the mid-1950's Richard was rapidly becoming the poster boy for juvenile delinquency, racking up some thirty-six arrests as a minor for various misdemeanors: vandalism, public drinking, and disorderly conduct. These were investigative arrests, in which a person suspected of an offense is questioned but not charged. The repeated offenses landed him in juvenile detention for a brief period.

Once an adult, Speck wasted no time establishing a record. On December 26, 1959, just three weeks after his eighteenth birthday, he was picked up by Dallas police and fined $20.50 for disturbing the peace. He managed to steer clear of trouble for nearly two more years, until October 5, 1961, when a property owner caught him throwing a brick through a window. He was arrested and fined $100 for malicious destruction of property.

The Texas State Fair, which opens every year on the last Friday in September, was in full swing that week. Right around the same time as his second arrest, twenty-year-old Speck met fifteen-year-old Shirley Malone at the fair. Malicious destruction was still in the air.

The two embarked on a rocky relationship, with Shirley becoming pregnant almost immediately. The couple married on January 19, 1962 and Shirley gave birth to Speck's only child, daughter Robbie Lynn, on July 5th. Richard was unable to visit his new baby girl in the hospital; he was behind bars, serving a twenty-two day sentence for public drunkenness and disturbing the peace.

He commemorated the occasion with a new tattoo on his upper right arm – "Rich and Shirley," with the initials "R.S." underneath, the initials of his new daughter Robbie Lynn Speck. The tattoo would last much longer than his tumultuous marriage, which was marred by wild fights and accusations of infidelity. The couple managed to stay together for a time. Shirley was employed at the Western Electric Company in Dallas, while Richard worked as a deliveryman for the 7Up Bottling Company. He held this job the longest, from August 1960 until July 1963, and was well liked by his supervisor, who considered him an honest hard-working man. But the boss didn't know about one of Speck's hijinx that he was fond of relating years later.

One of the stops on Speck's truck delivery route in Dallas was The Carousel Club, owned and operated by one Leon Jacob Rubinstein, better known as Jack Ruby, famed killer of Lee Harvey Oswald. Speck was fond of bragging how he swindled Ruby out of $36 by collecting payment on a beverage delivery that was short a few cases.

In September 1963 Speck, always an accident waiting to happen, was ready for prime time crime. Like the foolish kid who couldn't avoid climbing the rickety tree, he stole an employee's paycheck for $44 and forged the signature. This earned him his first serious charge for burglary and forgery.

After spending more time in a Dallas lockup, he was transported to the "big house," the state penitentiary at Huntsville, Texas, on November 19, 1963, just three days before America suffered its nightmare on Elm Street – the assassination of President John F. Kennedy.

Two days later, Speck's client, Jack Ruby, made his fateful entrance into the history books when he fatally shot Lee Harvey Oswald in the basement of the Dallas County Jail. At a time when both were still nobodies, the assassin's assassin had been cheated out of money by a mass murderer. True crime can be stranger than fiction.

Speck was released on parole on January 4, 1965, after serving just thirteen months into his three-year sentence. But freedom didn't agree with him. Just three weeks later he was picked up for aggravated assault for robbing a woman at knifepoint. This was a felony added to a parole violation, but resulted in a sentence of only 490 days (a little over one year plus four months), to run concurrent with his existing three-year sentence.

Mysteriously, he was paroled again due to good behavior, and in June 1965 he was caught forging another check, adding another felony and parole violation to his lengthening rap sheet. Parole for Speck was beginning to look like a bad idea, but either the prison system was overloaded or no one was doing the math. Just weeks later, on July 2, 1965, for reasons unexplained and inexplicable, he received a discharge from Huntsville.

Had Speck served out his full three-year term he would have been safely esconced in prison until November 1966, four months past the date of the mass murder. But destiny, in the form of judicial clerical error, had other designs. In spite of numerous parole violations and re-offenses, Speck was given another ill-advised shot at freedom.

During this same time period a repeat offender in another state continued to miraculously violate parole without serious consequences, as if law enforcement, or some other powerful agency, was deliberately allowing him to run wild, leaving drugs, death, and destruction in his wake. That convict's name was Charles Manson.[4]

Less than three years later, in August 1969, a new "crime of the century" would be christened in Tinseltown, thanks to Manson and his band of raggedy followers. This mass murder claimed the lives of actress Sharon Tate, hairdresser Jay Sebring, Wojtech Frykowski, Steven Parent, coffee heiress Abigail Folger, and the night after, Leno and Rosemary LaBianca.

Discharges from prison were granted on condition that the convict maintain a good pattern of behavior, and for a time Speck complied. He got a job as deliveryman with the Patterson Meat Company on Forrest Hill Boulevard in Dallas. Like his 7Up delivery job, he was entrusted with collecting cash on delivery, sometimes up to $1,000 a day. It is remarkable that an ex-convict with a history of burglary and theft would be entrusted with such a position, but background checks were unknown in those days.

For a time, Speck proved himself a reliable employee, and his supervisor thought well of the polite, soft-spoken young man. He held this job from July 17, 1965 until October 7, 1965, when the company let him go - not for theft, but for reckless driving; he had caused several accidents by speeding around town in the company truck. Even when all was going well, he still managed to foul things up for himself.

Richard Speck's home life had begun to mimic his relationship with his abusive stepfather. Shirley ended the rocky marriage in January 1966 and filed for divorce. She took off with their daughter Robbie Lynn and a new boyfriend, whom she married in March 1966, just days after the divorce was granted.

Speck had long suspected that Shirley cheated on him while he was in prison, and the divorce and abandonment for another man infuriated him. Days after Shirley filed for divorce, he got into a heated barroom argument with a man, stabbing him several times. Somehow the charge, aggravated assault, was downgraded to disturbing the peace, with a fine of only $10.

His overindulgent mother and favorite enabler, Margaret, had successfully pleaded with the court to reduce the charge to a misdemeanor. Speck, ignorant of his own dumb luck, remained a free man – free to commit another crime, which would be his last in Texas. But not before he spent another three days in the local slammer for refusing to pay the $10 fine. If the Gang That Couldn't Shoot Straight had run the streets of Dallas, Speck would have been their undisputed leader.

On March 5, 1966, Speck purchased a 1954 Plymouth that he owned for only one day. He loaded up the trunk with 70 cartons of cigarettes stolen from a grocery store and was caught trying to pass them off to local bootleggers. A warrant for his arrest issued on March 8th. A day or two later he took a bus bound for Illinois.

It was the last day Richard Speck would ever spend in the State of Texas. The convict born on the eve of Pearl Harbor was now en route to his own date with infamy.

Now back in his home county of Warren, Speck made another attempt at reform. His older siblings, who had remained in Monmouth, were respectable, well-regarded members of the community. Richard was the proverbial black sheep, yet his family members were still willing to help him change his ways.

One sympathetic sister was Martha Jean Speck Thornton, who lived on Chicago's north side with her husband Eugene and two teenage daughters. The Thorntons were a respectable couple; Eugene worked as night switchman for the railroad, and Martha had been a pediatric nurse. They worried that Uncle Richard, boastful of his colorful criminal past, was a bad influence on their two teenaged daughters. They limited his visits to a week or less.

Older brother William Howard Speck, 35, a carpenter in Monmouth, former Marine and Korean war veteran, found work for Speck as a carpenter's apprentice for one month. Howard also put Speck up at a friend's house. Things got off to their usual good start, but then Speck began missing work time, preferring to hang out at the local tavern.

He failed to complete the apprenticeship, and around the 25th of March he left the friend's house and took a room at the local Christy Hotel. He was a frequent customer at Frank's Place, a bar on Third Street in Monmouth. During this time two violent events occurred that have been linked to him.

On April 2nd, a sixty-five-year-old woman, Mrs. Virgil Harris, was attacked and raped in her home on South D Street in Monmouth. She had returned home at 1:00 AM from a babysitting job to find a burglar rifling through her possessions. She described the burglar as having a Southern accent; Speck spoke with a soft Southern drawl.

On April 9th, thirty-two year old Mary Kathryn "Kay" Brasche Pierce, a barmaid who worked at Frank's Place, went missing. She was last seen leaving the tavern around 12:45 AM. On April 13th, while out walking her child in a stroller, Mary Kay's sister noticed something protruding from under the door of a hog shed located behind the tavern. It was the nude, beaten body of Mary Kay. She had been viciously kicked in the abdomen, and one rib, broken in the attack, had punctured her lung.

Building hog sheds was part of Speck's carpenter training, and he was known to hang out at Frank's Place. Police questioned him on April 15th but no charges were brought. On April 19th police went to his hotel room for a second round of questioning but he had already packed up and left town, headed for Chicago.

The police reportedly found items stolen from Mrs. Harris and other area burglaries in Speck's room at the Christy Hotel. He had apparently left these incriminating items behind. Speck never returned to Monmouth.

Speck headed back to the Thornton's apartment in Chicago, where he stayed from April 19th until April 30th. Gene Thornton, a Navy veteran, urged Speck to sign up with the Coast Guard for a seafaring job. Speck was a constant drain on the Thornton's money and patience, and it was time for him to find his own way.

Gene Thornton was a close friend of Monmouth Chief of Police Harold Tinder. If Speck was a suspect in the burglary, rape and murder cases, he could have been easily tracked down at Thornton's home. However, no charges were ever filed against Speck in the Monmouth cases.

A curious item surfaced in an investigative report filed by Detective John Boeger, who tracked down Speck's movements in Monmouth during the month of April 1966. This report has been summarized in Appendix B.

Thornton drove Speck to the Chicago branch office of the Coast Guard where he filed an application on April 25, 1966. His file contains an unusual entry about an incident that was not reported elsewhere. An informal handwritten note, dated July 22, 1966, stated the following: "the 1965 agg assault & the 1963 Indecent Exposure – probably would have resulted in denial until rehabilitated."[5]

There was no mention of a 1963 charge of indecent exposure in Speck's Dallas police record. However, it seems that had the Coast Guard known about the aggravated assault and indecent exposure, they would not have offered him employment. This oversight joins the ever-growing list of slips through the cracks, just like his puzzling parole status.

On April 30, 1966, Speck joined the crew of the S.S. Clarence B. Randall, a Great Lakes ore freighter operated on behalf of Inland Steel. He was assigned menial tasks on board ship, like swabbing decks and routine maintenance, and he enjoyed the work. But, just four days later, after another promising start, fate sharply intervened in the form of acute appendicitis. This time, the foul-up was beyond Speck's control.

He was rushed to St. Joseph's Hospital in Hancock, Michigan where he received an emergency appendectomy. There he was assisted by several nurses, including Judy Sorensen Laakaniemi, a 28-year-old nurse's aide. Speck made a full recovery and new friends as well. He sent "Thank You" notes to all the nurses who had helped him, and even sent them postcards after he returned to Chicago.

Although their relationship was platonic, he forged a special bond with Judy during his recovery. Both of them had just undergone painful divorces. She related that he was a perfect gentleman at all times, and he made a good impression on her mother as well.

The only crack in the veneer was, predictably, a barroom scuffle that was precipitated by a man being rude to Judy. Speck immediately reacted by pulling his knife. Although unnerved at first, Judy wisely diffused the situation. The man apologized and Speck's temper subsided. The three of them calmed down and raised a glass together. One pattern evident in Speck's behavior was to initiate a barroom confrontation with someone over some minor offense, only to end up befriending his adversary, often buying him a drink afterward.

Judy and the knife were of particular interest to the prosecution team later on, who hoped to use her as a prosecution witness, but they were in for a surprise.

On May 20th, fully recuperated from surgery, Speck left Michigan to regain his position on board the Clarence B. Randall. There he befriended an older man, Robert Gerrald, nicknamed "Red," one of the ship's cooks and a heavy drinker who could match Speck's capacity for alcohol.

As was his custom, Speck performed his duties well during this second term on the Randall, until he didn't. On June 12th, he got into an argument with a ship's officer and was relieved of his duties after only twenty-six days on board ship. The Coast Guard discharged him, but in spite of this infraction he was still eligible to apply for work through the National Maritime Union.

Speck began to frequent the area around East 99th Street and S. Ewing Avenue, where he signed up for a room at the St. Elmo, a seedy establishment named for the patron saint of sailors, its main clientele. The place was a dump, a shameful namesake for a saint, but it housed a cozy tavern, Pete's Tap House, and with its bowling game and juke box, Pete's became Speck's favorite watering hole.

He knocked around the area waiting for another shipping assignment, but true to his restless nature, he couldn't stay put. He had stayed in touch with Judy Laakaniemi, and around June 22nd he took a train back to Michigan to visit her. True to her caregiving nature Judy had offered to help him find work, but he wasn't accustomed to making sensible decisions. He returned to Chicago on the 27th, once again crashing at the Thorntons.

He wore out his welcome several days later, after regaling his nieces with wild stories of his imaginary exploits as a drug runner for a Mexican cartel. The Thorntons suggested that he find lodging elsewhere in the city until a seafaring job became available. Gene Thornton gave him $25 to tide him over and dropped him off at the St. Elmo flophouse.

He spent the night of the 10th at the St. Elmo, but there were no vacancies for the rest of the week, so he meandered over to Pauline's boarding house at 3028 E. 96th Street, in the Vets Park neighborhood, where he rented a room for the night of the 11th.

Accustomed to slumming from place to place, Speck's needs did not extend far beyond bed, board, booze, and sex. He subsisted on a cheap diet of hamburgers, potato chips, candy bars, soft drinks, and hard liquor. Fast food outlets, in their heyday in the 1960s, made this possible; at the "Top Boy" burger chain, you could get a hamburger, French fries, and a milkshake for less than 60 cents.

Speck finally received an assignment on the SS Sinclair Great Lakes, a bulk ore freighter due to ship out the next day from East Chicago, Indiana. Two acquaintances from the NMU, Dante Bargellini, ship steward, and George Mackey, ship's engineer, drove him over to East Chicago, but when they arrived just after 5:00 PM Speck was told that the job had already been assigned to someone else. A disgruntled Speck complained all the way back in the car, much to the displeasure of his traveling companions.

It was now early evening of the 12th; he had no job prospects and no place to stay. Barzellini and Mackey dropped him off near the NMU, which was already closed for the day. With nowhere to hang his hat, he walked to the nearby Manor Shell gas station on S. Torrence to inquire whether he could leave his two pieces of luggage there overnight.

The station owner obliged, and Speck found refuge in a vacant apartment building on East 103rd Street that was under construction. He spent an uncomfortable night on the hard floor, using his shoes and jacket as a makeshift pillow. The high heat and humidity gave way to a torrential thunderstorm that evening, and he stayed put for the duration.

The Day Of

At 7:30 AM the next morning he found his way back to the Manor Shell gas station to pick up his bags. Mechanic Dennis Ryan recalled that he complained bitterly about missing out on the Great Lakes job. Ryan also recalled that New Orleans came up in the conversation, one of the destinations along the route of the Sinclair Great Lakes freighter.

Always meticulous in appearance, Speck used the men's rest room to shave and change clothing, and with his bags in tow, he headed back to the NMU to apply for another job. Sam Barger, a clerk, found him sitting on the steps in front of the building before the 8:30 AM opening time. Barger assisted him with the job application and recommended that he seek lodging at the Shipyard Inn, just over a mile and a half east on S. Avenue N.

Assignments on shipping freighters played out like a game of musical chairs. The labor pool for seamen was heavily populated with alcoholics and transients. No-shows were inevitable, so seafaring jobs, like the airlines, were often overbooked with the expectation that some would not show up for their assignments. Still, it was odd that Speck was even accepted into the Coast Guard in the first place, and still eligible to work after his fracas with the ship's officer. Taking these instances into consideration, along with his numerous yet unpunished parole violations and early release from prison, gives us something to wonder about.

Around 9:30 AM sister Martha and brother-in-law Gene met with Speck in front of the NMU, where they gave him another $25. They talked in Thornton's car for about half an hour. At 10:00 AM, Speck, with his two bags in hand, walked the mile and a half over to the Shipyard Inn and registered for a room with the Inn's manager, Mrs. Agnes Budak Goze. The Inn had ten clean rooms, a tavern, and a pool table, which would keep Speck occupied until the next shipping job came along.

The Inn drew its main business from workers coming off their shifts at the nearby shipyards, factories and steel mills. Unsure of his job prospects, he paid one week in advance, and Mrs. Goze gave him two keys – one for Room #7, and one for a door on the side of the building leading to a hallway where the rooms were located. It was now just twelve hours from a date with an awful destiny.

Mrs. Goze noted that Speck was very neat, polite, and soft-spoken, with a thick Southern drawl. He was also a good customer, shelling out $9 on whisky and cola drinks that afternoon alone. But that wasn't all. Sometime that afternoon he got hold of some street drugs, "red birds" as they called them, and popped six of them at once, chasing them down with a drink.

Speck had begun popping pills while still an unruly teenager on the streets of Dallas, where kids would sniff glue and swallow "red birds," "goofballs," or "yellow jackets" in search of brain-buzzing highs. Red birds were downers, yellow jackets were uppers, and goofballs were an incongruous combination of the two, causing bizarre or unpredictable behavior in people, thus, their name.

In an effort to portray Speck as an untamed, crazed beast, the prosecution claimed that the six "red birds" he had taken were amphetamines, chemical agents that stimulate the central nervous system. They were actually the opposite. "Red birds" was the street name given to sodium seconal, a barbiturate that sedates the central nervous system. Sodium seconal is a main ingredient in sleeping pills, which were marketed under the brand name Seconal. Many celebrities of the day, including Marilyn Monroe and Natalie Wood, routinely took Seconal for the treatment of insomnia.

After paying for his room and a few late morning beers, he still had money left over from Gene's donation of $25, which he supplemented with $11 in pool winnings. He was set for an evening of his favorite pastimes, drinking and playing pool. The only thing missing was sex, but somewhere between Pete's Tap and the Shipyard Inn that was about to change.

Ella Mae Hooper, a fifty-three year old barfly with a withered figure and straggly bottle blond hair, was no stranger to the watering holes on Chicago's southeast side. The two met up during Speck's round robin of bars, and went back to his room at the Shipyard for some afternoon delight.

Ella Mae had something else that Speck wanted. While she was getting dressed he saw a gun in her purse and promptly stole it. The two scuffled, and Ella Mae walked out in a huff, leaving Speck and the gun behind.

The gun, a black Röhm .22 caliber revolver, had been Ella May's birthday present to herself. She had purchased it for $16 via mail order from a West Virginia gun manufacturer. It was registered in her name, and therefore traceable. The revolver played a crucial role in the story of the mass murder, but just two days later any plan of entering it into evidence would backfire.

Blue Bottle Blackout

What happened next has largely remained a mystery. It sounded like just another one of his wild stories. In his own words, the night of the murders went like this:

" I don't know nothing about anything from 8 o'clock that night till I came to, about eleven o'clock the next day. All I remember is I met three sailors in the afternoon. We had some drinks, then we went off someplace and had a fix – a shot in the arm…. it wasn't heroin. It was something in a blue bottle, I think. I don't remember a thing after that. I couldn't tell you or anybody what any of those nurses looked like."[6]

Speck believed that he received the injection before darkness fell - "it was getting dark, but still light."[7] Based on the following timeline, he most likely got the shot between 7:00 and 8:00 PM.

After getting high on the mystery substance, Speck, clad in a red shirt, dark slacks, and brown work boots, trudged over to Kay's Pilot House, where he made the acquaintance of Murrill Farmer and his wife, Gerdena, a couple who tended bar, waited tables, and cooked short order meals. The two men engaged in friendly banter. Farmer, noticing Speck's fair complexion, light hair and eyes, and tattoos, though Speck was a German sailor at first, until he heard Speck's soft Southern drawl.

His description was accurate; Speck was of German descent, had a fair complexion, sandy blond hair, and light blue eyes. Farmer also noticed Speck's red polo shirt, and the tattoo on Speck's right arm showing the names "Rich & Shirley".

Speck left Kay's Pilot House around 8:30 PM and ambled back down to the Shipyard Inn, where he played pool with Michael Compateso, a welder from the nearby American Shipbuilding factory. Compateso remembered that the pool game lasted from 8:40 to 8:57 PM because he was on a regularly scheduled break from his evening shift. He also noted that Speck was wearing brown work boots, just like his own.

After Compateso left, Speck sat down at a table near a group of friends: Patrick Walsh, a construction worker, his fiancée, Dwella Stevenson, and two brothers, Michael and James Walsh. Also seated nearby was Army Sergeant Richard J. Oliva, who was on leave from a tour of duty in Vietnam.

Both parties saw Speck drop a knife on the floor, and when he bent down to retrieve it he eyed the couple suspiciously. "What are you looking at?" he growled. He also flashed the gun and knife in Oliva's direction, but no one was impressed by the childish display. Words ensued, but then Speck noticed that Walsh had a cast on one leg, the result of a work-related accident, and he immediately backed down.

"Sorry, I didn't see you had a broken leg," he mumbled to Walsh. All was forgiven. Speck offered to buy drinks for his new acquaintances. He joined them in forgiven. Speck then joined then in their booth where they chatted for several minutes. Speck spoke fondly of his daughter, Robbie Lynn, and angrily of his ex-wife Shirley, still bitter over their divorce and her quick remarriage. During this emotional exchange Speck spilled a drink on his red shirt.

Last Call

Between 9:30 and 10:00 the Walsh party got up to leave, as Dwella had to report early for work in the morning. Speck escorted them to the front door, where they shook hands and bid their goodbyes. Walsh introduced Speck to Richard Oliva, joking that they both bore the same first name.

Agnes Goze, the Inn's manager, saw Speck leave the bar sometime around 10:20, as did three men seated at the bar. He had gotten two room keys, one for the room door itself, and one to open a door on the side of the building that gave direct access to the hallway of rooms. Thus it was possible to leave the bar but enter his room through a separate entrance on the side of the building. It was most likely this time that Speck used the outside entrance to go to his room and change from the soiled red shirt to the black shirt. It is not known whether he also changed from the brown work boots to black leather shoes.

If he left the bar around 10:20, he had barely enough time to change his shirt and begin the 1.6 mile trek across East 100th Street to the townhouse at 2319, and according to the official story, that is how the night of horror began.

Richard Speck appeared to have the makings of a murderer: he was a career criminal who drank to excess and became belligerent and aggressive when intoxicated. He took drugs indiscriminately, unconcerned about their content or consequences. He often behaved impulsively and seemed incapable of staying out of trouble. The majority of his crimes were theft, robbery, and burglary. Burglars are also known to commit other acts of violence, like tying up, raping, and even murdering their victims.

Speck was quiet, soft-spoken, and polite with his acquaintances, who were mostly bartenders and hotel clerks, but he had no real friends. His former employers liked him, but something always went wrong, and he couldn't hold down a job for long. If he was a master at anything, it was the art of self-sabotage.

Speck had the perfect Jekyll and Hyde type of personality, an accident waiting to happen. We were told that accident finally happened on the 13th and 14th of July. But did this misfit ex-convict from Texas really manage to perpetrate "the crime of the century" all on his own? My first rip-roaring rodeo was far from over.

CHAPTER THREE

DAY OF INFAMY

Wednesday, July 13, 1966 began like any other day in the life of the eight nurses who occupied unit 2319. A few nurses enjoyed a day off, while the others worked the 7:00 AM–3:30 PM shift at South Chicago Community Hospital (SCCH), located just a mile north. A van sponsored by the hospital would pick them up for work at 6:30 AM and bring them home by 4:00 PM every day.

Three of the nurses – Merlita Gargullo, Valentina Pasion, and Corazon Amurao – were from the Philippines. They had arrived in Chicago only ten weeks earlier as part of a federal program enacted by President Lyndon B. Johnson. Under the Nurse Training Act of 1964, nurses from the Philippines were invited to practice in U.S. hospitals to address a severe shortage of American nurses.

Merlita, Valentina, and Corazon already had their nursing degrees, but were sharing the small townhouse with five American nursing students. They had not had much time to form friendships with their American housemates; relations were cordial but not close. Bonded by their culture and their native Tagalog language, the three Filipina nurses shopped, studied, and dined together, and wrote letters home nearly every day.

After returning from their work shift, the Filipina nurses took brief naps, dined around 4:30 PM, and began their evening activities of studying and writing letters. A couple of doors down, in Unit 2315, a few student nurses sat around the kitchen table, burning the midnight oil in preparation for upcoming exams. Gloria Davy and Suzanne Farris were out for the evening, but expected back in time for the 12:30 AM curfew.

2319 was an end unit, bordered only by 2317, which was rented by a private couple, Mr. and Mrs. Bert Weisz. The Weisz' happened to be vacationing that week in Elkhart Lake, Wisconsin, leaving the townhouse next door vacant on the night of the murders.

Housing regulations required that both front and back doors be kept locked at all times. Each nurse had her own set of keys to both front and back doors. Both front and back doors had button locks on the doorknobs and bolt locks on the door frames. Both doors had an exterior screen door.

Both doors also had doorbells with dissimilar rings so that the occupants would know which door to answer when someone came calling. Because of its proximity to the rear driveway and parking lot, the back door was used more often. A light above the back door was left on for those who came home after dark.

Corazon spent the evening at the living room desk writing letters. When finished, she checked to ensure that the front door was locked, but she did not check the back door. She then went upstairs to prepare for bed.

With only 1434 square feet, the townhouse was small and cramped, with a kitchen and living room downstairs and three small bedrooms and one bathroom upstairs. On the evening of Wednesday, July 13, 1966, the second floor would host an indescribable horror.

Corazon described the sequence of events as follows, taken directly from her trial testimony.[8]

10:30 PM

Corazon shared the small east bedroom with fellow Filipina nurse, Merlita Gargullo. The room was very small, hosting only one bunk bed, one small closet and one dresser. Merlita wanted to say her evening prayers, so Corazon left the light on, locked the bedroom door, and climbed into the upper bunk bed.

Four other nurses were on the second floor at this time – three in the south bedroom, which was the largest, and one in the west bedroom adjacent to Corazon's.

With the overhead light still on, Corazon drifted off to sleep.

<u>11:00 PM</u>

Suddenly there were four knocks at the bedroom door. Corazon climbed down from the top bunk to see who was there. Upon opening the door she saw a tall man, clad all in black, pointing a gun at her. His breath reeked of alcohol.

"Where are your companions?" he asked. Corazon stood looking up at the man for a minute or two; in the bright room light she could see the tall stranger clearly. The man said that he wasn't going to hurt them; he only needed money to go to New Orleans.

Keeping a gun pointed at their backs, the intruder then marched Corazon and Merlita at gunpoint outside their room, rousing Nina Jo Schmale from the adjacent west bedroom.

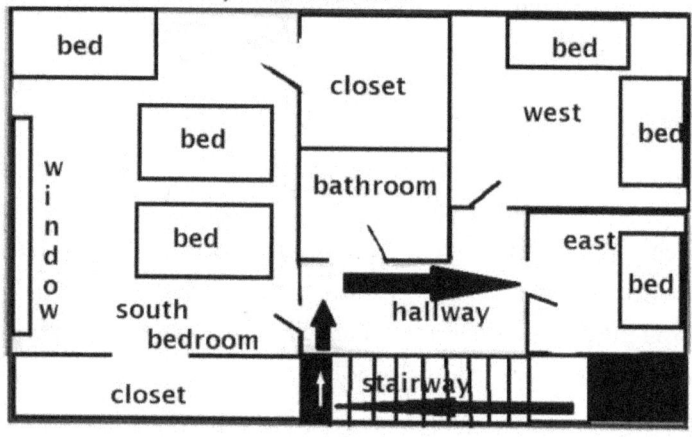

Diagram of Second Floor Bedrooms

He then marched them down the hall where they entered the south bedroom, awakening the three nurses who were in bed there. He ordered the six nurses to sit on the floor.

Suddenly Corazon, Merlita, and Valentina raced across the room and ran into the far closet, desperately pulling the doorknob closed to prevent anyone from entering. The intruder showed no reaction; he did not fire the gun, call out to them, or force them out of the closet.

After a few minutes one of the nurses reassured them that nothing would happen if they just gave him their money. The three slowly filed back into the room. The intruder then commanded them all to sit on the floor in a half circle, facing him with their backs to the dresser and the large picture window.

The large picture window overlooked the rear parking lot and Luella Park. A large curtain drape hung clumsily across half of it, blocking full view into the bedroom from outside.

The intruder spoke in a soft voice and a friendly manner, reassuring them that he would not hurt them. He just wanted money to go to New Orleans. The nurses whose wallets were in the bedroom got up and handed their money to him and then sat down again.

The wallets of Nina Jo, Corazon, and Merlita were in the west and east bedrooms. The intruder then marched all six nurses, single file, down the hallway to those bedrooms to collect the money from their wallets. All then returned to the south bedroom. All the while he kept the gun pointed at their backs.

The door to the south bedroom was just steps from the stairway, which they had to pass in order to go down the hallway, but no one tried to run down the stairs and get help.

The intruder then pulled a sheet from one of the beds and, producing a knife, began cutting the sheet into long strips, which he draped around his neck like a collar. While engaged in this activity he placed the gun on the floor, chatting all the while in a friendly, relaxed manner.

11:40 PM

Gloria Jean Davy returned from a special date with her fiancé. She was accosted by the intruder as soon as she entered the south bedroom. He was in the process of tying up each of the nurses, binding their feet together and their hands tightly behind their backs. Gloria gave him $2 from her purse and he then tied her hands and feet with the white cloth strips like the others. She sat on one of the bunk beds while the others remained on the floor.

12:10 AM

Fellow nursing student Tammy Sioukoff, who resided in 2315, had been up late cramming for exams and stopped to take a break. There was no bread in the kitchen for a sandwich, so she walked over to the back door of 2319 and rang the doorbell. By now the intruder had tied up all of the nurses except Corazon and Merlita.

The intruder forced Merlita and Corazon at gunpoint down the stairs to see who was there. He kept the gun pointed at their backs to ensure that they would not run or signal for help. But, recognizing the doorbell ring tone, Corazon deliberately escorted him to the front door, not the back door where Tammy was waiting. Finding no one at the front door, they returned upstairs.

After several unanswered rings, Tammy looked up at the second floor window. The south bedroom was dark and she assumed that all had already gone to bed. Tammy returned to 2315 and phoned in an order for a pizza from Aldo's Pizzeria, just down the block at 2435 E. 100th Street.

After returning to the south bedroom, Corazon and Merlita were the last to be tied up with the white cloth strips. Corazon stated that her hands were tied very tightly behind her back.

12:15 AM

Kathy Emmons, a fellow student nurse residing in 2311, drove through the rear parking lot hoping to stop in 2319 to return a typewriter that she had borrowed from Nina Jo Schmale earlier that day. But the house appeared dark, so she assumed that all had already gone to bed, and she continued on to 2311.

Both Kathy and Tammy had noted that there was no light on in the south bedroom at 12:10 and just minutes later at 12:15 AM.

Suzanne had been spending the evening with best friend and future sister-in-law Mary Ann Jordan, a fellow nursing student. They had spent the last hour chatting with Pat Waddington, a student nurse in 2311. Suzanne had wanted to discuss a problem she was having with one of her nursing instructors, but it is unknown whether such conversation took place.

Mary Ann lived in Chicago with her family, but had decided to spend the night with Suzanne at 2319 so that the two could discuss Suzanne's forthcoming wedding to Mary Ann's brother Phil. This well-intentioned but tragic decision proved to be devastating for Mary Ann and her family, who would never see her alive again.

12:25 AM

With just minutes to go before the 12:30 curfew, Suzanne and Mary Ann left 2311 and walked down to 2319, where they entered through the back door and headed up the stairs.

The intruder had just untied Pam Wilkening's ankles and was pushing her down the hallway into the east bedroom, where he stabbed her once through the heart. Corazon heard only the sound of Pamela gasping, "Ah!"

As Suzanne and Mary Ann reached the top of the stairs the intruder startled them. He demanded that they go into the east bedroom where Pam Wilkening had just been stabbed. The intruder then felled them one by one, side by side, in a frenzy of vicious stab wounds. Suzanne was also strangled with a nurse's stocking. Corazon heard some commotion, and what she called "yelling in low voices."

She stated that the intruder-turned-killer spent about 20 minutes in the east bedroom with Mary Ann and Suzanne. She then heard the sounds of running water in the bathroom.

Between 12:30 and 12:55 Tammy Sioukoff, back in unit 2315, heard a scream but was unsure of its origin. She walked toward the rear of 2319, but seeing that the house was still dark, she returned to 2315.

12:50 AM

The pizza deliveryman from Aldo's drove up to the townhouse complex, confused about the house numbers. He was about to ring the front doorbell at 2319, but saw that the house was dark; only one light was on in Corazon's east bedroom. He also noticed a faint light coming from the living room. Corazon had turned that light off, but someone, possibly Gloria, had turned it on when she came in.

He then realized that he was at the wrong address - the correct delivery address was 2315, not 2319. He delivered the pizza to the waiting Tammy and returned to Aldo's just before their 1:00 AM closing. Neither party had any inkling of the methodical massacre that was in progress on the second floor of 2319.

1:00 AM

The killer removed the ankle ties from Nina Jo Schmale and walked her to the west bedroom, where he strangled her on her own bed. Corazon heard her gasp, "Ah!" Once again the killer ran the water in the bathroom. He was gone for 20 minutes.

The four remaining nurses tried to wiggle underneath the bunk beds in the south bedroom, but petite Corazon was the only one to successfully secrete herself far enough under a bunk to avoid detection. The fifth nurse, Gloria Davy, remained atop one of the bunk beds.

The remaining nurses tried to roll underneath the beds and hide. Corazon managed to wriggle all the way underneath one of the beds, pressing her face and body against the floor. She was unable to free her hands from the tight restraints behind her back.

1:20 AM

Next the killer came for Valentina Pasion. He lifted her up by her bindings and carried her off to the west bedroom, where she was brutally stabbed. The killer once again was out of the room for 20 minutes, and was again heard running the water afterward.

1:40 AM

Merlita Gargullo was next lifted up and carried to the same west bedroom. She too was heard to cry out "Ah!" and "Masakit," in her native Tagalog, meaning, "It hurts." The killer spent 30 minutes with Merlita, whom he strangled with one of the white cloth ligatures. He again ran the water in the bathroom.

Merlita's body was placed across Valentina's in a criss-cross pattern.

2:10 AM

The killer untied Pat Matusek's ankles and walked her from the south bedroom to the bathroom, where he strangled her. Corazon estimated that he was gone from the room for from 35 to 40 minutes.

2:50 AM

The killer awakened Gloria and began unzipping and removing her slacks and underwear. Now intent on raping her, he removed the rest of Gloria's clothing.

In a polite tone of voice the killer asked Gloria if she would please wrap her legs around his back.[9] He sexually assaulted her on her bed for about 20 to 25 minutes. Corazon couldn't see this from under the bed but heard the creaking sound of the bedsprings.

The killer then carried Gloria down the stairs into the living room, depositing her on the couch. Corazon heard no screams, shouts, or conversation. The killer spent 45 minutes with Gloria and left her on the living room couch.

3:35 AM

His gruesome task completed, the killer went back upstairs to survey the carnage. Six nurses – Pam Wilkening, Mary Ann Jordan, Suzanne Farris, Nina Jo Schmale, Valentina Pasion and Merlita Gargullo - lay dead in the upstairs west and east bedrooms, and Pat Matusek lay stretched across the bathroom doorway. They had all been either stabbed, strangled, or a combination of both.

The killer flipped on the overhead light in the south bedroom and looked around, failing to notice Corazon underneath the bed. He then turned off the light and proceeded down the stairs.

5:00-5:30 AM

In an eerie conclusion to the nightmare, the nurses' alarm clocks began to ring at 5:00 and 5:30 AM. Corazon finally managed to wiggle out from under the bed and free herself from her bindings. She walked into the hallway and saw Pat Matusek lying across the bathroom doorway, deceased. She then entered her east bedroom, where the maimed bodies of Mary Ann Jordan, Suzanne Farris, and Pamela Wilkening lay in streams of blood.

Fearing that the intruder was still in the house, Corazon didn't run downstairs to call for help. The house telephone, in the kitchen, was the only phone, and the nurses, held hostage all night on the second floor, could not get to it.

Corazon sat on her bed and yelled out the window for help. It was almost 6:00 AM and the neighborhood was just beginning to stir. No one heard her cries, so she ripped the screen from the window and jumped out onto a ledge just below the window frame. She yelled for help until passersby on East 100th Street and a policeman patrolling the area took notice.

"Help! My friends are all dead! I'm the only one alive!"

6:00 AM

Patrolman Daniel Kelley had just reached the intersection of Crandon Avenue and E. 100th Street in his cruiser when he noticed the commotion in front of the townhouses. Student nurse Judy Dykton, who had come outside to see what was going on, was calling out to Corazon to come downstairs.

Finding the front door locked, Kelley went around to the back door, which was open. Upon entering the living room he noticed the lifeless body of Gloria Davy. He recognized her, as he had dated her sister Charlene. He immediately wired in for assistance, while Judy Dykton helped a shaky Corazon down the stairs and out of the townhouse.

6:10-6:30 AM

A flood of detectives began pouring into the townhouse, horrified at what lay before them. There was no consideration to preserving the crime scene; several detectives and officers, Commander Frank Flannagan, and Chief of Detectives Michael Spiotto, all tramped through the townhouse to survey the carnage. News reporters, with their notebooks, cameras, and recording equipment, started pulling up in their trucks, further attracting crowds of shocked neighbors and passersby.

Among the lead detectives were Byron Carlile and Jack Wallenda, who was related to the famous high-wire and trapeze artists known as the Flying Wallendas. He was right at home with the circus act that followed.

7:30-9:30 AM

At 9:15 Coroner Andrew J. Toman made all death pronouncements, and crime technicians began transporting the bodies to the Cook County morgue for autopsy. Toman had never seen anything close to such a massacre. He emerged wide-eyed from the townhouse to address a gaggle of reporters, declaring, "It is the crime of the century!"[10]

10:15 AM

The nurses' bodies arrived at the morgue where pathologists E.H. Tapia and J.E. Henry conducted the autopsies, which were completed within a matter of hours.

CHAPTER FOUR
THE POLICE STATEMENT

As sole survivor and witness, Corazon Amurao possessed an uncanny ability to recall the intricate sequence of events on the night of the murders, right down to the timing. But there are notable differences between her initial statement to police, of July 14, 1966, and her trial testimony of April 4-5, 1967.

In her statement to police Corazon stated that the intruder tied up everyone in the room, and when Mary Ann Jordan and Suzanne Farris came in later he tied them up as well. Everyone was tied up.

But at trial, she testified that the intruder approached Mary Ann and Suzanne and forced them down the hall into the east bedroom. She also described an intense exchange between them:

"After a few minutes, Miss Jordan and Miss Farris came in. I saw them in the door coming in the south bedroom. They rushed up to Miss Pasion's bed. They were dressed in Bermuda shorts....Then I saw Speck following Miss Jordan and Miss Farris. Then Speck was standing near the sliding door closet near the entrance door and he talked to Miss Jordan and Miss Farris. "You two come here." The gun was still in his hand. The gun was pointing toward Miss Jordan and Miss Farris. They were very reluctant to go towards Speck. But later on, Speck called in a more louder voice. He told, "You two come here," and then Miss Jordan and Miss Farris came towards Speck....When I saw them they went out of the big bedroom. Speck was behind Miss Jordan and Miss Farris. He went out together with them. The gun was pointing toward them."

In this version, they were not tied up.

In her statement Corazon also described how the first nurse to be removed from the bedroom was Gloria Davy. But at trial, the story changed. After everyone else except Corazon was gone, the intruder removed Gloria's clothing and raped her for 20 to 25 minutes. He then carried her downstairs and spent another 40 to 50 minutes with her on the living room sofa.

Gloria Davy was now the last victim, not the first. Corazon's police statement did not include any mention of the prolonged sexual assault. This later became a highly controversial issue at trial.

Corazon did not mention a knife in her initial statement. When she went over the statement a second time with police she realized her error. She then described the knife as a "small knife, about three to four inches long."

Corazon was assisted by a Tagalog interpreter when she gave her initial statement, but nine months later she testified at trial without the aid of an interpreter. During the nine months following the murders she had been kept sequestered in the company only of her mother and cousin and law enforcement. The extensive details given in the trial testimony, and the improvements in her spoken English, suggest that she was heavily prepped and coached prior to trial.

She often provided much more information than what was called for – "They were dressed in Bermuda shorts; then Speck was standing near the sliding door closet." The addition of extraneous information often signals that the speaker is trying to sell a story by providing extra details. But much remains to be deconstructed before reaching any conclusions.

A few other things bothered me about Corazon's story:

- Her impeccable recollections of the timing: the killer spent

20 minutes with Pam Wilkening, 20 to 25 minutes with Gloria upstairs, about 45 to 50 minutes with her downstairs, 30 to 35 minutes with Pat Matusek, five minutes in the closet, one to two minutes staring into the face of the intruder, etc. Corazon was wearing a wristwatch, but her hands were tightly tied behind her back. There was an alarm clock on the dresser in the south bedroom, but she couldn't see it from underneath a bed. And even if she could, this was a home invasion - why continue to make note of the time in such a threatening situation? It speaks of a memorized script.

- Corazon testified that she heard the intruder unzip Gloria's slacks prior to raping her. Gloria had been tied up, so we have to assume that he cut off all of her bindings before removing her clothes. She was found nude but with her hands once again tied behind her back. This discrepancy, and others, will be reviewed further under Evidence.

- Corazon stated that the light in the south bedroom was off for the duration of the evening. Between 12:10 and 12:15 witnesses Kathy Emmons and Tammy Sioukoff also noted that the south bedroom was dark. However, the south bedroom was control center for the intruder, where he made everyone sit on the floor, cut strips from a bedsheet and tie the hands and feet of several women. The four women who shared the room also retrieved money from their purses. And all this activity took place in the dark? There was some ambient light from the parking area, but a large drape across the picture window blocked much of the incoming light.

- The killer spent an inordinate amount of time with each

victim – 20 minutes, 30 minutes, 40 minutes. If this was a robbery turned murder, wouldn't he need to get out as fast as possible? Tammy Sioukoff's doorbell ring would have signaled to him that there were other student nurses and possible witnesses close by – not a good place to linger for four and a half hours.

CHAPTER FIVE
THE CRIME SCENE

Mass murders usually conjure the image of a crazed gunman firing wildly into a crowd, or a bomb going off on a city street. Mass shootings at schools, places of worship, and office buildings have become an epidemic in this country, and while often planned in advance, the outcome is always chaotic, with victims' bodies, furnishings and debris strewn about the crime scene. Often the perpetrator is killed during the siege by police or by his own hand.

The mass murder of the eight nurses was anything but chaotic, right down to the positions of the bodies. This was not a wild massacre, with women running through the house screaming and trying to escape, and many have asked, why didn't they?

I have no credentials in crime scene analysis, profiling, or interpretation; all remarks come from my own observations. I could be on the right track, or I could be way off. I have not seen any analyses of this crime scene, so hopefully, someone with more knowledge and experience will also take a closer look.

The Neighborhood

Jeffery Manor was a quiet, safe area with a low crime rate. Three townhouses on East 100th Street housed 24 nurses; Luella Park was behind them, where neighbors would walk their dogs and kids would play on the swings. On their summer days off the nurses would tan in the sun and enjoy picnic lunches. Some nurses complained of being hassled in the park by occasional gangs of kids, but nothing more serious ever came of it.

Across the street from the townhouses was an elementary school, which was vacant for the summer, and nearby was a Tastee Freeze ice cream stand. At the east end of the same block, 2335 E. 100th Street, was the National Maritime Union, the employment center for Merchant Marines and seafaring workers like Richard Speck.

Like Speck, some of the men had criminal records. Twenty-four nurses lived in the townhouse units and men visiting the NMU may have noticed them. The proximity of the NMU to the townhouses could have provided fertile ground for a stalker, and law enforcement believed that one such stalker was Richard Speck.

The townhouse was the end unit of a row of six, with unit 2319 being closest to the NMU. The unit next door, 2317, was unoccupied the week of the murders. On the other side was an alleyway that connected the rear parking lot to East 100th Street.

Directly behind the townhouse was an area allowing for one row of cars to park. Behind this lot lay Luella Park. A few street lamps lit the parking lot area. Unit 2319, the end unit where the murders took place, is marked with a star.

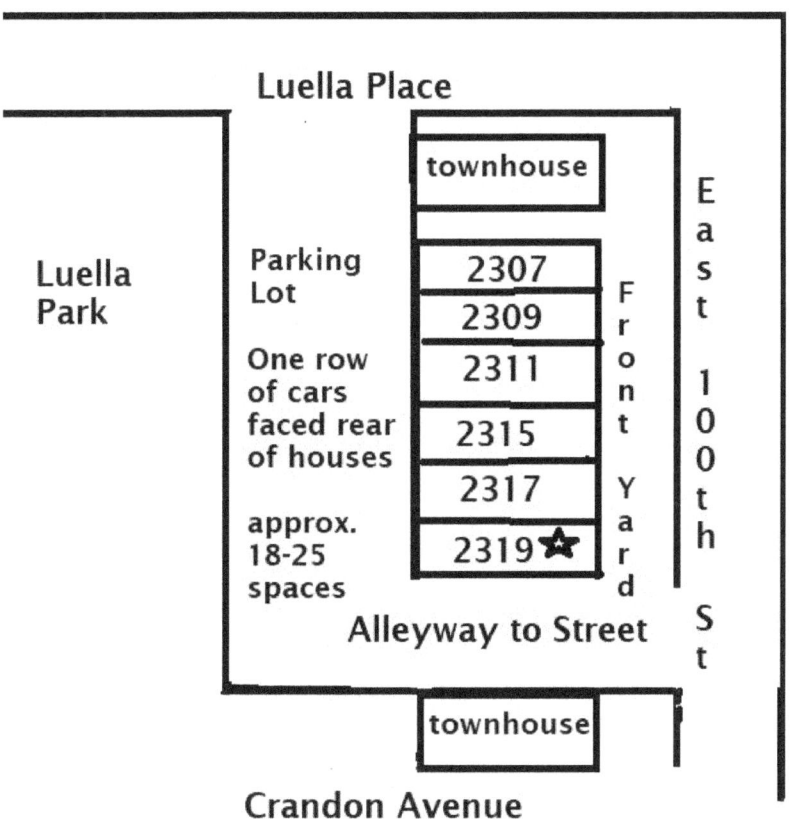

The nurses in 2319 did not own cars. The lot was used by other tenants, visitors, or nearby neighbors. People came and went at late hours, and the alleyway next to 2319 provided a quick and easy way out of the parking area and onto the street.

Causes of Death

The causes of death were either asphyxia due to ligature strangulation, stabbing, or in one case, a combination of both. No one was shot. There is a distinct variety in the murder methods. The knife wounds were of varying depths; some bore patterns of small knife wounds or punctures on the neck or back.

In the east bedroom:

Pamela Wilkening died from one stab wound to the heart.

Suzanne Farris was strangled, but also suffered eleven stab wounds to her upper back and seven stab wounds to her neck and chest.

Mary Ann Jordan received one stab wound to her left eye and three other stab wounds to her neck and throat.

In the west bedroom:

Nina Jo Schmale was strangled, no knife wounds.

Valentina Pasion's throat was violently slashed.

Merlita Gargullo was strangled, with small knife wounds.

Outside the bathroom:

Pat Matusek was strangled, no knife wounds.

Downstairs:

Gloria Davy was strangled, no knife wounds.

In all, four women were strangled by ligature, one was strangled and stabbed numerous times, and three were stabbed, two multiple times and one with one stab wound.

Based on the crime scene photos, a diagram of which follows, the bodies were laid out neatly side by side.

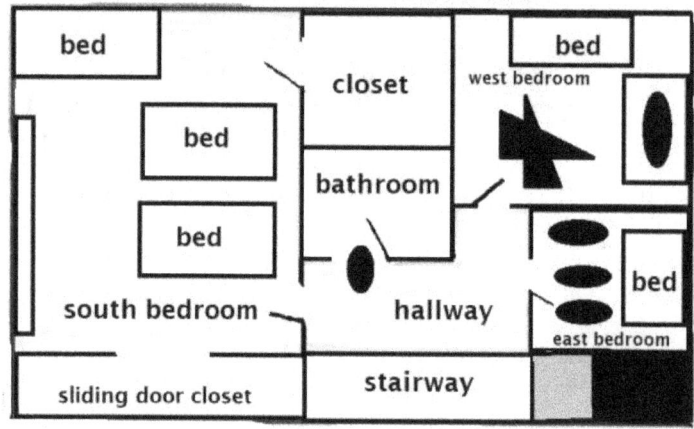

Positions of Bodies Found on Second Floor
(shown in oval and triangular shapes)
One near bathroom, six in east and west rooms

- In the east bedroom lay Pamela Wilkening, Suzanne Farris, and Mary Ann Jordan. These were the first three nurses to be killed, and they were laid out in that order, from east to west.

- Pam was on her back, Suzanne was face down, Mary Ann was on her back. Their heads faced north. The floors were covered with blood. Blankets and bedding had been placed over the upper portion of their bodies.

- In the west bedroom, from east to west, lay the bodies of Nina Jo Schmale, Valentina Pasion, and Merlita Gargullo. This too follows the order in which they were killed: after Mary Ann, Nina Jo was next, then Valentina, then Merlita, who appears to have been thrown across Valentina's body, forming a criss-cross pattern. They are shown by the crossed triangular shapes in the diagram.

- Valentina was face down and Merlita was face up, across Valentina's back. Nina Jo was face up on her bed, her head facing west and hands tied behind her. The others were on the floor with their heads facing north. There was a pillow across Nina Jo's face, and a bloody floral quilt covered the upper bodies of Merlita and Valentina. Merlita's hands and feet were tied; Valentina's feet were tied.

- Pat Matusek, who was taken after Merlita, lay across the bathroom threshold in the hallway, face up, her head facing west. Her hands were tied behind her back and her feet were not tied. She was not covered.

- Gloria Davy was found face down on the living room sofa, her head facing south. She was the only one on the first floor. Her hands were tied behind her back and her feet were not tied. She was not covered.

No gun or knife was found at the crime scene. The pathologists' reports are discussed in more detail in Part II.

- The following items of jewelry were found on the nurses' bodies:

Pam – one white ring with a black stone

Pat – a Winton watch, yellow metal ring with white stone, religious medal on necklace

Mary Ann – high school graduation ring

Nina Jo – pearl earrings

Suzanne – ring with white stone, possibly an engagement ring

If this was a robbery, one wonders why such valuable items were left behind.

CHAPTER SIX
ILLOGICAL LOGISTICS

Logistics is defined as a detailed, coordinated effort to direct a complex operation involving the movement of many supplies, facilities, or people. The words logistics and logic both derive from the Greek word *logos,* meaning reason, something that is sensible. The overtaking of nine healthy young women, who were subdued, bound, taken from one room to another and systematically killed one by one, save for the sole surviving witness, certainly qualifies as a complex operation.

But little was reasonable about the way in which the crime was described. It would have presented a stiff challenge even to a well-equipped, professionally trained killer, let alone a lone gunman, who was intoxicated, under the influence of multiple unknown drugs, and inexperienced in killing. There are many red flags in the path of the official story, beginning with Richard Speck's first steps toward the townhouse.

Door to Door

The townhouse was located 1.6 miles west of the Shipyard Inn; Speck would have had to leave there by about 10:25 PM to reach the back door, break in, and then make his way up to Corazon's east bedroom by 11:00. If his true intent was to commit a burglary, there were residential neighborhoods much closer to the Inn.

To reach his target destination he had to walk across the 500-foot long Calumet Bridge spanning the Calumet River and continue on through several blocks of vacant industrial lots, passing an Edison power substation, salt fields, and a Ford auto plant. Speck knew the route, as he had made this trek in reverse when he walked from the NMU to the Shipyard Inn earlier that day.

The temperature was in the mid seventies, but as the story goes, he wore a black rayon-lined corduroy jacket to hide his tattoos, although it was hot outside and pitch dark. Later on, this part of the story will change when other clothing is introduced.

Having reached his destination, he then broke in through the back door – or did he?

"Belliedout"

Law enforcement explained that intruder broke into the nurses' dorm by prying a screen off the back kitchen window with a knife, then reaching around through the open window to unlock the door. The intruder then had to pass through the living room to reach the stairway leading to the three bedrooms on the second floor. The foot of this stairway was opposite the front door. At the top of the stairway was the door to the south bedroom.

There were three separate panels on the kitchen window, but only one screen had to be removed in order to reach in and unlock the door. The next morning that screen was found underneath the kitchen window, leaning against the house.

The July 14th Supplemental Police Report of lead Detectives Byron Carlile and Jack Wallenda, CPD Area 2 Homicide, explained it in an unusual way:

"An examination of the premises was made and it was found that the rear screen of the window closest to the back door, which leads into the kitchen had been removed and further, the screen which is made of metal, showed the frame work to have "Belliedout" indicating that it had been forced in an outward direction."[11]

It took a minute for me to realize that "Belliedout" was the combination of two words, "bellied" and "out," and described the protruding shape of a window screen after it has been forced out of its frame. The bent or protruding part of the screen is the "belly."

A crime scene photo (not pictured) showed the screen resting against the house underneath the back window. The screen appeared flat and intact. There was no apparent damage, no evidence of a bent, buckling or protruding screen – no "belly."

None of the witnesses noticed the screen under the window, or if they did, didn't mention it. But in his book *The Crime of the Century: Richard Speck and the Murders That Shocked the Nation,* prosecutor William J. Martin revealed (italics mine): "Pushy reporters were on the scene, *one of whom had removed the screen from the back window* and stuck his head inside to try to see what was going on."[12]

> then made by theses Officers
> r. A general call was then plac
>
> es was made and it was found tha
> ow closest to the back door, whi
> een removed and further, the
> ame work to have "Belliedout"
> tward direction. The sore on had
> described. This could have been
> as at the time of the arrival
> No other means of a forced entry
>
> , 20 yrs., a student Nurse re-
> reet was interrogated and she re-
> out 0010 hrs., 14 July 1966 she
> 100th. street, to borrow some

In other words, it was a reporter who removed the back window screen, not the intruder. In spite of this discrepancy, the July 14th police report stayed with the broken screen theory:

"This could have been the means of entrance made by the assailant, as at the time of arrival of the Police the window proper was open. No other means of a forced entry could be found."

So how did the intruder get in? Maybe he just walked in, or maybe he was let in; Corazon had not checked the back door before going to bed. I'll go with a "no forced entry" for starters. The first action taken by the intruder, memorialized in true crime literature, did not happen as we were told. On its own, this isn't that important, except that in this story it is only the first of a long chain of toppling dominoes.

Stairway to Hell

The diagram below shows the first floor of the townhouse. The intruder entered through the back door and had to make his way through the kitchen and living room in order to reach the stairway leading to the second floor.

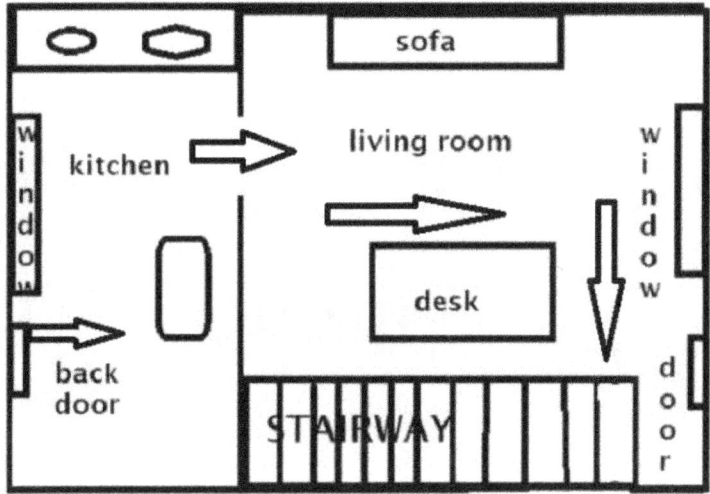

He then went directly up the stairs. The following diagram shows the layout of the second floor. The arrows indicate the path that he took to reach Corazon's east bedroom, where he knocked on the door.

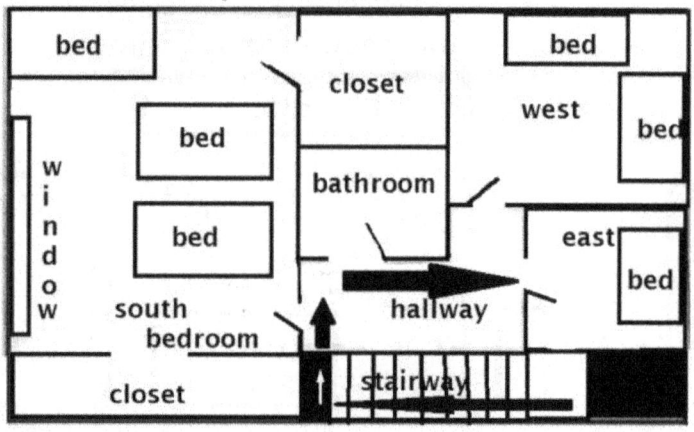

As shown in the diagram, the stairway led to the door of the south bedroom where Pam Wilkening, Pat Matusek, and Valentina Pasion were in bed. Their door was open, allowing a perfect opportunity for the intruder to enter the south bedroom, rob the women, and beat a hasty retreat back down the stairs and out the front door. Yet he bypassed two open bedrooms, filled with the nurses' belongings, including pocketbooks, purses, and wallets, and went to the one door at the farthest point of the hallway that happened to be closed and locked?

The intruder was lucky to have gained entry into the townhouse with no effort, so why knock on a locked door, inviting trouble? Richard Speck was not the sharpest pencil in the box, but his thefts were crimes of impulse and opportunity - smash, grab, and run, not knock, wait, and enter.

There are now two questionable methods of gaining entry - first, to the townhouse, and second, to Corazon's room. The next steps in the series introduce more weirdness into the mix.

The One Who Knocked

The intruder knocked four times on the east bedroom door. Corazon, who had fallen asleep, clambered down from her upper bunk to answer the door. I wonder why; Merlita, still awake in the lower bunk, was closer to the door. From this point on Corazon consistently took control of the situation as much as possible.

In her trial testimony Corazon described the moment that she opened her bedroom door to the intruder:

"STATE: What did you do after you heard the four knocks at the door?

CORAZON: Then I got up and I answered the one who is knocking on our door.

STATE: And will you describe what happened when you went to the door?

CORAZON: I went up to the – I went to the door and I unlocked it and I started to open it and at once there's somebody who is pushing the door....Then I saw a man standing near, on the center of the door holding a gun in his right hand.... I stared at him for about one to two minutes."[13]

One to two minutes is a very long time to stare directly into a stranger's face, especially when he is pointing a gun at you.

The intruder then marched Corazon and Merlita out of the room, pulled Nina Jo out of the bedroom next door, and walked them all at gunpoint down the hallway into the large south bedroom where Pat, Pam, and Valentina were already in bed.

At this point the nurses remained calm, at least outwardly. When conversation took place, it was relaxed and friendly, lending a surreal atmosphere to the situation.

Corazon's Call to Arms

Once herded into the south bedroom, Corazon and her two Filipina housemates raced through the room and dashed into a closet, shutting the door and pulling tightly on the doorknob to prevent entry. But when a voice called out "Come out, he won't harm us," they relented and exited the closet.

The troubling question of why they didn't try to escape has plagued many people over the years. In May 1970 an attorney for South Chicago Community Hospital posed this same question to Corazon, now Mrs. Atienza:

"When Kincaid asked why the girls didn't try to escape after Speck led them to one bedroom of the townshouse (sic), Mrs. Atienza said she told another nurse, "Let's untie ourselves and escape," but said they did not have enough time."[14]

There are problems with this statement. The women were obviously not tied up when they ran into the closet. And she testified that they were in the closet for about five minutes, enough time to plan some quick action to divert the intruder and rush down the stairs.

Everyone was in a terrifying situation, and my intent is not to victim blame Corazon. But I challenge her closet story because she changed it several times and none of the changes made sense. More inconsistencies follow.

Out On A Ledge

If a picture is worth a thousand words, the crime scene photos are worth an encyclopedia. They expose the official story in a single word: Implausible.

The photo on the next page shows the bunk bed shared by Corazon Amurao and Merlita Gargullo in the east bedroom. It is directly underneath the window facing north across E. 100th Street. Due to limited space the nurses would place their belongings on top of their beds until bedtime and then place the items underneath the beds.

This photo was taken just after the nurses' bodies were removed. Crime lab technicians had removed the bloody blankets from the bodies of Mary Ann Jordan, Suzanne Farris, and Pamela Lee Wilkening and placed them on the bottom bunk.

Corazon stated that she got out of bed at 11:00 PM and opened the door to the intruder. Then the night of horror began.

Merlita never returned to the room. Corazon, having escaped the slaughter, returned several hours later, yelled out the window for help, then broke the screen, jumped out the window onto the second floor window ledge, and yelled for help again.

The beds should therefore look exactly as they were left when the intruder came upon the scene. But Corazon's bed is loaded with newspapers, papers, a purse, books, and other items. Merlita's bed is also cluttered. These beds were not slept in.

This begs the questions:

- Where was Corazon when the intruder came?
- Why say that she was in bed when she wasn't?
- Did the intruder arrive at 11:00 PM?

- Did the intruder knock on her door?
- Why didn't the intruder take her money then and there? Corazon described how the intruder marched everyone to Nina Jo's room to steal her money, but her own room, which was right next door, was not mentioned.

The broken screen on this window is a much better example of a "bellied-out," bent screen than the intact, unbroken screen found outside the back door – the one that was popped out of its frame by a nosy reporter.

Three women were violently stabbed in the room, but no blood spatter or castoff is visible on the mattress, bedding, or items on the bed, or on the clean white nurse's uniform shown just to the right in the photo, which was hanging outside the closet.

For argument's sake, I considered that someone may have placed the items on the bed before the photographers arrived. Let's check the timeline:

6:00 AM: Corazon steps on her bed, breaks the screen, and goes out onto the window ledge to call for help.

6:10-7:00 AM: Police and crime scene techs arrive on scene.

9:15 AM: Coroner makes death pronouncements.

9:30-10:15 AM: Bodies transported to morgue, arrive at 10:15 AM. Photos taken of beds.

Sometime between 6:15 and 7:00 AM the blankets were removed from the bodies of Mary Ann, Suzanne, and Pam in order to view their injuries and make death pronouncements.

This leaves us with only one other possibility – that Corazon, who entered the room and climbed out the window around 6:00 AM, placed the items on the bed. But why? Her immediate priority would have been to call for help, not tidy up the bedroom in time for company.

The lower mattress of a bunk bed is usually much higher from the floor than a conventional mattress. Photographs of the nurses' bunk beds show about a foot in distance between the bottom mattress and the floor. As previously mentioned, the nurses used the floor space under the beds for storage, so the space was easily accessible and spacious enough to accommodate piles of textbooks, bags, and other personal items.

I don't believe the bunk beds offered any viable hiding place, even for petite Corazon; there was too much space between the mattress and the floor, and anyone hiding there could be plainly visible. Corazon claimed that she hid behind a portion of a blanket that was hanging over the edge of the bed, but even a portion of a blanket was not enough to shield her whole body from view.

If the killer was meticulous enough to tie everyone up, wash up after each murder, and survey the south bedroom before leaving, how did he forget about Corazon, the nurse who had opened the door, stared him in the face, and walked downstairs with him?

Here is an interesting note. This photo of Corazon's room appeared in many publications, but did not appear in the first edition of prosecutor Martin's book, *The Crime of the Century,* in 1993. But in the second edition, published in 2016, a different photo of this same bed appeared, showing the broken screen in the background. But in that photo the bed is completely clear and free of clutter.

The state of Corazon's bed casts a giant question mark over her account of the evening and raises another red flag.

Bloody Shoeprints?

Another item in the west bedroom would have garnered serious interest today, but back then was ignored: bloody shoeprints.

There were prints from two distinctly different types of shoes; one with a straight line grid pattern, commonly worn by medical professionals. The other had a special grid pattern often seen in military issue footwear. These prints were made when the blood was still fresh enough to make impressions of the entire soles, possibly by the killers.

The type of footwear worn by Richard Speck came under scrutiny, but only for purposes of identifying what he wore on the murder night. Michael Compateso, a defense witness, stated that Speck was wearing brown work boots when they played pool between 8:40 and 8:57 on the night of the murders. These boots would have left a specific grid type impression.

However, Corazon Amurao testified that the killer wore black shoes, which would have left a flat sole print, not a specific pattern marking. Bloody footprints could have helped identify the killer, but once police and medical technicians began streaming into the townhouse all bets were off.

No bloody footprints in the hallway or south bedroom were noted. This is hard to believe, given the extent of the bloodshed and the fact that the killer had to have walked back and forth between the rooms several times.

The absence of evidence spoke as loudly as the evidence at hand. But the crime lab techs were just beginning their collection of evidence, and another volley of red flags awaited.

Prophecies on the Wall

There was a bulletin board above Nina Jo's dresser with items that turned out to be eerily prophetic. One was a poster proudly declaring: "Sleep well tonight – Your National Guard is awake!" Ironically, embattled Mayor Richard J. Daley had called in 1,500 National Guardsmen to restore order to the beleaguered city just hours after the murders took place. Sadly, the National Guard was awake, but none of the nurses would sleep well that night.

Next to the poster was a diagram of a cross-section of the female reproductive system. Resembling a page from a medical textbook, it had an uncanny connection to this story.

Female reproduction was a hot topic of the day. The feminist movement was gaining traction in the mid-sixties, championing women's right to choose. Birth control and abortion were extremely polarizing subjects of discussion in political, social, and religious circles, and what they represented – the suppression of life itself – fed into certain extreme ideologies which, in my opinion, are the key to why these murders may have taken place.

Like the other eerie signposts along the way, this innocent poster was telling us something. How it all ended up in the mass murder of eight nurses is the subject of a later chapter.

CHAPTER SEVEN

THE WITNESSES

There were six townhouses in the block, three of which – 2311, 2315, and 2319 – housed student nurses. The remaining townhouses were rented by couples or families. Immediately next door to 2319 was 2317, rented by Mr. and Mrs. Bert Weisz, who ran a business at 8820 S. Stony Island Avenue, just a mile north.

The Weisz couple, as next-door neighbors, could have proven invaluable ear- and eyewitnesses to the horrific events of that evening, but they happened to be vacationing at Elkhart Lake in Wisconsin during the week of the murders.

Bill McCarthy, a neighbor, told police that he had to drive around the lot a few times to find an open parking space. Finally someone drove off at 1:30 AM and McCarthy parked in the vacated space. He did not recall what type of vehicle had previously occupied the space.

The police report of July 14th included this statement from another eyewitness in the neighborhood:

> "... he was sitting on his front porch and saw two of the girls enter the back door at approximately 0030 hours 14 July 1966. (Witness) stated that the girls got out of a 1963 dark gray Pontiac bearing Illinois plates and that the driver of this auto went around the block twice and through the alley to the rear of the girls' apartment. At the west end of the alley (Witness) stated that the driver parked the auto for several minutes before driving away. (Witness) further stated that the lights were on in the rear bedroom until 0115 hours."

This statement is intriguing. We know that Suzanne and Mary Ann entered the townhouse just before 12:30 AM, but they were not in a car; they had been visiting with fellow student nurse Pat Waddington in 2311, and then walked the short distance from 2311 to 2319, four doors down.

So did the witness notice the two nurses on foot, or did two other individuals actually get out of a car and enter the townhouse? If he saw two individuals at 12:30, wouldn't he also have seen Mary Ann and Suzanne at that same time, or did he just miss them moments before? Unfortunately the report didn't indicate exactly how long the witness was watching the townhouse.

The behavior of the driver – circling the townhouse twice, then stopping for several minutes before departing - is suspicious, and happened right at the time that the two nurses, or two other persons, entered the townhouse. Lampposts in the parking lot apparently provided enough light to detect the car's make, color, and license plate.

The witness also noticed the light in the south bedroom. Corazon stated that it was off all night, until the killer took a quick look around before leaving. Kathy Emmons and Tammy Sioukoff stated that the south bedroom was dark between 12:10 and 12:15. However, the witness, who saw the two figures at 12:30, said the light was on until 1:15, which suggests that it was on at least since 12:30 when he saw the two nurses and the car. The approximate 12:30 AM time will become more significant shortly.

The witnesses' observations show that there was a fair amount of activity behind the townhouses late at night, and introduce the possibility of other individuals coming and going from the townhouse between 12:30 and 1:30 AM. However, these leads were not fleshed out. And the mysterious 1963 Pontiac that circled the block twice and hovered in the area for several minutes disappeared into the shadows.

CHAPTER EIGHT

THE NURSES

In the theater of true crime the perpetrators always get top billing. They receive fancy nicknames like the Killer Clown, the Lipstick Killer, the Zodiac, and the Green River Killer, as if they were circus performers and not dangerous psychopaths. And who wants to think of a band of drug-crazed killers as the Manson "Family?"

I was glad that the nurses' murders weren't given a catchy nickname. Even so, it is Richard Speck whose name rings famous in true crime, not Gloria Jean Davy, Merlita Gargullo, Valentina Pasion, Nina Jo Schmale, Patricia Ann Matusek, Suzanne Bridgett Farris, Mary Ann Jordan, or Pamela Lee Wilkening. Yet I found their lives more inspiring than the accounts of Speck's aimless antics in and out of bars, burglaries, and jails.

Pamela Lee Wilkening – born August 2, 1945

The daughter of John, a pipefitter, and Lena, a homemaker, Pamela Lee "Pam" Wilkening grew up in a small Cape Cod house on Commercial Avenue in south Lansing, Illinois. She was active in the Brownies and the Girl Scouts.

Pam graduated from Thornton Fractional High School, Calumet City, Illinois, in 1963, where she was active in the Nurses Club, Pep Club, Dramatics Club, and several singing clubs, both choir and *a cappella* style. A diligent and hard worker, she also held down a part time job in a bakery while attending school.

Pam was off from work on July 13th and spent the day with friends in Michigan City. She told them that her boyfriend, who was in the military, had just been stationed in San Francisco.

Pam was quiet and reserved. As the youngest nurse in the group she kept to herself, content to remain in the background while her housemates let off steam by playing pranks, like blasting loud classical music while zipping around the living room on roller skates.

Pam's older brother Jack, seven years her senior, raced cars, and she became a muscle car enthusiast, attending many of his races. Pam was looking forward to her 21st birthday on August 2nd when she expected to get her first car. I felt sad when I read this. I got my first car when I turned 21, my mom's old green Ford Falcon that she deeded me for $1. It was a special moment, one that Pam Wilkening never got to enjoy.

After one of Jack's races he watched his sister wave goodbye, promising to meet up again soon. That was in June 1966. He never saw her alive again.

Pam Wilkening is interred at Mount Hope Cemetery, Cook County, Illinois.

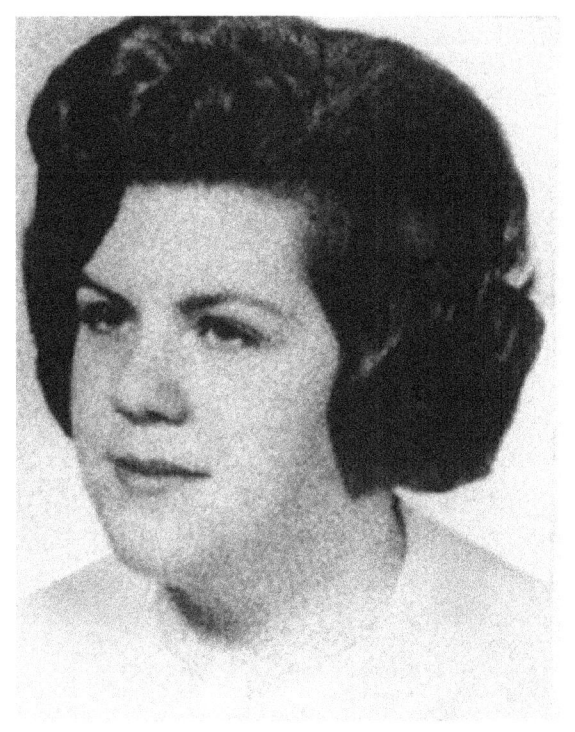

Pamela Lee Wilkening

Patricia Ann Matusek – born December 8, 1945

Patricia Ann "Pat" Matusek was the daughter of Joseph and Bessie Matusek, both of Czech descent. Joe owned Joe Matusek's Club, a tavern in the 10800 block of South Michigan Avenue. She had one sister, Betty Jo, who attended Catholic elementary school with her. Betty Jo suffered from scoliosis, an abnormal curvature of the spine, and Pat proved to be a kind, dependable caretaker for Betty. Inspired by her strong dedication to children, her goal was to join the staff of Children's Memorial Hospital as a pediatric nurse.

Always energetic and lively, Pat's hobbies provided an outlet for her athletic, competitive nature. An excellent swimmer, she participated in swim meets, and she also trained in water ballet, which required skill, patience, and timing. She played volleyball as well. Pat was engaged to Robert Hinkle, a male nurse, whom she planned to marry after her graduation from SCCH.

Pat's interest in nursing was inspired by the illness and early death of her cousin Tommy, whom she used to visit at Roseland Community Hospital after her classes at Fenger High School in Chicago. Nurturing came naturally to Pat; she would hold Tommy's hand, smooth his bedding, tell stories, and comfort him. She sometimes left Tommy's bedside in tears, but the experience only served to strengthen her motivation to enter nursing.

Pat had the day off on July 13, 1966, which she spent with best friend Arlene. At the end of the day Pat invited Arlene in for coffee, but Arlene was tired and took a raincheck. The two planned to get together the following Friday for a visit to Chicago's tony Gold Coast. Instead, Arlene would learn the next morning of Pat's tragic murder.

Years later, sister Betty Jo would name her daughter Patricia Ann in Pat's honor. Her father, Joseph, attended all of Richard Speck's parole hearings to ensure that he would never be released from prison. Even in his declining years, Joe Matusek religiously attended the parole hearings in a wheelchair, determined that Richard Speck never see the light of day.

Patricia Ann Matusek is interred at St. Mary's Catholic Center, Evergreen Park, Cook County, Illinois.

Patricia Ann Matusek

Merlita Ornado Gargullo – born September 1, 1942

Merlita was the oldest of nine children born to a family on Mindoro Island, the seventh largest island located in the west-central area of the Philippines. Her father, A.G. Gargullo, was a doctor, and she carried on the family tradition of healing. Quiet and shy, she was a hard worker and an efficient student, receiving her nursing degree from Avellano University in Manila.

In addition to nursing, Merlita's other talents included singing, and she would serenade the dorm while cooking or doing household chores. She sent many letters home to her family about her experiences and impressions of America.

Merlita was Corazon Amurao's roommate. The two had become friends after traveling together to Chicago to commence their nursing careers several weeks earlier. They shared the tiny east bedroom, which housed one bunk bed, one small closet, and one dresser. Merlita slept on the bottom bunk. A devout Catholic, she was in the process of saying her evening prayers when mayhem reportedly came knocking at their bedroom door.

The caskets of Merlita and Valentina were flown back to the Philippines on July 17, 1966. The next day John Patrick Cardinal Cody held a solemn mass in Chicago for them.

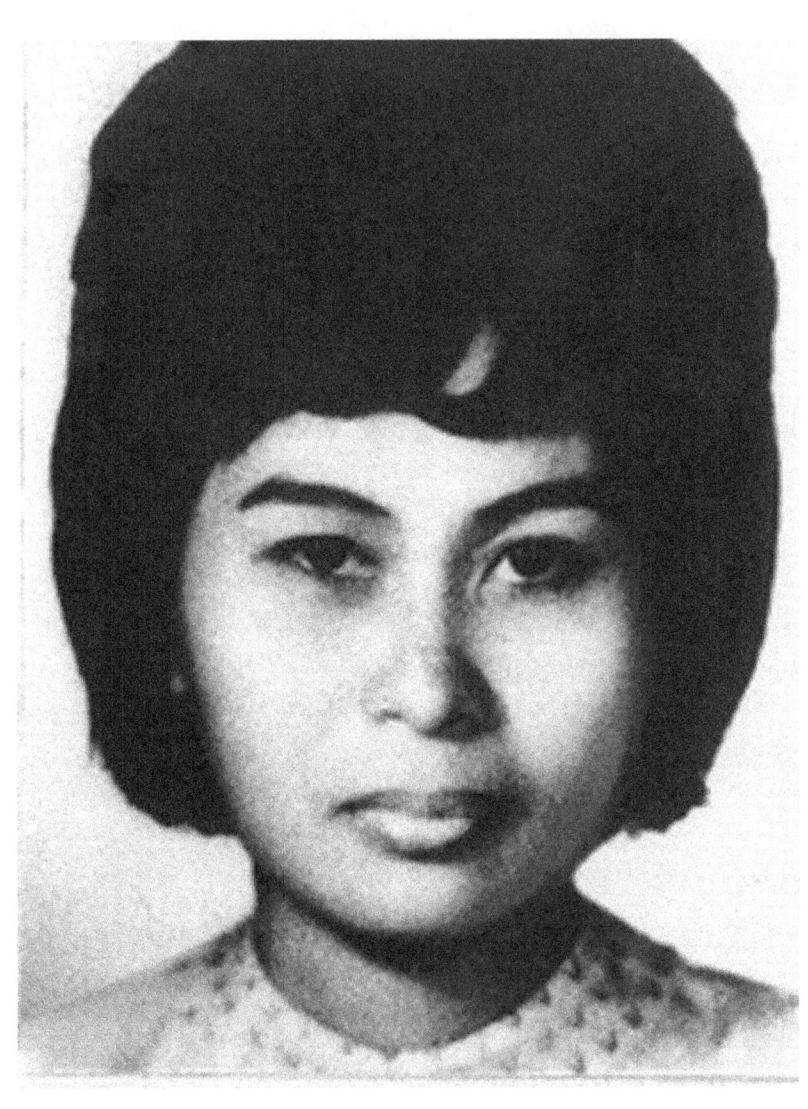

Merlita Ornado Gargullo

Valentina Pasion – age 24

"Tina" came from a poor family of six children in Jones City, Province of Isabela, Island of Luzon, about 150 miles north of Manila, the country's capital. Pretty, petite, and friendly, she attended Manila Central University School of Nursing where she ranked among the top ten in her class.

Tina was excited to have the opportunity to work in the United States. Once here, she hoped to make a new life for herself, but that dream was viciously cut short. Her father, Luis, took an agonizing sixteen-hour flight from Manila to Chicago to identify her body.

Tina was especially fond of American singer Jerry Vale, whose songs "Arrivederci, Roma" and "Be My Love" were very popular at the time. In the weeks preceding the murders she attended a Jerry Vale concert with friends and sent one of his records home to a friend in the Philippines.

Tina and Corazon often attended Our Lady Gate of Heaven Roman Catholic Church just blocks from the townhouse, and they did their grocery shopping together at nearby Grocerland. She enjoyed preparing Philippine cuisine as much as her housemates enjoyed devouring it. One specialty, "pancit," consisting of noodles, pork and vegetables, was a special favorite.

The bodies of Valentina Pasion and Merlita Gargullo were flown to Manila International Airport on July 17th. Over a hundred mourners lined the tarmac to welcome them home.

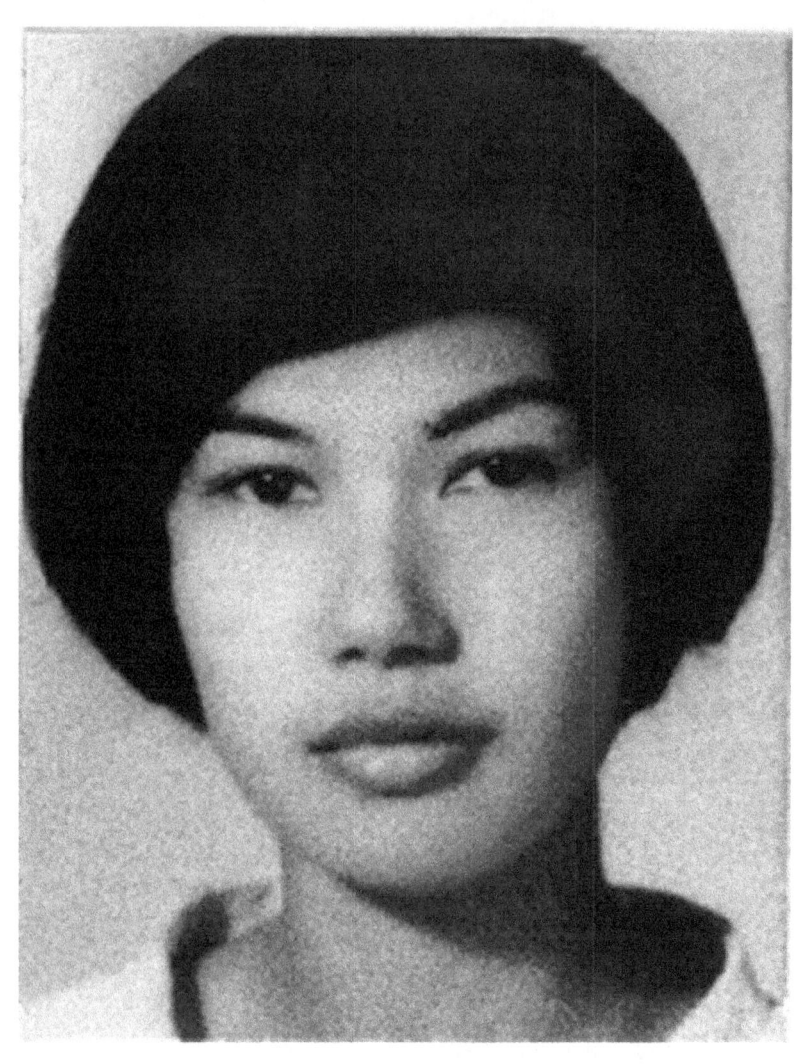

Valentina Pasion

Mary Ann Jordan – born October 4, 1945

Mary Ann was born to Philip Sr., a civil engineer, and Mary Jordan, who had four boys and two girls. Her youngest brother Billy was born with Downs syndrome and required special care. Big sister Mary Ann was only too happy to help out. The two developed a very close and loving relationship, and from this experience Mary Ann knew she was destined to be a caretaker. Her grandmother, Grace, had been a high-ranking surgical nurse in Michigan at the turn of the century, so it seemed only natural for Mary Ann to follow in her footsteps.

And a natural she was. Caring for Billy paved the way for her career, and she set her sights on becoming a pediatric nurse. Like Gloria Davy, she was a member of the Future Nurses of America.

Mary Ann was no slouch when it came to sports: she enjoyed swimming, baseball, roller skating in the summer, ice skating in the winter. A 1963 graduate of Aquinas Dominican High School in Chicago, she was scheduled to graduate from nursing school on August 7, 1966, along with three of her housemates.

Fate took a cruel twist for Mary Ann that night. She did not live in the townhouse but had decided to stay over with her best friend, Suzanne Farris, so that they could discuss Suzanne's upcoming marriage to her brother, Phil Jordan.

Earlier that night Mary Ann borrowed the family car. She and Suzanne went out for burgers and cokes at a local Burger King with fellow student nurse Pat McCarthy, who lived in 2311. After they returned they parked the car and visited with Pat in 2311 until 12:25 AM, when they walked back to 2319 for the final time. Pat McCarthy was overcome by strange feelings as she watched Suzanne and Mary Ann take their last fateful walk down to 2319 that night. It was the last time she would see them alive.

Mary Ann Jordan is interred at Riverside Cemetery, Three Oaks, Berrien County, Michigan.

Mary Ann Jordan

Nina Jo Schmale – born December 27, 1941

Nina (pronounced NIGH-NA and not NEE-NA) was the daughter of John and Dorothy Schmale. John, a cement finisher, was of German descent, and Doris' heritage was Czech and English. She had an older brother, John Jr.

Raised on a family farm in rural DuPage county, near Wheaton, Illinois, Nina Jo's first school was a rustic one-room schoolhouse called the "Queen Bee" that she and John walked down country roads to attend. She was known for her cheerful attitude and good sense of humor. In honor of times past when her family owned property with its own road, she kept a street sign, "Schmale Road," in her room. Her older brother John was also drawn to medicine, and became a physician while Nina Jo pursued her nursing degree.

At Glenbard Township High School in Glen Ellyn, Illinois, Nina Jo participated in the Pep and Y-Teens clubs. She graduated in 1959, as yet uncertain of her career path. Secretarial work wasn't to her liking, so she tried volunteer work in a skilled nursing home and there she found her calling. She enjoyed assisting the elderly and infirm, and brought them gifts during the Christmas holidays. Her supervisors held her in high esteem for her kindness and patience. From this experience came Nina Jo's goal to become a psychiatric nurse.

An inspirational message, written on the cover of one of Nina Jo's notebooks, reveals her passionate commitment to nursing:

"For the community nurse, the ability to give of herself for another's benefit is a way of life ... her involvement with her patient is but an overflow of her inner plentitude and of her richness of being."[15]

At 24, she was a little older than her nursing colleagues at SCCH, and the age difference initially gave her cause for concern. But she got along well with her classmates, who appreciated her maturity and self-confidence as well as her quirky sense of humor. Surrounded by Roman Catholics in the dorm, she proudly wore a necklace declaring "I Am Lutheran!"

Nina Jo and her boyfriend of seven years, Peter McNamee, a schoolteacher who also served with the Coast Guard, planned to marry after she obtained her nursing degree. Among her other loves were cats and Elvis Presley.

After Nina Jo's death, her mother Dorothy set aside boxes of photos and slides showing a cheerful Nina having fun with friends and relatives. Her brother John found these many years later and had them published. Dorothy had thoughtfully labeled them "Nina Jo" on a sheet of pink paper. Pink was Nina Jo's favorite color.

To honor his sister John Schmale and his wife created the Nina Jo Schmale Scholarship Fund at Wheaton College. Nina Jo is interred at the Wheaton Cemetery, in DuPage County, Illinois.

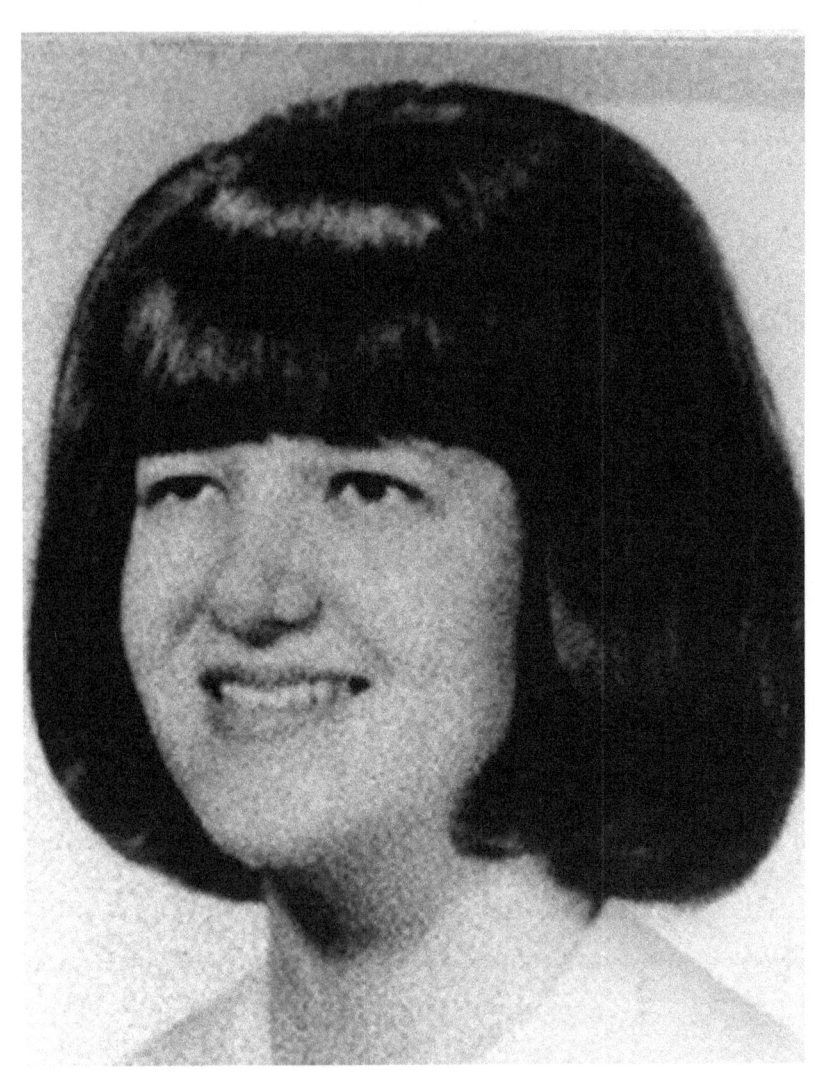

Nina Jo Schmale

Suzanne Bridget Farris – born September 10, 1944

Suzanne, 21, was the daughter of John and Mary Farris and the sister of John Jr. and Marilyn. John Farris, a superintendent for the Chicago Transit Authority, affectionately nicknamed his daughter "Cookie." Suzanne grew up in the South Side neighborhood of Fair Elms and graduated from Aquinas Dominican High School in 1962. Always perky and outgoing, the caption underneath her yearbook photo read: "... way out yonder ... spirited."

Nursing was not in Suzanne's plans when she first graduated. But she was a people person with a knack for nurturing. While both parents were busy working, she took exceptional care of her younger brother John, who felt safe and protected in her presence.

Suzanne was engaged to Philip Jordan, Jr., 28, a member of the Coast Guard; the two planned to marry in June 1967. Philip was the brother of Suzanne's best friend, Mary Ann Jordan, a fellow nurse who tragically perished beside her. Fellow nurses Gloria Davy, Nina Jo Schmale, and Pat Matusek were included in the wedding party.

Suzanne loved children and planned to go into pediatric nursing. Online photographs of Suzanne show her dancing, dressing up in costumes, playing pranks. Known as an avid clothes horse, yet mindful of the tight family budget, she was adept at sewing and made her own clothing. She had a trim, athletic figure, and enjoyed volleyball and roller skating; on a lark, some of the nurses once let off steam by roller skating through the first floor of the nurses' dorm to the tune of loud classical music.

A devout Roman Catholic who attended mass frequently, Suzanne is interred at Mount Carmel Catholic Cemetery, Hillside, Cook County, Illinois.

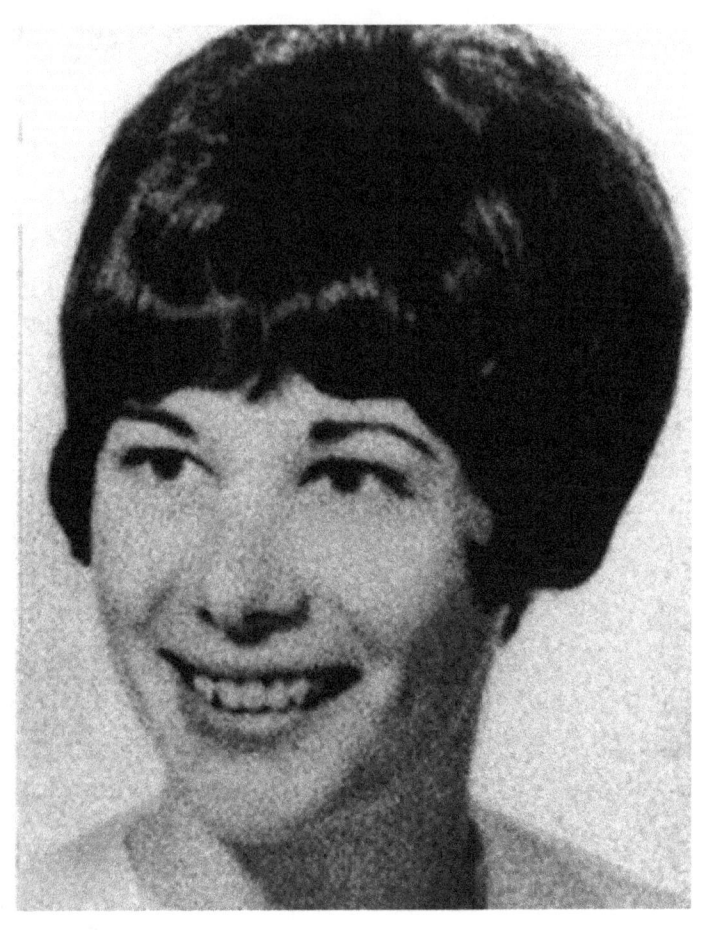

Suzanne Bridgett Farris

Gloria Jean Davy – born 1944

Gloria was born in Dyer, Indiana to Arline and Charles Davy, who had four other daughters and one son. Charles Edward "Chuck" Davy, a former Marine, was a manager at Republic Steel in Dyer, where the family had moved in order to be closer to his job. On July 14th, while attending a business meeting in Pittsburgh, he learned of his daughter's gruesome murder from a news broadcast.

An enterprising young woman with strong leadership skills, Gloria was the head of the cheerleading squad at Saints Peter and Paul High School, where she also won the title of Future Farmers of America Sweetheart. After graduating in 1961, she briefly worked as a nurses' aide at Our Lady of Mercy Hospital in Dyer before attending Northern Illinois University, where she pledged to the Alpha Xi Delta sorority. Always a leader, Gloria served as President of the Student Nurses Association from 1965 to 1966.

She had a flair for fashion and entertained thoughts of becoming a model, but instead decided to pursue her nursing degree. Gloria's desire to contribute to her community led her to write a column for teenagers in a local newspaper. She received a scholarship to South Chicago Community Hospital, and was set to graduate just three weeks following her death. On August 7, 1966, her younger sister Lori proudly but sadly received Gloria's diploma.

Gloria's outspoken, sometimes sassy nature was well known to her friends. She wasn't the type to blindly follow the others, and if something displeased her she wouldn't let it pass. She was the type of person you'd want on your side in a conflict.

Gloria was able to command the cooperation of others. A heavy sleeper, she often enlisted the aid of her roommates to help her wake up in the morning. If shaking her didn't do the trick, they were to make her sit upright in bed, ignoring any cranky objections from sleepy Gloria.

Gloria was engaged to Robert Stern, a well-to-do executive nine years her senior, with whom she enjoyed a dinner date on her last evening. When Rob dropped her off at the rear door of 2319 he was one of the last people to see her alive.

Gloria is interred at Holy Cross Cemetery and Mausoleum in Calumet City, Cook County, Illinois.

Gloria Jean Davy

Corazon Amurao, Sole Survivor – born March 26, 1943

Corazon Pieza Amurao was born in San Luis, a village in Batangas Province, Philippines, about 42 miles south of the capital city of Manila. Like Richard Speck, she had seven brothers and sisters and, like Speck, she was no stranger to hardship. Father Ignacio, 60, ran a small clothing store, which was the main source of support for the struggling family of ten.

Corazon, nicknamed "Zony" by her friends, was serious, determined, and hard-working, earning her nursing degree from Far Eastern University in Manila in 1964. She spent eight months working at San Sebastian General Hospital in prestigious Lipa City, then called "the Little Rome of the Philippines," renowned for its many Catholic schools and churches. But fate intervened. A new two-year nursing exchange program became available which would change the course of Corazon's life: She was going to be a nurse in America.

Signed into law by President Lyndon B. Johnson on September 4, 1964, the Nurse Training Act of 1964 was created to address a severe shortage of nurses in the nation's hospitals. The Act was specifically intended to bring thousands of trained nurses from the Philippines to the U.S.

This legislation was the most sweeping reform made to the profession of nursing, and Filipino emigrants were quickly filling nursing positions around the country. By 1966 there were 325 Filipino nurses on staff in Chicago hospitals alone. Already in possession of their nursing degrees, they shared community housing in the dormitories together with the American student nurses. Their average monthly salary was $350, almost $3,300 by today's standards, and they often sent money home to assist their families.

Corazon's determination and resourcefulness never served her so well as when, on the night of July 13-14, 1966, she shimmied under a bunk bed to escape the massacre of her fellow nurses. As sole survivor, she was singly responsible for identifying Richard Speck as the intruder who broke into 2319 E. 100th Street, robbed nine nurses, and perpetrated one of history's worst mass murders.

As the State's star witness and sole survivor, Corazon Amurao helped to convict Richard Speck as the mass murderer of eight student nurses. She is regarded as a heroine in the annals of true crime. But the more I studied the crime, the more I doubted her story.

Some Thoughts on the Nurses

The nurses were all between the ages of 20 and 24. They were all attractive, vibrant young women with everything to live for. Several of them were engaged to be married; four were about to graduate nursing school. Patricia Matusek was a champion swimmer; Suzanne Farris played softball and enjoyed roller skating; Mary Ann Jordan was also active in softball and volleyball. These women displayed a competitive nature and they were in excellent physical shape. Nina Jo Schmale and Gloria Davy also showed strong leadership qualities.

These energetic women were no shrinking violets. So I found it irksome to continually read the same story of the nurses remaining passive in the face of mortal danger. These accounts portray them as meek little lambs being led to their slaughter, and this did a serious disservice to their spirited natures.

It was said that this passivity was part of their training, and that is why no one resisted or tried to escape: They were taught to remain calm to prevent a threatening situation from escalating.

This is good advice when dealing with an irate or irrational patient, maybe even with a burglar. No one challenged the intruder when he entered the house, took their money, even when he tied them up. No one wanted to provoke an angry outburst at the point of a gun, and if they did what he asked, they believed he would eventually go away. That part made sense.

But this explanation only works up to a certain point – the point of a knife. It's one thing to diffuse a hostile situation by remaining calm, but once a knife is being swung at you with deadly force, self-preservation automatically takes over. The fight-or-flight response doesn't care what was taught in training class. The story that the women did not scream or fight back against an intruder who was outnumbered nine to one begs for deeper examination. One could argue that several of them were tied up, but even that statement pales under closer scrutiny.

NOTES
PART I: THE CRIME

Introduction: "The Broken-Hearted"

1 "Eight Student Nurses Slain," *Chicago Tribune*, July 14, 1966.

This is not the exact article that I read that morning. A copy from the local newspaper could not be located, but this article contains the same information.

Chapter One: "The Long, Hot Summer"

2 John Gavin, "Police Tell How Riot Started on West Side," *Chicago Tribune,* July 16, 1966.

Chapter Two: "Nowhere Man"

3 Jack Altman and Marvin Ziporyn, *Born to Raise Hell: The Untold Story of Richard Speck,* (New York: Grove Press, Inc., 1967), 39.

4 Tom O'Neill with Dan Piepenbring, *Chaos: Charles Manson, the CIA, and the Secret History of the Sixties,* (New York: Little, Brown and Company, 2019).

5 This application for employment is contained in Speck's file with the U.S. Coast Guard, obtained through FOIA request, file reference 5720/377548 2022-CGFO-00688.

6 Altman and Ziporyn, *Born to Raise Hell,* 14.

7 Altman and Ziporyn, 197.

Chapter Three: "Day of Infamy"

8 "Nurse's Story of Death Night: Tells Jurors of Mass Murder," *Chicago Tribune,* April 6, 1967.

All quotes from the trial testimony of Corazon Amurao were published as excerpts in the cited edition of the *Chicago Tribune.*

9 "Summer of Slaughter," *Murder Casebook: Investigation Into the Ultimate Crime,* no. 81 (1991): 2887.

10 Dennis L. Breo and William J. Martin, *The Crime of the Century: Richard Speck and the Murders That Shocked the Nation,* (New York: Skyhorse Publishing, 2016), 10.

Chapter Six: "Illogical Logistics"

11 Byron Carlile and Jack Wallenda, "Supplementary Report," Area 2 Homicide, Chicago Police Department, July 14, 1966. This comprehensive report of the crime scene is often referenced in this section and is referred to as "the July 14th police report".

12 Breo and Martin, *Crime of the Century*, 68.

13 "Nurse's Story of Death Night," *Chicago Tribune*, April 6, 1967.

14 "Atienza's Lawsuit," *Central New Jersey Home News*, (New Brunswick, New Jersey), May 20, 1970.

Chapter Eight: "The Nurses"

15 "Crime of Century Three Years Old," *Daily Calumet,* Chicago, Illinois, July 12, 1969.

PART TWO

THE EVIDENCE

CHAPTER NINE

DRAGNET

The Morning After

As law enforcement began arriving on scene the hospital van driver, unaware of the horror that had occurred the night before, pulled up to drive the student nurses to their 7:00 AM shift. But there were no passengers on this miserable day. The familiar comfort of normal everyday routine quickly gave way to shock and chaos.

On duty were lead homicide detectives Byron Carlile and Jack G. Wallenda. Both were tasked with tracking down the monstrous murderer and protecting Corazon Amurao from the ravenous media for the next ten months.

With police now on the scene, a shaken Corazon was quickly whisked into unit 2315, where she was comforted by Laura Bisone, the resident housemother, and Josephine Chan, her nursing supervisor, who also acted as Tagalog interpreter. In the presence of Officer Kelley and the detectives Corazon then gave a statement of the harrowing events of the night before, which is referred to here as her "initial statement," or her "police statement". This statement is included in Appendix A.

Although suffering from shock, she held up well under questioning, and spoke with police for nearly two hours, until 8:30 AM. Police then escorted her to South Chicago Community Hospital, where she was examined by physicians and placed under sedation.

The media, reveling in the scoop of the murders, released reports that she was too hysterical to be questioned, that she had to be heavily sedated, that she suffered a nervous breakdown, that she was rushed to the hospital. None of these were accurate. Corazon proved durable and resilient beyond any expectations. She quickly gained the admiration of law enforcement. Wallenda, a World War II veteran, had served with the U.S. Army tank division in the Philippines, and immediately took a protective attitude toward the petite Filipina survivor.

Doctors at South Chicago Community Hospital examined Corazon for injuries. She had lain in very uncomfortable positions underneath a bed for over three hours with her forehead squeezed against the floor or a wall in an attempt to hide from the killer. She had writhed and struggled to break free, managing to do so only after the massacre was over. She described her ligatures as being very tight. In spite of this prolonged ordeal, doctors found no injuries on her body. This was another red flag.

Fearful of subjecting Corazon to more pressure, police did not show her photos of offenders until the next morning. She spent the night in the hospital, sedated and under police guard. She did not return to the townhouse.

The FBI Files

Marlin W. Johnson and John P. Quinlan, Special Agents of the Chicago office of the FBI (no. 88-10194), quickly reached out to FBI Headquarters in Washington, D.C. to request assistance in the tracking and apprehension of the killer. Homicide Commander Frank Flannagan passed information to the local FBI agents, who then relayed the information to FBI headquarters.

I received many FBI files in response to my FOIA Request No. 1512360-000 covering the period from July 1966 until January 1967. To my amazement, the files contained one startling item after another, none of which ever turned up in any other reports. And some of those items were bombshells.

<u>Bombshell #1</u>

A teletype from Chicago Special Agent Quinlan to Director J. Edgar Hoover, dated July 14, 1966, made the following observations about sole surviving witness Corazon Amurao:

"... surviving victim engaged unsub approximately thirty minutes in conversation but she lacks sufficient fluency with English, being native of the Philippine Islands, to be of any genuine assistance regarding identity of unsub."[1]

That Corazon engaged in a 30-minute conversation with the intruder is mind-boggling. No such conversation was ever mentioned in her police statement or trial testimony.

Intrigued by the implications of this 30-minute conversation, I searched for confirmation in the FBI files, and found it in a memo dated July 21st. I have entered the redacted names in brackets, as I know that Flannagan was the commander and Corazon Amurao was the witness.

"TITLE: Richard Franklin Speck

CHARACTER: Unlawful Flight to Avoid Prosecution – Murder

> .... On July 15, 1966, Commander [Frank Flannagan] advised that ... the surviving victim, [Corazon Amurao], a transfer student nurse from the Philippine Islands, made a positive identification of Richard Franklin Speck, FBI Number 967 004 D, as the person with whom she talked for approximately 30 minutes at approximately 12:30 am

on July 14, 1966, at the residence of the deceased nurses, and the person she observed take the other victims from their rooms after binding them."[2]

Here was my confirmation. Two separate FBI memos reported that Corazon engaged in conversation with Richard Speck at 12:30 AM for approximately 30 minutes. This revelation knocks the timeline, and the official story, way off kilter, not to mention, Corazon's credibility.

The timeline tells us that the killer finished tying everyone up before 12:30 AM. He then brought Pam Wilkening into the east bedroom and stabbed her, and then ambushed and killed Suzanne Farris and Mary Ann Jordan after they reached the second floor landing at 12:30. Obviously 12:30 AM was not the most auspicious time for Corazon and the killer to engage in a 30-minute chat.

If the conversation took place, then the timeline collapses, as well as the rest of the story. If the conversation didn't take place, then why did Flannagan inform the FBI that it did? The mysterious 30-minute conversation never made it into the official story.

It's also noteworthy, if not xenophobic, how little confidence Flannagan placed in Corazon's language skills or her ability "to be of any genuine assistance regarding identity of unsub." A Tagalog interpreter had sat in on her sessions with detectives to prevent any language difficulties. However, her inability to be of genuine assistance would change in a New York minute.

Bombshell #2

Another piece of information threw another wrench into the works. Continuing on in the same July 21st memo:

"... survivor states that unsub knocked on second floor bedroom door of two victims at approximately midnight instant, demanded money and advised he was en route to New Orleans."[3]

Corazon maintained throughout that the intruder came knocking at 11:00 PM. But here it was "approximately midnight," which again distorts the timeline. The report called to mind one of my favorite songs of the Sixties, "Does Anybody Really Know What Time It Is?" Of course, the name of the band was none other than Chicago.

Errors in an investigation happen, but here the contradictions go off the rails. The above memo continues: "... subject took total of eight victims to one room, removed clothing, ravished and then murdered victims."

No one except Gloria Davy was naked, and none of the nurses were "ravished," an odd choice of words to imply a brutal sexual assault.

The FBI files proved useful yet unsettling. Here were primary sources that clashed with each other, the stuff of massive headaches for even a seasoned investigator, which I certainly was not. What do I believe – the police reports with their multiple errors, the inconsistent official story, or the FBI files that contradict both sources?

Other newspapers had even reported that the killer, wearing a bloody t-shirt, was captured trying to board a Delta Airlines flight bound for New Orleans, and this was reported just hours after the murders were discovered. Someone was having too much sick fun with the story, and that included the police. Soon after the murders one of the first responders was interviewed on WIND-Radio Chicago and described how he found the bodies of seven nurses, all of whom were nude and had been molested.[4]

The contradictions and inconsistencies in this case signaled significant cracks in the veneer of the official story. They called to mind two mottos from a favorite TV show of mine, *The X Files*. *Trust No One*. By now I didn't feel very trusting of any official statements. But it was the other motto that kept me going: *The Truth Is Out There*. I decided to keep digging.

Overnight Baggage

It was still early morning when patrolmen began canvassing the area of Jeffery Manor. They were on the lookout for a tall slender man with dark hair and a crew cut who was headed for New Orleans.

"Survivor describes unsub as WMA (white male American) age twenty-five, six feet, one hundred seventy-five pounds, short dark hair," announced the July 14th teletype from Chicago FBI to FBI headquarters. The age, height, and weight were close to those of Richard Speck, but not the hair. Speck wore his sandy blond hair in a longish, slicked-back style.

And that was all they had to go on. Corazon Amurao did not give a description of the killer's face; a composite sketch would not issue until the next morning. Detective Wallenda's July 14th report summarized the man they were looking for as:

"One M/W (male/white), 25-26 yrs., 6'0" tall, slender build, wearing a black suit coat, black pants, black shoes. Had been drinking. Carried a small black revolver and knife.

Offender's clothing possibly badly blood stained."

A patrolman stopped at the Manor Shell gas station at 9954 S. Torrence Avenue, six blocks east of the townhouse, and asked the mechanic on duty, Dennis Ryan, if he had seen anyone of that description. Ryan remembered that a tall man had shown up early the previous morning of the 13th to pick up two bags he had left there the night before.

Ryan recalled that the man had complained about missing out on a freighter bound for New Orleans. The officer, suspecting that the man was a seaman looking for work, then headed up the street to the National Maritime Union at 2335 East 100th Street, just down the block from the nurses' townhouse at 2319.

There the officer met clerk Sam Barger, who recalled that a man had been there the previous day complaining about losing out on a shipping assignment with a Great Lakes freighter. The freighter was bound for New Orleans.

Barger had found the man sitting outside the building waiting for the NMU to open so that he could apply for another assignment. The two men briefly conversed. Barger suggested that the man book a room at the Shipyard Inn, a tavern and rooming house about a mile and a half east at 10063 S. Avenue N until another assignment became available.

The officer then questioned NMU Supervisor William O'Neill to ask if he had recently dealt with a man who wanted to ship out to New Orleans. In an amazing turn of events, O'Neill looked in his wastebasket and retrieved an application that had been filled out and discarded.

It listed the applicant as one Richard Franklin Speck, 24 years old, 6 feet one inch tall, 160 pounds. He had filled out the application on July 13th, some fifteen hours before the mass murder. The application listed his residence as 3966 N. Avondale, in the Old Irving Park section of north Chicago. This was the address of Martha and Gene Thornton's apartment, where Speck had spent the previous week.

The police were discovering vital information at record speed. By 11:00 AM on Thursday, July 14th, they had a promising name and an address for their suspect. Richard Speck shot quickly to the top of their "Persons of Interest" list - probably the one and only time he ever ranked highly for anything.

At that same time, in room 7 of the Shipyard Inn, Richard Franklin Speck was just rousing himself from a dense, drug-induced slumber. America was about to be introduced to one of its first, and most despised, mass murderers.

Ebbing Tide

Richard Speck recalled that he had awakened at 11:00 AM in a fog. "The next thing I know I was back in my own room and it was morning. I had a gun and I don't know where I got it. I just sat there wondering where the hell I got that gun."[5]

Things were out of sorts. He had blood on one hand, but there was no injury. The other hand held a gun. And he awoke wearing a black shirt and black pants, as if he had passed out flat on his back, fully clothed.

Confused and groggy, he cleaned up and went about his usual business of the day: binge drinking and bar hopping. He went downstairs to the Shipyard Inn bar for a few beers and a game of pool.

Within minutes a patrolman canvassing the bars on the southeast side stopped by the Shipyard Inn to ask the bartender, Valie Blair, if he had seen a man about six feet tall with short hair. Blair replied that he hadn't seen anyone of that description. The patrolman glanced around the bar and left, while Speck, pool cue in hand, stood just a few feet away, unaware of the dragnet that was tightening around him.

News of the murders began bombarding the airwaves. Speck recounted the moment when he first heard of the murders: "In the afternoon I heard them talking about the murders on the radio. I remember saying to the guy next to me at the bar, 'I hope they catch the son of a bitch.'"[6]

Restless as usual, Speck headed north up S. Avenue N and found himself at another watering hole, the Ebb Tide Tap, where he ran into a friend from his brief shipping days on board the Clarence S. Randall – Robert "Red" Gerrald, fellow seafarer and drinking buddy.

It was now the early afternoon of Thursday the 14th. A couple of miles west, the autopsies of the eight student nurses were under way, Corazon was under watch at South Chicago Community Hospital, and police were busy at the townhouse gathering evidence. Speck and Red Gerrald wiled away the hours drinking, to the point where a wasted, wobbly Gerrald could not manage to walk the several blocks back down to the Shipyard Inn. Speck called a cab. The driver remembered that Speck appeared sober and well-groomed, while Red was drowning in his cups.

Back at the Shipyard, Speck let Gerrald clean up and rest in his room for an hour or so. Gerrald later told police that Speck's bed had been slept in, and that there was no blood anywhere in the room - on the bedding, towels, sheets, or Speck's clothing.

The Ruse

Speck's discarded job application listed Martha Thornton as next of kin and included her address and phone number. The police decided to trick Speck into coming down to the National Maritime Union for a non-existent job. When he showed up a detective would be on site to take him in for questioning. A phone call was made to the Shipyard Inn. Speck, still there with Gerrald, took the call. He was offered a job but had to show up by close of business at 4:30 PM to claim it.

In an odd sequence of events, Speck packed his suitcase and called for a cab at 3:25 PM to pick him up at the Shipyard Inn. But Gerrald asked to be driven to his rooming house first, which was farther uptown at 95th and Ewing. After Gerrald was dropped off, Speck mysteriously told the driver to bring him to a low-income housing project in Old Town.

Speck appeared to be on the run, having left behind a room that had been prepaid for a whole week. He later explained that he noticed policemen patrolling the area and was fearful of being picked up on his warrant from Texas.

He was dropped off at the Cabrini-Green housing project, a predominantly African-American neighborhood, where he was quickly noticed. Toting his tan suitcase and black-and-red plaid zipper bag, he ambled over to the Raleigh Hotel at 648 N. Dearborn, where he checked in at 4:45 PM, reportedly under an assumed name, David Stayton.

The Raleigh was one more pit stop along Speck's tortuous spiral downward. Built in 1882, it was one of Chicago's first luxury apartment buildings, an elegant high rise of eight floors, a considerable height in those days. But by the 1960s, years of decline and neglect had relegated the once admired structure to a transient flophouse. Speck was assigned room 806 on the top floor. There was nowhere to go but down.

Pink Twistin' the Night Away

The Raleigh Hotel manager, Otha Hullinger Roemer, was impressed by her new guest's politeness and soft-spoken manner. He was talkative and friendly, and insisted on bringing her a coffee whenever he went out to get one for himself. But later that same night, he would incur her wrath.

The Raleigh Hotel was close to N. Clark Street, an area rife with Speck's preferred recreational pursuits. Seedy, run-down bars hid behind bright, colorful names, like the Pink Twist Inn, Club Erin, the Shamrock, and Queen's Paradise, and prostitutes were in no short supply.

Speck drank away several hours at the Pink Twist, where he met up with a woman who agreed to entertain him in his room at the Raleigh. During the wee hours, after their interlude, the young woman anxiously approached the front desk, manned by the night clerk, Algy Lemhart.

Once again, Speck's encounter with a prostitute had gone sideways, once again because of a gun. She told Lemhart that her client seemed like a nice guy, but he had a gun in the room. When Otha Hullinger took over the morning shift she called the police to report it. Angry that her new guest had broken the house rules by entertaining a prostitute, she read the riot act to Speck, who feebly apologized and promised not to do it again.

Another strange turn of events occurred when the police finally arrived. Officers Robert Ratledge and Clarence Shuey asked the startled hotel guest for his identification and demanded that he hand over the gun. Although he had allegedly registered under the name

David Stayton, he identified himself as Richard Speck, and engaged the officers in friendly banter. He told them he was going to spend the week at the Raleigh.

Incredibly, word had not yet spread to the officers about the frantic manhunt for Richard Franklin Speck. Ratledge improperly seized the gun and the officers left the hotel. They both agreed that the guy with the gun seemed harmless.

The case of the disappearing gun is another one of the mounting curiosities in this story. Ratledge seized the gun, but recorded in his report that the report of the gun was "unfounded." There was no gun.

However, a gun finally did materialize. Ratledge hadn't felt like filling out the extra paperwork to report a handgun seizure, so he didn't. He didn't have a warrant to seize it in the first place. The unfounded gun was later turned in. Tainted by the illegal seizure, the gun could not be admitted into evidence. Where it eventually ended up is anyone's guess.

This was the account of Richard Speck's intended week-long stay at the Raleigh, which lasted all of one night. His meanderings through Old Town were fast approaching the end of the line.

Lost in Translation

Corazon Amurao had been kept overnight under observation at South Chicago Community Hospital. Now she was ready to view mug shots of prospective persons of interest. It was 9:30 AM on Friday July 15th, just twenty-four hours after her slain housemates were pronounced dead. Police feared that Corazon was still in too fragile a state of mind to view photos of possible suspects, but again she came through remarkably well.

Thanks to the discarded application in the National Maritime Union wastebasket, word was already out that the police were looking for an unemployed deck hand. They quickly compiled photos of men who had registered for employment with the Coast Guard. Deputy Chief of Detectives Michael Spiotto presented Corazon with over 100 photographs.

Mixed into the batch was Richard Speck's Coast Guard photo from the application he had placed on file back in April. Corazon selected this photo as being "similar" in appearance to the killer. This ID photo is shown on the next page.

She then met with the police sketch artist, Otis Rathel. A Tagalog interpreter, Myrna Foronda, sat in on the session to bridge any language difficulties. The three spent almost an hour discussing the killer's facial features, but what resulted was a very plain nondescript composite sketch. This became one of the more hotly contested aspects of the case. The sketch as it appeared in the Chicago PD Bulletin is shown in the following pages.

Speck had sandy blond hair combed back and deep, pitted acne marks on his face. These distinctive features, unmistakable in all of his photos, were missing in the composite sketch. The image is that of a dark-haired male with a crew cut, normal skin, and dark eyes. The sketch captured the shape of Speck's long face but little else. Corazon fared better regarding his physique. She described a man about six feet tall, 175 pounds, and 25 years old; Speck was six feet one, weighed 160, and was 24.

In the end Otis Rathel fell on his sword and took the blame for not asking Corazon for more specifics on the facial features. Corazon insisted that she told Rathel about the longish hair and the acne scars but he failed to draw them. She was certain that she never described Speck as having a crew cut, although the sketch clearly shows crew-cut hair.

Eyewitness identification is an important piece of direct evidence, but often people have trouble remembering and describing faces. This is especially true in cross-racial identification:

"A cross-racial ID occurs when an eyewitness of one race is asked to identify a particular individual of another race. The last half-century's empirical study of cross-racial IDs has shown that eyewitnesses have difficulty identifying members of another race, though the degree to which this difficulty affects the accuracy of an eyewitness ID is not certain. Likewise, it is unclear whether all races are affected."[7]

Corazon had been in the States for only ten weeks, a very different racial environment than her native Philippines.

Having an interpreter present had not made the identification process any easier. The contradictory results of the composite sketch added weight to Commander Flannagan's doubt in Corazon's ability to identify the unsub. But within nine months she would become a formidable witness for the prosecution, and her testimony was regarded as good as gospel.

In connection with the composite sketch, it is worth noting that Corazon did not give a facial description of Speck until she viewed his Coast Guard photo ID, which she considered "similar" to the killer. The photo was not shown to sketch artist Otis Rathel.

Coast Guard Photo of Richard Speck, April 1966

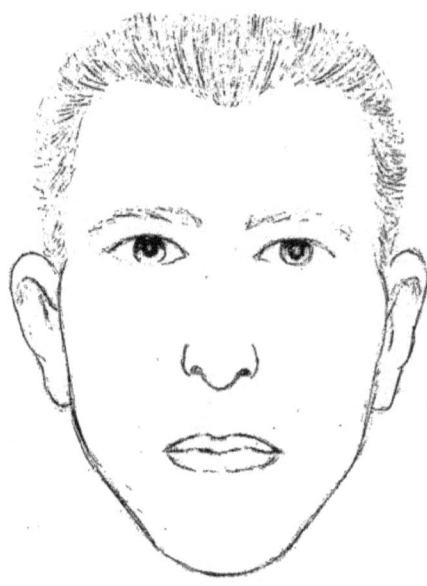

Stakeout

The police's first ruse to lure Speck to the National Maritime Union had failed, but they were back at the NMU on Friday morning to see whether their suspect would turn up. Another team of three detectives headed north to the address of Gene and Martha Speck Thornton in hopes that Speck might be found there.

The stakeout at the Thorntons proved fruitful. Even though Speck never showed up, they gathered vital information about his appearance, his clothing, and his likely whereabouts. Gene Thornton told that he had lent some t-shirts and a black corduroy lined jacket to Speck just days earlier – all items that connected him to the murders. I have read that he also loaned Speck either a pair of black shoes or a pair of brown work boots, but could not confirm this claim.

Martha told police that Speck wore BVD and Fruit of the Loom t-shirts, men's size 38-40 Medium. The t-shirts wove a whole new texture into the official narrative and will be covered in the chapter on Evidence.

In an odd exchange, she also told police that Speck always combed his longish hair toward the back of his head in a "duck's tail" style; he hated crew cuts and never wore his hair that short. "He does now," retorted one of the detectives.[8]

There's a reason that I've harped on the inaccurate description of Speck and the kerfuffle over the crew cut. The evidence is discussed in a later chapter, but one crucial item now requires review.

The comprehensive July 14th police report described the body of Valentina Pasion as follows:

"Found clutched between the thumb and forefinger of the left hand of Valentina Pasion was found a single strand of short black hair. This was called to the attention of the Lab Techs, and they took possession of it."

Also found underneath Valentina Pasion's fingernails were minute particles of human skin – Valentina had scratched her killer and pulled a short black hair from his head. Therefore, her killer must have had black hair that he wore in a short hair cut, like a crew cut. He must have left the crime scene with a visible scratch or injury to his head or face. And Valentina could not have done this if her hands were tied together. But at trial, Corazon stated the following:

"CORAZON: The next time I saw him Speck was dragging Miss Pasion going out of the big bedroom.

STATE: Would you describe the way in which he dragged Miss Pasion out of the south bedroom?

CORAZON: Speck hold (sic) Miss Pasion's arm on the side and then he dragged Miss Pasion out of the big bedroom.

STATE: Did he untie her?

CORAZON: He did not untie Miss Pasion."

Either he untied her right before killing her, which makes no sense, or she wasn't tied up to begin with. The red flag collection was growing by leaps and bounds.

The Boulevard of Forgotten Men

After the debacle with the prostitute and the police Speck wanted to make amends with Otha Hullinger. He had booked the room for a week in advance and it wouldn't help to be on the outs with the manager. He brought her a coffee and a newspaper, and they sat in the hotel lobby watching the latest news of the murders on television.

He showed her the afternoon edition of the *Chicago American*, which featured a description of the killer and the composite sketch of a man with short dark hair and a long face. Together they commiserated on how awful those nurse murders were.

Tension was escalating in the streets outside the Raleigh Hotel. After a series of violent clashes with rioters, police were out patrolling the area with rifles. The local El line had been shut down and streets were closed off to keep innocent bystanders out of the line of fire. At the same time, detectives were canvassing the area in search of the monster who had killed eight student nurses. Speck, growing more and more nervous at the sight of police, kept on the move.

Restless as usual, he drifted over to the Ebb Tide Inn, where he ran into two men drinking on a street corner. One of them was Claude Lunsford, a haggard hobo with a penchant for drinking and hopping freight cars to get from place to place.

Lunsford, forty-nine going on eighty, wore the distressed look of the classic wandering hobo. Glaring from behind his straggly hair and rough, ruddy face, was his one good eye. He had lost the other in a boiler room accident, which added to his unsettling appearance. It was strangely appropriate that some local newspapers mistakenly referred to him as "Claude Munster."

When in town Lunsford frequented the sleazy bars of Skid Row, financing his drinking with occasional stints as a day laborer. He had been staying at a fleabag called the Starr Hotel since July 8th under the alias B. Brian.

Speck was impressed with his new drinking pal. The two idled at the Ebb Tide, drinking away the afternoon and their meager savings. By day's end, though, Speck's boastful and boorish behavior began to get on Lunsford's nerves.

Lunsford found Speck's appearance equally unsettling. When not talking trash, he would often lapse into silence and stare blankly into space, eyes glazed over and mouth half open. Lunsford nicknamed his new companion "Fish Mouth."

Ground Zero

The odd couple swirled their way down to the dregs of Skid Row, heading west toward the Starr Hotel at 617 W. Madison. This decrepit neighborhood was memorialized by poet Carl Sandburg as the "Boulevard of Forgotten Men."[9] It was so feared an area that even census-takers avoided it. The Starr was just blocks away from another location - the intersection of Madison and State Streets, the starting point of Chicago's numbered grid structure, known as "point zero."[10]

The layout of Chicago is based on a pattern of blocks of numbers beginning at 400. This numbered grid system, invented in 1909, was designed to facilitate navigating Chicago's irregular network of streets and neighborhoods.

Speck's erratic wanderings would soon pass from point zero to ground zero. Although he had booked a whole week at the Raleigh, he accepted Lunsford's offer to crash at the Starr. In another inscrutable move, he trudged back to the Raleigh, gathered some clothes and toiletries, and departed, leaving his tan suitcase and other items behind. He told Otha Hullinger that he was taking his clothes to a laundromat.

Police arrived moments later, just missing him. Hullinger confirmed that the man in the Coast Guard photo that police showed her had just left. Speck never returned to the Raleigh Hotel.

Not far from point zero the Starr Hotel stood as a monument to decrepitude. Ninety cents a night got you a dank five by seven cubicle, equipped with a mangy mattress, a stool, and a small footlocker. Sheets of rough unfinished plywood divided the individual cubicles. In place of a ceiling, sections of tacked-down chicken wire bridged the plywood partitions to provide ventilation, allowing fetid odors to spread freely among the cubicles.

Speck forsook the relative comfort of the Shipyard Inn and the Raleigh and stayed the night. On the morning of the 16th Claude Lunsford arose at sunrise to report to a day job. He invited Fish Mouth to join him, but his lethargic friend complained of feeling sick, and spent the day lounging in his cubicle.

Police were now targeting bars on the southeast side, and they knew that Speck was staying at the Shipyard Inn. On Friday afternoon, police fingerprint technician Bill Scanlon rummaged through Room 7 looking for evidence. He hit pay dirt. On the nightstand he found an empty beer can bearing latent fingerprints. He dusted the can, lifted the prints, and hurried back down to the police lab. If the prints belonged to Richard Speck, the police were in business.[11]

Due to an issue with the chain of custody police were unable to use the fingerprints on file with the local Coast Guard. The FBI had to dispatch a set of Speck's prints by jet from Washington, D.C. There was nothing Chicago PD could do but wait for the official prints, but in the meantime they had the prints from the beer can to work with.

The official prints dispatched by jet finally arrived at police headquarters at 7:30 that evening; an airline strike had caused travel delays. Fingerprint expert Lieutenant Emil Giese and others worked through the night comparing sets of fingerprints. By 5:30 AM on Saturday the 16th, the police rejoiced. Three fingerprints matching

Speck's turned up on a door in the nurse's townhouse – the door to the south bedroom where the night of horror began. The door was removed by senior fingerprint analyst Burton Buhrke and taken into evidence.

Although Speck's room at the Shipyard Inn was not a crime scene, the prints taken from the beer can strangely factor into one of the State's most powerful, yet suspicious, pieces of evidence.

Presumed Guilty

The net was now tightening around the shiftless seaman. On the afternoon of Saturday the 16th police issued a local and national stop order for one Richard Benjamin Speck, a.k.a. Richard Franklin Speck. The physical description and the composite sketch were circulated to all districts and areas, and police radio put out an "all call wanted," or BOLO (Be On The Lookout) message:

"Richard Franklin Speck, age 25 yrs., DOB 12/6/1941. 6'1" tall, 160 lbs., brown blond hair slightly longer than crew cut. Blue eyes...."[12]

The Stop Order finally got the description of Speck right - "brown blond hair slightly longer than crew cut." In spite of their findings, police never sought a man with short black hair.

Police Chief O.W. Wilson appeared on television armed with the composite sketch and Speck's Coast Guard photograph. Police now know the identity of the killer of eight student nurses, he solemnly declared, and his name is Richard Speck. Wilson went one step further and revealed that detectives had found over 30 fingerprints in the townhouse that matched Speck's.[13]

His first statement was improper, but the second was flat wrong. Thirty-two, or thirty-three as some references have it, was the total number of fingerprints found in the townhouse, of which only three partial smudged prints were attributed to Speck.

Chief O.W. Wilson's behavior matched the promise of his initials. His premature judgment of guilt tweaked the State's Attorney's office; the Chief had just violated Speck's constitutional rights on live television for all to see. State's Attorney Ward quickly followed up the gaffe with a radio interview to reassure the public that "...we will conduct ourselves properly, in accordance with the ethics and the requirements of the law. There will be an ethical observance of the requirements of the law."[14]

That horse had already left the barn, but no one was especially bothered by Wilson's premature verdict – all they knew was that the police had their man. Life in the beleaguered city could begin to recover some shred of normalcy.

Wilson's verdict would be echoed in another mass murder that followed just three years later, when President Richard M. Nixon announced in the news media that Charles Manson, on trial for the Sharon Tate mass murders, was guilty. Wilson's bold announcement set a worrisome precedent, but the murders were so heinous that few gave it a second thought.

Hooked

Lunsford returned to the Starr from his day job at 6:30 PM on Saturday the 16th. He found an incoherent, mumbling Speck stretched out on the mattress in his cubicle. Rather than summon for help, he beat a hasty retreat to another flophouse. A few hours later he placed a call to the police to inform them that Richard Speck, the man wanted for the murder of eight student nurses, was lying in Room 584 at the Starr Hotel, bleeding to death. Speck had apparently cut his right wrist and his left elbow in a suicide attempt.

It is not known why Lunsford waited hours to make the call, especially if he thought Speck was bleeding to death, but by then he must have seen the news bulletins displaying Speck's photo and description. He surely noted the $10,000 reward offered by South Chicago Community Hospital to anyone with information leading to the perpetrator's capture.

Lunsford's call put to the test a new two-million-dollar communications system that Chief O.W. Wilson had proudly had installed on his watch. All incoming distress calls would be entered onto a card by the dispatcher, who would then relay the request to officers on patrol. Officers were obliged to respond to each and every call with the results entered onto the dispatch card, thus creating a physical record for every incident.

But this time the expensive new system didn't work. No one showed up at the Starr to rescue the city's most wanted man. In the meantime, Fish Mouth raised the concern of other occupants at the Starr, who noticed a bleeding man babbling incoherently in his cubicle. Someone finally told the desk clerk to call the police.

This time the new system worked - patrolmen Burns and Krause arrived on scene and carted the injured man off to Cook County Hospital. But it was too late for Claude Lunsford. The faulty two-million-dollar communications system cost him his shot at the $10,000 reward.

It was just after midnight on Sunday, July 17th. Gloria Davy had been laid to rest the previous morning. The remaining five American nurses would be buried the following day, and the coffins of Merlita Gargullo and Valentina Pasion flown back to the Philippines. Those messy hours in a putrid cubicle at the Starr would be Richard Speck's last as a free man. Fish Mouth was finally hooked.

Bombshell #3

On Saturday the 16th, Special Agent Quinlan filed a complaint with Judge Julius J. Hoffman for the issuance of an interstate non-bondable arrest warrant for the apprehension of one Richard Franklin Speck. The teletype read: "At ten A.M. this date subject in Chicago wearing short-sleeved gray-blue, dirty shirt and similar pants." The Stop Order that issued that same day also described Speck as wearing a grey-blue shirt and slacks outfit.

How did the local FBI know what Speck was wearing that morning? This suggests that someone, possibly Lunsford, had recognized Speck and contacted police. Why he wasn't picked up until fourteen hours later, and only after the emergency call from the desk clerk, remains a mystery. It was another conundrum, brought to us courtesy of the FBI files.

All Stitched Up

Police quickly transported the delirious man to the emergency ward of Cook County Hospital. He was bleeding from his right wrist and left elbow. Police theorized that he had cut his right wrist with a razor blade and slashed his left elbow with a jagged piece of glass. In an ironic mix-up, the clerk gave police the name B. Brian, his drinking buddy Lunsford's alias. But one of Speck's infamous tattoos would soon straighten things out.

The doctors in attendance at the hospital described both wounds as superficial. In response to the grisly rumors of a suicidal bloodbath Detective Jack Wallenda grumbled "there wasn't enough bleeding for a blood test."[15] When admitted to the hospital he was in serious condition, but not due to the bleeding or the arm injuries; doctors discovered that he was also suffering from pericarditis, an inflammation of the heart lining marked by fatigue, shortness of breath, pain, and fever.

The wound to the left elbow was surgically repaired with four stitches by Dr. William Norcross, chief surgeon at the hospital. The injury to the right wrist was a straight-across slice running perpendicular to the length of his arm just inches from the palm of his hand. Neither wound was life-threatening.

Doctors in attendance noticed the two-and-a-half inch scab on his chest. Police attributed this to the struggle with Valentina Pasion, whose fingernails contained minute particles of flesh. They did not note any other injuries on his body, including his hands, arms, neck, or face.

Speck was then examined by hospital resident Dr. Leroy Smith, who noticed the "Born To Raise Hell" tattoo on the inside of his left arm. He recalled the newspaper reports that the number one suspect in the nurse murders, Richard Speck, bore this tattoo. Smith called the police. At 1:50 AM on Sunday, July 17th, Suspect Number One was photographed, fingerprinted, and placed under arrest for the mass murder of eight student nurses.

Bridewell and Gloom

Following surgery, Richard Speck was brought to Room 324 of Cermak Memorial Hospital, also called "the Bridewell hospital," a correctional facility hospital that provided medical and psychiatric care for inmates from both the Cook County and the Bridewell jails. While the larger Cook County jail served the entire county, the Bridewell, as it was called, housed inmates who had committed crimes in Chicago.

Located at 2800 S. California Street, the Bridewell was built in 1952 to house 4500 inmates, but the numbers quickly increased in direct proportion to the exploding crime rate in the city. Mental health disorders, considered contributing factors to the spread of crime, were also on the rise.

To address both ends of the problem the state established Cermak Memorial Hospital right next door to the Bridewell. It was the first penal hospital to be accredited by the Joint Commission on Accreditation of Hospitals and the only penal hospital licensed by the board of its respective state.[17]

Speck's presence thrust Cermak Memorial into the national spotlight, which now housed and treated a despised mass murderer. Dr. William Norcross, director of surgery who had operated on Speck's left elbow, ran interference between his notorious patient and law enforcement until Speck was well enough to return to his jail cell.

July 18th is the date of the Festival of Saint Camillus, the patron saint of nurses and hospitals. But nothing was festive about this date in 1966. The bodies of Nina Jo Schmale, Suzanne Farris, Mary Ann Jordan, Patricia Ann Matusek, and Pamela Lee Wilkening were laid to rest in their respective hometowns. Gloria Jean Davy had already been buried on Saturday. The murders took place on the anniversary of Saint Camillus' death and many of the nurses were laid to rest on his feast day. This year the revered saint's holy days were touched by the hand of evil.

Shown Up

Speck's arraignment in felony court was scheduled for Tuesday, July 19th at 2:30 PM, but Norcross objected, claiming that his patient was still too weak to appear in court. But even before the arraignment, Norcross was faced with another more urgent dilemma – a visit to Speck's hospital room from none other than the surviving witness, Corazon Amurao.

Law enforcement felt that the only way to nail down the identification of Richard Speck was for Corazon to view him face to face. This procedure is known as a "show up," where an unsuspecting suspect is shown to a witness, either in a car or at a distance, for purposes of identification.[18] It is different from a typical line-up, where five or six subjects appear before an anonymous witness who is safely concealed behind a one-way mirror.

In a show up the police will surreptitiously drive past a suspect without his knowledge. But Corazon and the accused murderer would now come face to face, less than a week after the murders. It was a risky proposition, and incredibly, Corazon was not forewarned. The police were thrusting the lamb into the lion's den.

At 1:30 PM on July 19th Corazon, dressed in a nurse's uniform, gingerly entered Speck's room, flanked by Chief of Detectives Michael Spiotto, Assistant State's Attorney Martin, and Dr. William Norcross. She quietly viewed Speck for an anxious moment, careful not to draw attention to herself. Upon leaving the room, she confirmed that Speck was indeed the man who had robbed and murdered her colleagues. Speck appeared oblivious, showing no reaction to the visit by the one nurse whom he had let get away.

In my opinion, the show up served a purpose other than to simply identify Speck. Corazon Amurao's initial description of the killer had left open too much room for doubt. This face-to-face viewing would help to fix his image firmly in her mind.

Up to that point Speck, dull and detached from the buzz around him, had languished in a hospital bed, speaking only to doctors and nurses. During his three days in the hospital he had been arrested, publicly declared guilty of the murders, and positively identified in a face-to-face show up.

Fearful of violating the new Miranda rule established by *Miranda v. Arizona 384 U.S. 436 (1966),* Police Chief Wilson gave explicit instructions that no one interrogate Richard Speck. Under the Miranda ruling an individual placed under arrest is entitled to remain silent and not incriminate himself. The individual is also entitled to an attorney. Wilson did not want his police force to risk committing a technicality that might allow Speck to go free. It is ironic that he showed such concern for the Miranda ruling when he had just proclaimed Speck's guilt on television, violating another legal tenet, that all are innocent unless proven guilty.

The circumstances of Speck's arrest are unclear. He remained under arrest in the hospital for three days without benefit or appointment of counsel, so he either waived his right to counsel, or he just didn't bother to ask for an attorney. That omission was remedied by Judge Daniel J. Ryan of the Felony Court, who proceeded with Speck's arraignment in his absence and appointed Public Defender Gerald Getty as defense counsel. Meanwhile, law enforcement assured the public that "both Speck's medical condition and his constitutional rights were being scrupulously guarded."[19]

There's Something Happening Here

On Wednesday, July 20th, police, armed with a warrant, searched room 806 at the Raleigh Hotel. Speck had left behind his tan suitcase. Neatly tucked inside was one BVD t-shirt, men's size 38-40M, slacks, shoes, the infamous black jacket, socks, and other sundries. They were seeking items stained with blood, and were successful, but only briefly.

Having completed the search, Sergeant Vic Vrdolyak and Assistant State's Attorney Joel Flaum triumphantly returned to headquarters bearing a t-shirt with blood on it. It was exciting evidence that Speck had gotten blood on himself during the murders, and it supported their t-shirt theory. But later that day Flaum, experiencing a crisis of conscience, admitted to Martin that the blood was Vrdolyak's: While trying to pry open the suitcase, Vrdolyak had cut his finger on the latch, and a few drops bled onto the t-shirts. When confronted by Martin later, Vrdolyak admitted the same, and the shirt was discarded.[20] Flaum's conscience prevented one case of evidence tampering, but other opportunities would present themselves.

The search was not a total loss. Vrdolyak had pulled three editions of a newspaper from underneath the mattress, with their headlines announcing Speck's guilt. Police quickly ascribed the newspapers to Speck's consciousness of guilt. But during his one-day stay at the Raleigh, Speck had shown the same newspaper to Otha Hullinger and they had talked about the murders. The front page featured the composite sketch of the killer, but she didn't make the connection. If Speck was indeed the culprit, he was brazenly flirting with danger.

It didn't make sense for him to purchase copies of three different newspapers and stuff them under the mattress. He didn't know that the room would be searched, so there was no reason to hide them. He was also a poor reader, barely able to make his way through the comics section of one paper. The story of the three newspapers tucked under the mattress, thought to show consciousness of guilt, joins the growing list of oddities.

Less than one week later, on July 26th, Richard Franklin Speck was indicted for the murders of Pamela Lee Wilkening, Suzanne Farris, Mary Ann Jordan, Nina Jo Schmale, Merlita Gargullo, Valentina Pasion, Patricia Ann Matusek, and Gloria Jean Davy. In the thirteen days since the night of the murders, a blinding flurry of activity had taken place. Speck was now housed in the Bridewell jail, where he would remain until the trial, scheduled for early 1967.

Speck's 25th birthday, December 6, 1966, coincided with the creation of an iconic song. Just the day before, the Sixties rock group, Buffalo Springfield, had recorded "For What It's Worth," written by Stephen Stills. The song had prophetic overtones. What was happening here wasn't exactly clear. The story of the man with the gun over there was suspicious. Confusion and chaos were in the air, and people had to beware.

CHAPTER TEN

DOCTOR DAD

Doc and Dick

The latter half of July marked the beginning of the end for Richard Speck. He was staring down a long dark tunnel illuminated by high voltage sparks from Stateville's electric chair. The murders took place on the 14th; he was arrested on the 17th and indicted on the 26th. The wheels of justice were grinding exceedingly fast.

On the 29th Speck was introduced to a new friend, courtesy of Cook County - Dr. Marvin Ziporyn, a forensic psychiatrist who became his closest confidante and briefly, his surrogate father.

Marvin Ziporyn was born in New York City in 1923 to Russian Jewish immigrants. A graduate of Northwestern University, he obtained his medical degree from the University of Chicago Medical School. He specialized in psychiatry at Illinois State Psychiatric Institute and taught at the University of Illinois as Assistant Professor of Psychiatry.

He was also a gifted concert violinist who performed in venues around the world, and served as dean of the American Conservatory of Music. Ziporyn had the education and the reputation that Speck's booze buddies could never dream of attaining, and he quickly earned his patient's admiration and respect.

Ziporyn was hired by Cook County in 1965 for the sole purpose of assessing the mental state of prisoners – whether they were suicidal, legally sane, and fit to stand trial. He attended the prison four or five times a year to conduct diagnostic interviews, mostly for defense counsel. A strong proponent of the temporary insanity defense, he was regarded as an outlier in more conservative medico-legal circles.

Defense counsel Getty planned to plead temporary insanity for his client, and gave Ziporyn the unenviable assignment of getting inside the head of Richard Speck. From July 29, 1966, until February 13, 1967, Ziporyn visited Speck every Tuesday and Thursday at the Bridewell lockup. The doctor kept track of all conversations by jotting down extensive notes after each visit.

Their visits lasted from one to three hours, much to Speck's delight; here was someone who listened to him with compassion, free of judgment. Speck anticipated the doctor's visits with a boyish enthusiasm, presenting him with a dessert that he had set aside for the occasion. He also set aside a designated cup only to be used for Ziporyn's instant jailhouse coffee. Speck took to calling the doctor "Doc," and looked forward to his scheduled visits like a child awaits Christmas. In return, Ziporyn called his patient "Dick." In all, Ziporyn logged over one hundred hours of visits over a span of six and a half months.

Ziporyn encouraged Speck to take up painting, and supplied him with the then-popular "Paint By Number" sets. Gradually Speck began to paint on his own, creating crude elementary scenes of a house, a yard, and a deer. Such art work, however bad, would command a high price even today, just for sporting the signature of an alleged mass murderer.

This fact was not lost on the families of the nurses and Corazon Amurao, who filed a civil suit against Speck under the Illinois Wrongful Death Act. Its purpose was to foil any attempt made by Speck to profit from his paintings. The verdict awarded 1.5 million dollars to Corazon Amurao and 250,000 dollars to each of the families.[21] The money was never collected, but the judgment ensured that Speck would never profit from his paintings or the sale of his story. But someone else would – his new friend Doc.

Born to Raise Hell

Unknown to Speck, and for a time, to the prosecution team, Ziporyn had entered into a collaboration with British journalist Jack Altman to write a book about the case. Assistant State's Attorney William J. Martin, who later co-wrote his own book (a reference for this work), had many well-placed spies in high places. Martin caught wind of the project and set detectives on Ziporyn's trail to try and prove that he was planning to exploit the case by publishing a best selling book about Speck.

Martin's fears were confirmed when he obtained proof that Ziporyn had taken a flight to England to consult with Altman regarding the book. The cat was now out of the bag. Ziporyn's intentions were revealed to the public and scandal followed, causing the book's original publisher, Hawthorn Press, to drop the project.

However, it was quickly picked up by Grove Press and published in the summer of 1967 to wide acclaim. *Born to Raise Hell*, named in honor of Speck's infamous tattoo, was an instant sensation. Both co-authors received lucrative deals to publish excerpts from the book in both American and British magazines.

The White Blank Wall

As the weeks passed, Speck shared more and more of himself with Ziporyn:

"Headaches ... I get them all the time. And get dizzy at the same time. I get this haze in front of my eyes – it's like a white blank wall," he confided.[22]

Speck ran into the white blank wall whenever he tried to remember the night of the murders: "I don't know nothing about anything from 8 o'clock that night till I came to, about eleven o'clock the next day."[23]

As the relationship between the two men grew the enormity of the murders began to sink into Speck's consciousness. He would sit with Ziporyn and stare at pictures of the eight nurses.

"I would give anything to turn back the clock and bring those girls back to life," he cried at one point.[24] As the months wore on, Speck was examined by a panel of six psychiatrists. Their questioning, probing and prodding took root like a metastatic tumor. Over time, the weak-minded and impressionable Speck resigned himself to the idea that he must have committed the murders after all. "Everybody says I did it. Must be so. If they say I did it, I did it."[25]

Ziporyn theorized that Speck suffered from the famous Freudian "madonna-whore" complex, placing certain virtuous women, like his mother Margaret, on a pedestal, while condemning others less virtuous as whores, human devils in women's clothing. Speck regarded the eight nurses as whores, and therefore felt no sympathy when killing them.

It also established a flimsy, but effective, motive. Gloria Davy and Shirley Malone Speck were both pert brunettes; both wore the shoulder-length "flip" popular in the day, and they even bore some resemblance to each other. Once Speck the robber saw Gloria, he was triggered into becoming Speck the murderer. By killing Gloria, he was symbolically killing his ex-wife Shirley, and the other nurses also had to die.

The problem with this motive is that the prosecution ultimately charged Speck with eight counts of first-degree premeditated murder, cancelling out their own theory that the murders were committed on impulse. So which was it? Law enforcement had to have it both ways.

With even his own trusted confidante believing in his guilt, Speck folded like a cheap tent. Like everyone else, he assumed he must have done it. Now he had to deal with its consequences: death by electrocution. If he had really committed these atrocities, he told Ziporyn, he deserved to die. And if he really had suicidal tendencies, it seemed as though certain parties hoped he would go through with them.

Having established a rapport with the warden, Speck was allowed to have razor blades for shaving. This was a curious move considering his recent failed suicide attempt with a razor and a broken bottle. Exposed water pipes extended across the ceiling of his cell. He often joked to Ziporyn that it would be a cinch to hang himself from the pipes above his head.

A more detailed look at the circumstances behind the alleged suicide attempt are discussed in Appendix C.

An Untold Story

Marvin Ziporyn's book, *Born to Raise Hell: The Untold Story of Richard Speck,* showed a human side of Richard Speck not seen by the public. During one bitter winter day a fire broke out in a Chicago apartment building, seriously injuring a little girl. She suffered severe burns over sixty percent of her body and would not survive without blood transfusions and skin grafts from compatible donors.

Speck, who watched the news of the blaze on the jail's small television, felt sorry for the little girl. He offered to donate his blood and skin and implored Ziporyn to take the matter up with jail warden "Big Daddy" Johnson, with whom Speck had developed a friendly relationship. Speck followed the story on television, making note of the medical center where donations of blood and skin could be made.

Ziporyn, fearful that the gesture would look like a ploy to engender sympathy, argued against it, but Speck stubbornly insisted that he would make the donation anonymously. It is not known whether Ziporyn ever passed the offer on to Warden Johnson, and nothing ever came of it.[26]

In Ziporyn's view, Speck was not a manipulative sociopath and therefore not clever enough to engineer such a scheme. Ziporyn also noted that Speck never told a panel of psychiatrists about the many head injuries that he incurred in childhood. This, he felt, showed that Speck did not possess the guile or the desire to create excuses for his behavior. Either he was correct, or Speck was indeed so clever that he managed to trick his own psychiatrist.

Ziporyn concluded that had Speck committed the murders during a spell of temporary insanity but was competent to stand trial. He attributed Speck's violent tendencies and loss of impulse control to brain damage. The final diagnosis was "organic brain defect – chronic brain syndrome associated with cerebral trauma."[27]

Speck's cherished time with "Doc," his surrogate father, finally came to an end on February 13, 1967, when prisoner No. 387443 was moved from the Bridewell to a jail cell housed in the basement of the Peoria County Court. Ziporyn was not called to testify on Speck's behalf; by then the scandal about his book had been exposed, and he was considered *persona non grata* by both prosecution and defense counsel.

Once Speck was transported to Peoria he would see Doc only one more time. Ziporyn's assignment was effectively over, and so was his job. Cook County authorities fired him on April 20, 1967, just days before his notorious patient was found guilty of the eight murders.

CHAPTER ELEVEN

THE SIX FACES OF THE PANEL

Ziporyn's diagnosis was a minor setback for the prosecution, but the matter was far from being settled. A star-studded panel, the best that psychiatry could offer, would come through for them. Judge Herbert C. Paschen instructed the prosecution and defense teams to each select three psychiatric experts who would examine Richard Speck, diagnose his mental condition, and evaluate his ability to stand trial.

Marvin Ziporyn, who was separately assigned to Speck on behalf of the defense, was not included in the panel of six. Several distinguished experts in the field provided additional consultation, bringing the total number of medical consultants to nine. All told, the medical and psychiatric personnel involved in the Speck murder case far outnumbered the attorneys for both sides combined.

The prosecution hoped for three outcomes from their panel: That Speck be found competent to stand trial, that he be found legally sane at the time of the crime, and that he be diagnosed a sociopath. The latter designation, as a pre-existing and permanent condition, would effectively bar any claim of temporary insanity.

Their first selection to the panel was Dr. William Norcross, a well-regarded physician and the only panel member without a degree in psychiatry. Norcross taught surgical techniques at two area hospitals, and served as associate medical director at Cermak Memorial Hospital since 1961, where he managed a staff of ten part-time physicians. Norcross was Speck's primary caregiver, having performed the surgery on Speck's slashed elbow, and the two had struck up a cordial relationship.

It was Norcross who shielded Speck from the prying eyes of the media. It was Norcross who arranged for Corazon Amurao to show up dressed as a nurse and enter Speck's hospital room with the express purpose of identifying him. And it was Norcross who somehow got Speck to recall the theft of the gun from Ella Mae Hooper.

"Norcross says I got it from some whore. I remember her now. Met her the day I was with the sailors."[28] After that session, bits and pieces of his memory drifted back into his consciousness, but there was no recollection of the nurses or the murders.

Dr. Vladimir G. Urse, supervisor of the Cook County Department of Psychiatry and director of the mental health clinic in Cook County Hospital, was the next panel member for the prosecution. Dr. Urse had served as lieutenant colonel in the Army, where he gained experience working with veterans, and he also served as chief of psychiatric services at Walter Reed Hospital in Bethesda, Maryland.

The third panel selection for the prosecution was Dr. Groves Blake Smith, of Alton, Illinois, psychiatric consultant to the Illinois Department of Safety and director of psychiatric services at Illinois State Prison. Smith had experience with hundreds of criminals. Assistant State's Attorney Martin believed that Smith would easily ferret out any attempt by Speck to con the panel, make excuses for his behavior, or fake any mental impairment.

Chief Defense Counsel Gerald Getty set his sights high in his panel selections: Dr. Edward Kelleher, Dr. Hervey M. Cleckley, and Dr. Roy Grinker. He had chosen the cream of the crop in the emerging field of psychopathy, hoping that his panel's evaluations would pave the way to a successful defense of temporary insanity. Unfortunately, the defense team had not adequately vetted its choices, and the plan went south.

Dr. Kelleher was a staff psychiatrist for the Chicago Municipal Court. His evaluation was curt, succinct, and sweeping: Richard Speck was a "sexual psychopath" who had committed "probably the greatest single sex crime in history."[29]

Kelleher's comment met the standard of hype characteristic of this case – "the crime of the century" doubled down as "the greatest single sex crime in history!" His knowledge of true crime history may have been lacking, but some aspects of the murders fit the criteria of a sex crime.

Multiple stabbings of three or more wounds occur more frequently in sex-related homicides.[30] Other criteria for designating a sex-related crime include the victims being nude or lightly clothed, sexual injury or mutilation, sexually suggestive placement of a body, the presence of semen on or near a body, and evidence of fantasy or masturbation.[31]

Dr. Hervey M. Cleckley was a distinguished Professor of Psychiatry at Emory University in his native Atlanta, Georgia. He was also a professor in the Department of Psychiatry and Neurology at Georgia Medical College in Augusta. Through his seminal work *The Mask of Sanity,* first published in 1941, Cleckley introduced psychopathy to mainstream America - a destructive mental disorder, characterized by antisocial, often criminal behavior and the inability to empathize with others.

A sociopath will often adopt the facade of an average, well-adjusted, productive citizen. They are not raving maniacs confined to mental institutions, like those exploited in bad B movies of the 1940s and

1950s; they exist in every walk of life, and due to their shrewdness and intelligence many are able to manipulate themselves into respectable positions in society.

Like Dr. Urse of the defense panel, Cleckley treated many war veterans suffering from post-traumatic stress disorder, then called "shell shock" or "battle fatigue." But his most famous patient was a housewife, Chris Costner Sizemore, who suffered from multiple personality disorder, now termed "dissociative identity disorder."

Cleckley memorialized his patient in his best-selling book, *The Three Faces of Eve*. The book was turned into a movie by the same name, starring JoAnne Woodward, who won an Academy Award for Best Actress in 1957. Both book, movie, and Cleckley received widespread critical acclaim.

Cleckley concluded that Richard Speck was not in a state of temporary insanity when he committed the murders. Getty's lineup was now oh-for-two in helping him secure a strategy for the defense. There was still one more panel member to consult who would hopefully issue a different opinion – one whose professional background gave Dr. Ziporyn a few sleepless nights.

At the time of his appointment to the panel Dr. Roy M. Grinker, the son of a neuropsychiatrist, held many distinguished titles. In 1951 he had founded the Institute for Psychosomatic and Psychiatric Research at Chicago's Michael Reese Hospital, where he served as director until 1976. He was also professor of psychiatry at the University of Chicago, clinical professor of psychiatry at the University of Illinois College of Medicine, and professor of psychiatry at Northwestern University. He edited the *Archives of General Psychiatry* for the Journal of the American Medical Association for seventeen years.

Grinker's background was distinguished by his training with the father of psychiatry himself, Sigmund Freud, while in Europe in 1933. He served as colonel in the U.S. Army in North Africa during World War II. Like his fellow panel member Hervey Cleckley, the bulk of his practice involved the diagnosis and treatment of psychiatric disorders in soldiers and veterans of the World Wars.

Prior to his selection to the panel, Grinker had handled only one other criminal evaluation – one that could have ruined his reputation. That was the case of Chicago's notorious "Lipstick Killer", so named because of a bizarre message found scrawled in red lipstick on one of the victim's mirrors.

"Catch Me Before I Kill More"

William George Heirens had a few things in common with Richard Speck: poverty, a troubled family background, and a propensity for theft. By his mid-teen years Heirens had committed over a dozen burglaries. Unlike Speck, he was good-looking, popular, and intelligent, enough to be granted the opportunity to bypass his senior year of high school and attend the University of Chicago. Heirens eagerly accepted the offer and began classes at the University in the fall of 1945. He worked at different jobs in order to support himself, but continued to burglarize local residences for money.

On June 26, 1946, seventeen-year-old Heirens was arrested for burglary, which sent his life careening into a deepening abyss. He was considered a suspect in the murder of two women, thought to be the work of a burglar, and the grisly murder of six-year-old Suzanne Degnan, whose body was expertly butchered, its pieces dumped in various sewers in Chicago. This crime horrified and angered the public, who demanded swift justice.

The police leaned heavily on Heirens, subjecting him to hours of interrogation and extreme abuse at the same Bridewell jail where Speck would later spend time. The abuse was not limited to law enforcement; doctors subjected the youth to endless hours of psychological and metabolic tests, including a very painful spinal tap that was performed without benefit of anesthesia.[32]

The weary and terrified Heirens finally broke down and confessed to the three murders, and in spite of questionable police procedure, sketchy evidence, medical abuse, and suspected prosecutorial misconduct, he spent the next sixty-five years in prison, becoming America's longest-serving inmate, first at Stateville in Joliet, then at Dixon Correctional. Heirens appealed his case and recanted his confession many times over the years, but remained imprisoned until his death in 2012 at the University of Illinois Medical Center.[33]

Besides the obvious comparisons, Heirens and Speck had two worrisome psychiatrists in common: Roy Grinker and William Haines. Haines was a psychiatrist at Cook County Hospital and had been a colleague of Grinker for many years, going back to the days of the "Lipstick Killer."

In 1952 Grinker revealed that in 1946, he and Haines had given William Heirens an injection of sodium pentothal – the so-called "truth serum" drug. Sodium pentothal does not automatically cause a person to tell the truth. It works by lowering the inhibitions, so that the subject will speak more freely and openly. It was often used by various three-letter agencies to extract confessions from suspected criminals and spies. Grinker and Haines questioned the boy under truth serum for three grueling hours in a desperate attempt to secure a confession to the three murders.

They failed. Grinker admitted that Heirens never confessed, nor did he implicate himself in the murders. The problem was not just the lack of a confession, which changed no one's mind anyway, but the fact that the procedure was done without a warrant or parental consent. I am not sure whether these were legal requirements back in 1946 but the actions of the two psychiatrists still show an overzealous and ruthless approach toward achieving their objective.

Marvin Ziporyn feared that the dodgy duo of Grinker and Haines had secretly injected Speck with sodium pentothal while he was recuperating in the Bridewell infirmary. But he was never sure of it. He had only the words of his patient:

"While I was still in the hospital at Bridewell, a girl came and stuck a needle in my arm. Some blood came out, then I began to feel real good and then dizzy. A little fat guy came in with a pen and a pad of paper, and he started asking questions about the murders."[34]

If this was the work of Grinker and Haines, as in 1946, nothing came of it in Speck's case either. He never remembered, or confessed to, the crime. It is recorded in true crime literature that he confessed, years later; that incident is discussed in Part III.

The panel decided, against Ziporyn's wishes, to give Speck an electroencephalogram (EEG) to determine the existence of brain damage. Although positive findings would support Ziporyn's diagnosis of "organic brain syndrome," he was mistrustful of the test.

EEGs were notoriously unreliable in those days, with less than a forty percent accuracy rate; it's a wonder such tests were even used. Ziporyn did not consider the equipment sophisticated enough to detect brain damage. But his objection held little weight; the panel went ahead with the test, and ruled that the findings were null for brain damage of any kind.

Speck's brain was removed and tested after his death in 1991. The tissue samples were lost, but photographs of them revealed evidence of extensive brain damage to the areas of the brain that relate to memory and impulse control. This time, the results of the EEG conducted in 1966 were reviewed by a neurologist, who confirmed the presence of extremely unusual abnormalities, the likes of which he had not seen before. Somehow these abnormalities went unnoticed back in 1966 when Speck's brain was judged as normal and free of defect.[35]

Aided by the outside help of Drs. Haines and Roland Mackay, a noted neurologist, the panel of six confirmed Speck's diagnosis: anti-social behavior and sociopathic personality, with alcoholism. Speck was judged responsible for his behavior.

All told, the panel spent about twenty-one hours examining and questioning Richard Speck. In spite of Ziporyn's hundred-plus hours of visitations, his observations and opinions held little sway. Adding insult to injury, the poor optics of his book deal cast a shroud of bad faith over him: He had exploited his patient for monetary gain. Interestingly, no one raised similar comparisons to Cleckley and his book and movie successes with *The Three Faces of Eve*.

As if the case were not top heavy enough with psychiatrists and medical experts, Judge Paschen also brought on board an independent consultant to interview Richard Speck. Dr. Ner Littner, originally from Canada, was a Freudian psychoanalyst and founder of the child therapy program at the Chicago Institute for Psychoanalysis.

There were only eleven hundred licensed Freudian psychoanalysts in the United States at that time. Paschen wanted the benefit of Littner's opinion on the mental state of Richard Speck, even though

Littner, a specialist in child psychiatry, had previously evaluated only one other criminal.[36]

Littner interviewed Speck for four hours in September 1966 and found that he suffered from a variety of phobias, which he summed up as "chronic personality disorders with neurotic features."[37]

Littner did not concur with Ziporyn's finding of organic brain syndrome. He acknowledged Speck's frequent throbbing headaches, dizziness, blurred vision, accident proneness, and drug and alcohol abuse, but dismissed the possibility that Speck suffered from brain damage. Nowadays it is well known that throbbing headaches, dizziness, blurred vision, and aggression may be symptomatic of neurological brain damage, also known as TBI or traumatic brain injury.[38]

Aided by some of his own questionable choices, the panel's conclusions dashed any plans of Getty entering an insanity plea. He abandoned his former strategy and decided to plead his client not guilty. From now on he would have to rely on discrediting the evidence against his client. If his past actions were any indication of his future performance, he was in for a resounding defeat.

CHAPTER TWELVE

CRY FOR ME, ARGENTINA

Here, There, and Everywhere

The public was understandably in a panic during those three terrifying days following the murders. Tips had come pouring in from all parts of the country, including the usual array of crank calls. Richard Speck had been sighted in Maryland, Arizona, New Mexico, and Pennsylvania, when in reality he was no farther than a filthy flophouse on Chicago's Skid Row.

Local tips fared no better. One woman reported that she knew a man who matched the description, but she hadn't seen him for two years, which was not helpful. Another called in a report of a suspicious man hanging around the local train depot, but by the time police arrived his train had left the station.

Another woman reported that a derelict had been seen wandering in her neighborhood. He resembled the sketch of the suspect, except that he had long hair and sideburns. Richard Speck, the maniacal mass murderer, was popping up everywhere. A $10,000 reward had been offered to anyone with information leading to Speck's capture, and leads rolled into FBI headquarters like tickets for the Irish Sweepstakes.

One tip had promise. A hospital employee reported that a window washer at the hospital resembled the man in the sketch. He might have been acquainted with the nurses, so this lead needed prompt attention.

A police office went to the nurse supervisor at SCCH, Josephine Chan, to pursue this line of inquiry. Ms. Chan informed him that he would have to contact the Personnel Department, (which we now call "Human Resources"), and gave him the contact information for Robert Moore, the Director of Personnel, but it is not known whether the tip regarding the window washer was ever pursued.

It didn't matter. Speck was always the man in the crosshairs, and so it remained. True to the bombshell FBI files, there was one other tip too big to be ignored, but it almost was - one that came from thousands of miles away, and nearly slipped through that gigantic crack mentioned before. Bombshell #4 took the form of a letter that, in my view, would prove prophetic.

"Richard Speck Es Inocente"

The letter, dated July 26, 1966, had been sent to State's Attorney Patrick J. Ward from Buenos Aires, Argentina and it relayed an intriguing message to "Mr. Word" in Spanish. A copy of the actual translation from the FBI files follows:

```
Mr. Word:
            Richard Speck is innocent. The real assasin
is a doctor, an intimate friend of [        ]. Richard
Speck, an ex-patient of this doctor, was used by him as a
weapon. [              ] knows very well what I say.
My brother politician, [        ] and I, approximately
10 days ago left Chicago, but we possess proofs that
affirm the innocence of Richard Speck.
                                    s/s [            ]
                                    7/26/66
```

Unfortunately, the names are redacted, but in other correspondence the FBI revealed that the "intimate friend" of the doctor was one of the student nurses, whose name went undisclosed. It's an intriguing, if not explosive, piece of information.

The writer had left Chicago ten days earlier, on July 16th, two days after the murders. The letter was dated July 26th, the same day that

Speck was indicted. But by then law enforcement already had their man, and no one wanted to chase down any more leads.

The letter was received at Pilsen Station, on S. Ashland Avenue, on July 29, 1966. The State's Attorney's office would have had the letter in hand within a day or two. However, the letter was not brought to the attention of the FBI until early January 1967, when preparations for Speck's trial were already well under way.

On January 10, 1967, the letter was attached to an internal FBI memorandum, stating:

"The State's Attorney's office has requested that the Bureau, if possible, have the writer of the letter located in Argentina and interviewed, noting that the Defense Attorney has knowledge of the receipt of the letter and lack of investigation of information alleging innocence could be legally embarrassing in the forthcoming trial."[39]

The "lack of investigation of information alleging innocence" would not only be "legally embarrassing", but illegal. The State's Attorney's office was certainly aware of its obligation to submit the letter to the defense, but instead held onto the letter for five months, taking action only after the defense had found out about it. They knew better; in 1963 the Supreme Court had ruled in *Brady v. Maryland 373 U.S. 83 (1963)* that the prosecution was obliged to disclose any possibly exculpatory evidence to the defense in pre-trial discovery.

But the strange matter took an even stranger twist. After conducting an investigation, the Argentine Legat advised FBI Director Hoover by cablegram dated January 27, 1967:

"[REDACTED], born [REDACTED], denies writing letter or any knowledge in this case. Her brother-in-law [REDACTED], and sister-in-law [REDACTED] also deny knowledge author of letter or facts this matter (sic)."

The parties, who provided sworn statements, also claimed that they had never visited the United States. The Argentine Legat then asked FBI headquarters to verify this claim by checking international travel records, but FBI Director Hoover instead let Chicago FBI know that he was not passing the request along to his field agents. Case closed.[40]

Like a juicy piece of gossip, the Argentine tip stirred my imagination. Was it a hoax, or a viable tip from someone who truly had inside information of the crime? Who was the doctor, which nurse was his "intimate friend," who were the visitors from Argentina, what did they know, and what proof did they have of Speck's innocence? And why would they make such shocking claims only to suddenly reverse course and deny them?

Upon closer review, I found an error in the translation of the letter and this added more fuel to the flames. The translated letter claimed that Richard Speck was a former patient of the mysterious doctor and was "used by him as a weapon" in the crime. But how was Speck used as a weapon? This suggests that Speck committed the murders on someone else's behalf, except that the letter also states that Speck was innocent. A magnifying glass came to the rescue.

The Spanish phrase, in scrawled handwriting, was read as "fué usado por el como cornado." The direct translation of "cornado" is "gored," like what a bull does with its horns. This was loosely interpreted to mean "weapon," but it didn't sound right.

When I double-checked the letter I was in for a surprise. The a's had been misread as o's. The phrase was not " fué usado por el como cornado" – it was " fué usado por el como carnada." This changes the translation significantly, from "used by him as a weapon," to "used by him as bait."

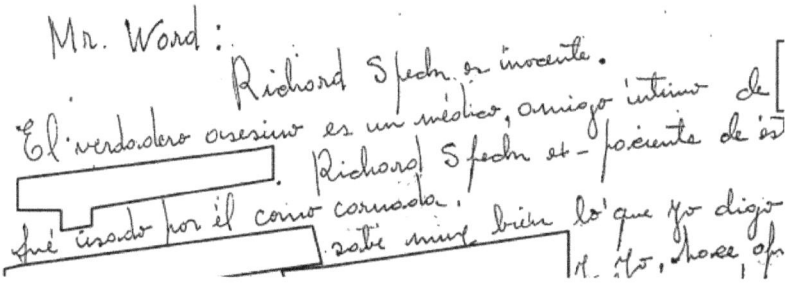

So the letter claimed that a doctor was the true killer of the nurses, and that Richard Speck was used by this doctor as bait. Something fishy was going on.

This lead required confirmation that Speck was acquainted with a doctor in Chicago sometime prior to July 1966 - a task that seemed well out of my reach. Amazingly, it wasn't, thanks to the U.S. Coast Guard files that I received in response to my FOIA request. In line with all the other weirdness of the case, that request bore the eerie file numbers RD 66646.

Encouraged by his brother-in-law, Speck filed an application with the Coast Guard for seafaring work on April 25, 1966. His application required a complete physical examination and a statement from a physician confirming that he was physically fit to perform the work.

Speck received a routine physical in late April and his medical clearance was approved and signed by a surgeon. Much like a doctor's prescription, the signature is impossible to read. However, the form establishes that Speck was indeed acquainted with a doctor in Chicago. South Chicago Community Hospital, just a mile north of the NMU hiring hall, routinely handled these requests. This document connected Speck with a local doctor, giving some traction to the tip from Argentina.

The idea of an Argentine politician being privy to such information seemed odd, but I learned that between the 1960s and the 1980s, Argentine citizens were emigrating from their country to the U.S. in large numbers due to political and social unrest. SCCH's staff reflected a diversity of nationalities, with doctors from Latin America, the Philippines, and Taiwan. It is possible that the politician was involved with immigration or other related matters in connection with some of the doctors at SCCH.

Whether genuine or not, the Argentine tip should have been pursued like the others. The fact that the letter was ignored by the prosecution for five months, then hurriedly investigated, with the sender then doing a complete 180, suggests negligence, or worse - that someone warned the sender to drop the matter entirely. One wonders whether the prosecution would have ever dealt with the letter had the defense not gotten wind of it.

But not all was lost. I would soon come to learn that a doctor's involvement in the murders was more likely than anyone would imagine.

CHAPTER THIRTEEN

UNTYING THE KNOTS

I purchased copies of six pathology and toxicology reports from the Chicago Medical Examiner's officer; two reports, for Mary Ann Jordan and Merlita Gargullo, could not be located. While my knowledge of human anatomy enabled me to understand the reports, my observations are not intended to masquerade as professional conclusions. They are listed in bullet points at the end of each section, and they are my opinions only. Where necessary, I did additional research to explore noteworthy or unusual findings.

The autopsies of the eight nurses were fast-tracked by the coroner and assigned to two Cook County pathologists, Drs. E.H. Tapia and J.W. Henry. The eight autopsies began at approximately 10:30 AM and most were completed by late afternoon.[41]

The reports were typed single-space onto 8-1/2 by 14 inch legal size paper. It was surprising to note that there were no diagrams of the bodies indicating the location of the wounds. There were other irregularities as well.

All of the nurses were fingerprinted in the morgue, but the pathologists made mention of the black ink on the fingers of only two nurses. Defensive wounds on the bodies of the nurses also were not noted; those who were not tied up could have raised their arms involuntarily during the attack, but such details were not provided. The absence of these details made it difficult to know whether these features simply did not appear on the bodies, or were overlooked.

Pamela Lee Wilkening

Dr. J.W. Henry conducted the autopsy. His report filled one single sheet of legal sized paper. Pam, 20 years old, stood five feet seven inches in height and weighed 155, with shoulder length brown hair and blue eyes.

Pam was found on the floor in Corazon's east bedroom face up, with her hands bound behind her back, her head pointing north. She was wearing what we used to call "baby dolls" – a popular style of women's pajamas that consisted of puffy panties and a frilly short-sleeved blouse.

A white cloth strip was found stuffed into her mouth with another strip tied across her mouth and around her head. One stab wound pierced her left lung and upper portion of her heart. The wound was four and one quarter inches in depth and was delivered with such force that it broke her third rib. "Stab wound of pulmonary artery" was the cause of death.

Pam's face contained multiple small petechial hemorrhages that were bluish or cyanotic in color. Petechiae appear as small red, brown, or purple pinpoint dots in the eyes, skin, or organs, and indicate minute bursting of the blood capillaries due to force or injury to the area. They are noted in deaths caused by "ligature or manual strangulation, traumatic asphyxia/chest crushing injury, plastic bag-ligature suffocation, carotid sleeper holds with a concomitant struggle...."[42]

There were two slightly depressed groove-like reddish blue to brownish red markings measuring over 9 centimeters, or 3-1/2 inches, from the right to the left side of her neck.

The toxicology report was negative for alcohol or barbiturates; tests were not done for the presence of any other drugs.

- The long groove-like markings on Pam's neck and the

- petechiae in her face show that some type of neck compression or manual strangulation took place first. She may have been rendered unconscious before being stabbed.
- If so, the killing was the work of two men, one who gagged and subdued her from behind, and one in front who wielded the knife.
- The knife wound to her heart measured four and a quarter inches deep. It had to have been delivered by a knife at least that long. This will become important in the chapter Evidence.

Suzanne Farris

Suzanne Bridgett Farris, 22, stood five feet eight inches and weighed 150 pounds, with curly dark brown hair and blue eyes. She was wearing a blouse, shorts, and sneakers. Her body was between Pam Wilkening and Mary Ann Jordan; their heads all faced north. Suzanne was face down, with no ligatures on either hands or feet.

The police report stated that her hands were behind her back and a white cloth strip was loosely draped across her wrists. However, the crime scene photo shows that her hands were at her side, with no cloth strip in sight. The police report makes no sense - if someone had tried to tie her hands but failed, the strip would be on the floor, not draped across her wrists while she was already down.

Dr. E.H. Tapia conducted the autopsy. The cause of death was "anoxia," or oxygen deprivation, due to "strangulation and stab wounds of chest." There were petechial hemorrhages in her eyes and a ligature mark around her neck. Suzanne was strangled with a white nurse's stocking.

She also suffered by far the most stab wounds - eleven to the front of the upper body and seven to the back, mostly around the right shoulder. The depth of these was not stated. Also noted was an irregular jagged t-shaped wound on the right side of her neck and six small punctures or stab wounds on the left side of the neck that ran parallel to each other.

There was lividity in the upper chest, consistent with her being found face down. Also known as *livor mortis*, lividity is a condition in which blood, through the action of gravity, settles in the lowest part of the body after death, leaving dark red or purplish areas on the skin that resemble bruises. Lividity reveals the position in which a person has lain for several hours following death, and can be helpful in estimating time of death.[43]

There were abrasions to both of Suzanne's knees. There was also a bruise on one side of her head measuring two centimeters, or about three quarters of an inch in width.

The tox report was negative for alcohol or barbiturates.

- Unlike the others, Suzanne was strangled with a white nurse's stocking; this was a departure from the white cloth strips used on the others. At the time Speck allegedly killed Suzanne, he still had plenty of cloth strips around his neck, which he used on the nurses who were strangled after Suzanne.
- The bruise on her head and abrasions to her knees suggest that she was punched in the head, fell to her knees, and was possibly dragged.
- The punch, the ligature strangulation, or the combination of both, quickly rendered her unable to fight back.
- The autopsy report did not indicate the presence of defensive wounds to her hands or arms. I assumed that this meant there were none. Given that she was not tied up, the

lack of defensive wounds suggests she was quickly overcome before she could fight back.
- Why did the police report differ from the crime scene photo in regard to the cloth strip?
- Again, this murder suggests two participants: one with the ligature, one with the knife.

Mary Ann Jordan

Mary Ann Jordan's autopsy report could not be located at the Medical Examiner's Office. She was 20 years old at the time of her death. She was wearing a white print blouse, yellow shorts, and brown sandals.

Mary Ann suffered four stab wounds: one to her left eye and three in her neck and throat. She was not bound.

It is hard to fathom how Mary Ann and Suzanne could have been brutally murdered side by side in the same room without screaming or signs of a major struggle, unless there were two – or three - attackers who immediately subdued them. Corazon Amurao's trial testimony tells us only the following:

"STATE: Did you hear anything after Speck took Mary Ann Jordan and Suzanne Farris from the south bedroom?

CORAZON: I heard a noise as if Miss Jordan and Miss Farris were resisting. I just heard a noise as if – they were talking in a low voice, but I don't know what they were talking. As if they were yelling but in low voices.

GETTY (defense counsel): I object. She wasn't sure. I would like to know whether they were yelling or whether it was a low voice or –

JUDGE: She said, "Yelling in a low voice," is what she said."[44]

Nina Jo Schmale

Nina Jo, 24, had long brown hair and brown eyes, stood five feet seven inches tall and weighed 130 pounds. She was found lying on her back in her bed with her hands tied behind her. She was wearing a multi-colored nightgown, which had been pulled up above the waist to reveal that she was not wearing underpants.

Dr. J.W. Henry listed the cause of death as strangulation, noting petechial hemorrhages and ecchymosis (bruising) in the eyes. A white cloth strip was knotted tightly behind her neck. On the right front side of the neck was a large brownish-red discoloration four inches long and a half-inch in width.

Also on the right side of her neck were three lacerations going in a diagonal pattern from top to bottom. The first was a quarter of an inch to the right of the midline of the neck. The second, below it, was one half inch from the midline, and the third, was one and one half inch from the midline. These lacerations were three eighths of an inch wide and penetrated to a depth of about two inches.

Nina Jo's toxicology report was negative for the presence of alcohol or barbiturates.

- The evenly-placed lacerations were done with deliberation, not as the result of a frenzied stabbing.
- Nina Jo's hands had been tied tightly behind her back but no ligature marks were noted – "the extremities revealed no evidence of trauma." Unfortunately, not all of the reports indicate the condition of the extremities.

Valentina Pasion

Valentina Pasion was 24 years old, with long black hair and brown eyes. She stood five feet one inch tall and weighed 120 pounds.

To add to the confusion surrounding the identities of the Filipina nurses, Valentina's report indicated that the autopsy was performed at 12:50 AM on July 14, 1966, which is impossible, as the murders were in progress at that time. It was more likely 12:50 PM on the 14th. The report was not signed off by Dr. E.H. Tapia until September 12, 1966.

Valentina was found on her back with her hands beneath her and her ankles bound together. Her throat was brutally slashed almost ear to ear, revealing her larynx through the gaping wound. The fifth cervical vertebra was severed.

There was a bruise on Valentina's chin measuring nearly two centimeters, or about three-quarters of an inch. I believe she was struck or punched in the chin. This was the same size as the bruise on Suzanne Farris' head, which I believe also came from a punch or blow to the head.

Pathologist E.H. Tapia attributed the cause of death to the gaping stab wound in Valentina's throat. The report also noted petechial hemorrhage in the eyes, an indication that strangulation or neck compression had also taken place. No ligature was found.

There were significant discrepancies in Corazon's statements regarding Valentina. Corazon had stated that:

- Valentina was in bed when the killer arrived.
- She was killed around 2:00 AM.
- Her hands and feet were tied up.

Wrong. Valentina was clothed in a white bra, black panties, a white blouse and yellow shorts. She was not dressed for bed.

Valentina's stomach contained a few cc of dark brown fluid, and her duodenum, which connects the stomach to the small intestine, contained a greenish-yellow grumose material. Grumose material is a lumpy, clotted substance, the residue of food as it is broken down during the digestive process.

The digestive process varies from person to person, but it generally takes from two to four hours for the stomach contents to empty into the duodenum.[45] The three Filipina nurses dined together at around 4:30 PM. If Valentina ate at 4:30, the food would have passed from the stomach into the duodenum by 8:30 PM. By 2:00 AM, a full nine and a half hours after eating, the duodenum should have been empty. The presence of grumose material in the duodenum suggests that Valentina was killed much earlier in the evening. If she had eaten a late-night snack, then this theory goes out the window, but there's still the fact that she was not dressed for bed, while almost everyone else was. This raises questions concerning the actual time of her murder.

In her sworn testimony Corazon stated that Speck picked Valentina up by her ankle and hand restraints and carried her out of the south bedroom. He never untied her. But as previously noted, the July 14th police report revealed:

"Clutched between the thumb and forefinger (of Valentina Pasion) ... was found a single strand of short black hair. This was called to the attention of the Lab Techs and they took possession of it."

How did Valentina manage to rip a single strand of short black hair from her attacker's head with her hands tied behind her back? Yet the short black hair found between her thumb and forefinger, a crucial piece of any forensic puzzle, was disregarded. After the crime lab took custody of the short black hair it was never seen or heard of again.

In addition to the short black hair, minute scrapings of human skin were found underneath Valentina's fingernails. She had put up a fierce fight before being rendered helpless, possibly by a blow that left the mark on her chin.

This finding indicates for certain that Valentina's hands were not tied, and contradicts the sworn testimony of the State's star witness - another red flag. Valentina's tox report was negative for alcohol or barbiturates.

Merlita Gargullo

Merlita's autopsy report could not be located. She was found face down in the west bedroom with her hands bound behind her and her feet tied together, and her body was lain across Valentina Pasion's body in a criss-cross pattern.

She was ligature strangled by a white cloth strip, and also had four puncture wounds on the left side of her neck. The ligature strangulation was forceful, causing a dislocation of her neck.

- Merlita had four laceration or puncture wounds on one side of her neck, like Nina Jo and Suzanne. Although their cause of death was strangulation, these lacerations or puncture wounds suggest that one killer poked a knife into some of the women after they were strangled, as if toying with them or punishing them.
- The placement of the Filipina nurses' bodies, in a criss-cross 'x' pattern, is curious. These two brutally forceful killings suggest rage against these women, and that Valentina angered her killer by scratching him and pulling his hair.

As a result, Merlita was thrown onto the floor and Valentina was thrown across her in a show of resentment and disrespect.
- Police would have been well advised to search for a suspect with a scratch on his head, face, or arms, but this detail was not included in any subsequent reports.

Patricia Ann Matusek

Pat, 20 years of age, stood five feet six inches and weighed 155 pounds, with long black hair and blue eyes. Dr. E. H. Tapia ruled the cause of death as ligature strangulation, as evidenced by petechial hemorrhages to the sclera and conjunctiva of the eyes, petechiae also in the lungs, heart, and other internal organs, and damage to the thyroid and cricoid cartilage in the throat area.

Dr. Tapia also noted dependent lividity in the back, which is consistent with her being found on her back.

He also noted "impression bands" on her wrists, probably referring to ligature marks. Dr. Tapia, a Cuban émigré, was not a native speaker of English, as shown by some of the unusual language in the reports. Pat's was the only autopsy report to indicate ligature marks on the wrists or ankles.

Her toxicology report was negative for alcohol and showed .26 mg of phenobarbital in her system.

The report noted hemorrhage in the duodenum, a c-shaped segment that connects the stomach to the small intestine. The coroner later testified that this injury was caused by a forceful kick or blow to the stomach area.

This forceful blow to the stomach is reminiscent of the unsolved murder of Mary Kay Pierce, whom Richard Speck was suspected of murdering in Monmouth in April. Mary Kay's nude body was found in a hog shed built by Speck during his short-lived carpenter apprenticeship. She was found nude and beaten to death, with evidence of forceful blows to her stomach. One forceful blow broke a rib that punctured her lung. Speck was a person of interest, but no charges were ever brought.

- Several nurses were found with their hands bound behind their backs, but Pat's was the only body that bore "impression bands" or ligature markings on the wrists. Was this detail simply omitted from the other reports, or were there no such markings on anyone else?
- Pat and Gloria were the only women to be killed by ligature strangulation alone; the others who were strangled also had seemingly uniform patterns of puncture or laceration wounds (Nina Jo, Merlita, Suzanne).

The inconsistencies mount, as do the red flags. And then there's Gloria.

Gloria Jean Davy

Gloria, 22, stood at five feet seven and weighed 140 pounds, with long dark brown hair and blue eyes. When compared with the official story, details of her death sent more flags flying than a NASCAR race.

Dr. E.H. Tapia marked the time of Gloria's autopsy as 3:10 PM on the afternoon of July 14th. This is odd because he marked the time of Suzanne's autopsy as 3:12 PM. The speed of the autopsy procedures evidently took precedence over accuracy and thoroughness. It was probably a clerical error, but it added another layer of curiosity to the reports.

Gloria was found face down, nude, on the living room sofa. Her hands were tied behind her with a strip torn from the purple-and-white blouse she had worn that evening. Around her neck was a tightly tied white cloth strip. The cause of death was ligature strangulation, evidenced by petechial hemorrhage and blue discoloration in the eyes, eyelids, face, and gums.

Dr. Tapia made a disturbing observation: Gloria's back showed "marked dependent lividity." She had to have lain on her back for several hours in order for lividity to become fixed in that position, yet the police report stated that she was "found lying face down" on the sofa. This raises a bright red flag:

"It is worth noting that lividity begins to work through the deceased within thirty minutes of their heart stopping and can last up to 12 hours. Only up to the first six hours of death can lividity be altered by moving the body. After the six-hour mark lividity is fixed as blood vessels begin to break down within the body."[46]

The lividity shows that Gloria had to have lain on her back for several hours; then someone turned her over before she was found. This also revisits the question of her time of death. Was it around 3:00-3:30, as Corazon testified, or was it before everyone else, as Corazon had initially stated, which made the time closer to midnight?

Another finding in Gloria's autopsy casts even more doubt on just when Gloria was murdered. She had attended a celebratory dinner that evening with her fiancé Robert Stern, with steak and champagne on the menu. She had enjoyed the champagne; her blood alcohol content was .111, just below the then-legal limit of .150.

As for the steak, her stomach contents included 150 cc, just over five ounces, of undigested food. Dr. Joseph Ksiazek, the forensic chemist who conducted the toxicology exams, did not analyze the stomach contents, but steak is a likely choice for the following reasons.

Animal protein can take from four to six hours to fully digest, and even longer if the individual is under stress.[47] I don't know what time Gloria ate dinner, but even if she dined as late at 8:00 PM, the digestive process should have been much further along if the true time of death was between 3:00 and 3:30 AM.

If the undigested food matter was not animal protein, it should have passed through her stomach even faster. In either case, this information changes her time of death, and again discredits Corazon's story.

Considering the undigested food matter and the state of lividity, death more likely took place around midnight, just after she returned to the townhouse. Even Corazon's initial police statement to detectives Carlile and Wallenda of July 14th confirms this:

"The victims gave him what money they had and at about this time, victim #1, Gloria Davy came into the bedroom. She was forced to join the others on the floor and she also surrendered some money to this man. He then bound all their hands and feet ....

This man then took the Davy girl out of the bedroom, leaving the others bound and on the floor.... After the man had taken the Davy girl out, he returned in a short time and took another of the girls out and he continued to take the girls out one by one until all had left the bedroom in question, with the exception of the witness."

In this harrowing account, Gloria was the first to be taken from the room and killed; she was even designated "Victim #1" in all the police reports. Subsequent legal actions that were filed on behalf of "Gloria Davy et al," always listed her as the first victim.

To fully realize the impact of Gloria's autopsy we have to jump ahead to some of the revelations made by witnesses at the trial of Richard Speck. Other aspects of the trial are covered in the chapter The Trial.

At trial Corazon testified at length on the two brutal assaults wreaked upon Gloria in her last hours; sordid details relating the attacker's removal of Gloria's clothing, his instructions to Gloria to wrap her legs around his back, followed by a gut-heaving description of the mattress bouncing up and down for the duration of the assault. The sickening sequence of events ended with a brutal sodomy downstairs on the living room sofa that took another agonizing 40-50 minutes.

The trial testimony of coroner Dr. Andrew J. Toman proved as shocking as Corazon's testimony. In a development that greatly angered the prosecution team, Toman refused to confirm that Gloria Davy had been raped. This shocker came just days after their star witness spent considerable time on the stand describing this specific assault right down to the cringeworthy details. Now back to Tapia's pathology report:

"The external genitalia are those of a normal female .... The vagina is dry. The internal genitalia are unremarkable." This does not sound like the effect of a prolonged sexual assault.

This contradiction took the courtroom by surprise. Even Speck's psychiatrist weighed in on the controversy: "An official report stated that Miss Davy's anus was mutilated, but the published autopsy did not refer to this."[48] The published autopsy instead stated: "The various cavities of the body are unremarkable."

According to law enforcement the anus, a body cavity, was "mutilated", but according to the pathologist who had examined the body, it was "unremarkable." It was this way - no, it was that way.

The coroner was invalidating the star witness' testimony right on the witness stand.

This startling contradiction appeared to fly right over everyone's heads. Undaunted, the prosecution maintained that the crime lab technicians had found semen inside the buttocks of Gloria Davy and on a nearby blanket, and held firm to its claim: "The crime lab had proven that the rectal swab taken from Gloria contained sperm, as did the cushion from the couch on which the body had been found. This undoubtedly was the sperm of Richard Speck."[49]

Considering that DNA technology was still decades in the future, this was a brash assertion. Note the pathologist's statement that "There is feces, formed and soft, in the anus," with no mention of any accompanying finding of semen. Ultimately the prosecution made a clever side-step of this evidence, later discussed in the chapter The Trial.

Notable takeaways from Gloria's autopsy:

- Her body was turned over and moved hours post-mortem.
- She was a known leader, sassy and outspoken. How could she have endured a prolonged, depraved rape without screaming or verbally attacking the rapist? It is unfathomable that Corazon heard not a single utterance from Gloria during her agonizing rape and sodomy, which allegedly lasted about 75 minutes.
- Gloria's stomach contents suggested a much earlier time of death.
- Her body showed no evidence of frontal or anal rape; sexual assault without penetration can't be ruled out.
- She was initially tied up with white cloth strips, then her clothing was removed (we have to assume that the

restraints were removed first), then she was allegedly raped, then carried downstairs, then her hands were re-tied with pieces of her blouse, then she was sodomized – this is a lot of busy work for one attacker. Total time elapsed: approx. 75 minutes. Much of this either makes no sense, or is unsupported by the evidence.

The Last Word

While they seemed rushed and incomplete, the autopsy reports brought forth astounding information that has not to date been taken into account in the story of this mass murder. The reports reveal numerous inconsistencies in the official story, introducing many new possibilities into the mix – that there was more than one killer, that the killers were angry or vengeful, that the killers subdued the victims by first rendering them unconscious, that at least one body was moved hours later, that the timeline of the murders was all wrong. Things didn't happen as we were told.

Not one to hold her tongue, outspoken Gloria was a force to be reckoned with even from beyond the grave. The state of her body screamed out that the timeline and the narrative were seriously flawed. And brave Valentina Pasion had fought with and scratched her attacker, providing law enforcement with crucial clues that sadly went ignored. Through the forensics the nurses had the last word, but back then no one was listening. I hope that someone is listening now.

CHAPTER FOURTEEN

THE EVIDENCE

Thursday, July 14, 6:30 AM

Compared to today's stringent protocols, the crime scene investigation at the townhouse resembled a free-for-all: Police, medical examiners, lab technicians, reporters, attorneys, and photographers began flooding (and compromising) the scene from the get-go. The townhouse probably had more visitors in just two days' time than the nurses had entertained in months. Few wore gloves, and none wore protective booties, which likely ruined blood stain patterns on the floor, as well as shoes.

Detective Jack Wallenda was understandably disturbed when he first set eyes on the horrific carnage; he was acquainted with some of the nurses through police business at the hospital and had found them kind and helpful. He knew Patricia Matusek since she was a little girl; father Joe ran a tavern that Wallenda patronized. He was especially distressed to see how tightly the ligatures were tied around the necks of the strangulation victims, so he took drastic and uncharacteristic action:

"The knots were tied very, very tight. They were all double knots and they were all done very professionally. I couldn't get my fingers between the cloth and the neck, and I had to cut the knots with scissors."[50]

Why cut the knots? The nurses were already deceased; no act of misplaced mercy could relieve their suffering. From the start, the evidence was in for a rocky ride.

Cutting the knots may have altered the evidence in more ways than one. The autopsies of Nina Jo Schmale, Suzanne Farris, and Valentina Pasion, discussed in the previous chapter Untying the Knots, made note of small uniformly patterned cuts or punctures on the victims' necks, evenly spaced apart.

Wallenda may have had trouble sliding the scissors between the tight ligatures and the skin, which would have already hardened from the effects of *rigor mortis*. Did he inadvertently jab the scissors into the flesh, leaving a few evenly-spaced incisions? In any case, Wallenda later testified that the crime scene photos represented the crime scene exactly as he had come upon it, cut-off knots notwithstanding.

The careless and haphazard treatment of the crime scene mirrored the messy state of the nurses' rooms. For the nurses, the disorder was understandable; for the police, it was unfathomable.

Thursday, July 14, 10:00 AM

While evidence was being collected, photographers from the Associated Press entered the townhouse at 10:00 AM and took photos. Crime lab technicians continued to dust for fingerprints and search for evidence while the photographers snapped away. No one seemed concerned about preserving the crime scene. One reporter later recounted how the sticky the soles of his shoes got from tramping across the blood-soaked floors.

Thursday, July 14, PM

A search of the basement of the townhouse yielded the butt of a plastic-tipped cigar. This was a promising piece of evidence; did the killer smoke a cigar in the basement, waiting for a good time to strike? The cigar butt was packaged and brought to the crime lab. Months later it came to light that one of the detectives had smoked a cigar while searching the basement, and had left the butt on the basement floor. Any hope of a promising lead was quickly extinguished.

The police report of July 14, 1966 listed the following inventory of items from the crime scene:

- All of the victims' clothing
- White strips of cloth
- One strand of hair
- One cigar butt
- One window screen

Like the official story, this list will undergo significant additions and subtractions.

As the miserable first day of the investigation drew to a close Captain Dan Dragel of the Chicago PD crime lab took possession of all clothing, bedding, and related items and brought them to the lab for further examination.

The police, satisfied that they had taken charge of all physical evidence, then asked the grief-stricken families of the victims to come to the townhouse to retrieve the personal effects of the slain nurses. Incredibly, police had the devastated families visit the crime scene on Friday, July 15th, just twenty-four hours after they were notified of the horrendous murders.

Friday, July 15, 10:00 AM

The heartbroken families had barely begun to register the enormity of what had just happened to their daughters and sisters, yet there they were, having to sort through piles of clothing, knick knacks, purses, and jewelry, like stunned survivors sifting through disaster wreckage. The visit by the families was not only devastating for them, but also counter-productive to the job at hand; crime lab technicians were still dusting for fingerprints. It is not known exactly when the crime scene cleanup took place. Hopefully, the dried puddles and streams of blood were washed away before the families set foot inside.

The search for fingerprints went on without interruption, but positive results would materialize only after another curious turn of events.

Law enforcement had trouble getting an official copy of Richard Speck's fingerprints for purposes of comparison. He did not have a criminal record in Chicago, and the Automated Fingerprint Identification System, or AFIS, the national fingerprint database, did not exist at the time. Speck's fingerprints were on file with the Dallas sheriff's department under the name Richard Franklin Lindbergh, with the Texas Department of Corrections under the name Richard Franklin Speck, and with the Coast Guard under the name Richard Benjamin Speck. Chicago PD would have to get the prints from one of these agencies, and the sooner the better.

The fastest way to obtain the prints was through the Chicago Coast Guard office. However, there was an issue with the chain of custody of the fingerprints on record. The State's Attorney's office then asked the FBI to obtain the prints from Coast Guard headquarters in Washington, D.C. The fingerprint cards had to be rushed by jet from Washington, D.C. to Chicago late Friday afternoon.

The following timeline of the sequence of events on Friday the 15th presents a shocking development in the desperate effort to find a match between fingerprints obtained at the crime scene and those of Richard Speck.

Friday, July 15, 3 PM

Technician Bill Scanlon searched Speck's room at the Shipyard Inn, where he discovered a beer can with latent partial prints on its surface. He lifted the prints with adhesive; they were then photographed and brought back to the crime lab.

Friday, July 15, 7:30 PM

Speck's fingerprint cards arrived by jet from Washington, D.C. and were brought to the crime lab by FBI Special Agent Marlin Johnson.

Friday, July 15, 9:45 PM

Chicago FBI made a revealing admission to FBI headquarters regarding the fingerprint search. Their July 15th teletype stated: "At nine-forty-five PM this date Chicago PD advised no positive identification made in fingerprint comparison."

The police already knew that the beer can prints were Speck's; they had received his fingerprint cards from Washington at 7:30 PM and were able to confirm that the prints on the beer can belonged to him. However, they had begun comparing the beer can prints to the crime scene prints as soon as they received the beer can prints in the afternoon. That left several hours to make the comparisons, but by 9:45 PM they still had not found a match. This implies that Speck's prints were not found at the crime scene.

The intrigue didn't stop there. The State's Attorney's office summarized the conclusion of the fingerprint search:

"By Friday night the technicians had found thirty-three prints at 2319. Five of the thirty-three prints were too smudged or lacking in detail..... Of the twenty-eight remaining prints found suitable for comparison, eighteen did not compare with anyone whose inked impressions were tried. Of the ten latent prints that had been positively identified, two belonged to patrolman Dan Kelly, and eight to the nurses. That left two prints yet to be compared."[51]

That did not leave two prints. Check the math:

33 minus 5 too smudged or lacking in detail = 28.

28 remaining prints minus 18 that did not compare = 10.

10 positively identified, minus 2 of Kelly, minus 8 of the nurses, does not equal 2 to be compared. It equals zero. 10 – 2 = 8, 8 – 8 = 0.

Was this just an error, or was Assistant State's Attorney Martin letting slip that there were no prints matching Speck's in the final tally? It's another stunner, another red flag to add to the list.

Saturday, July 16, 5:30 AM

Things were looking dark for law enforcement, but then came the dawn. At 5:30 AM excited police officials confirmed that they had found three partial prints in the townhouse matching Richard Speck's. "Too smudged or lacking in detail" was an accurate descriptor for what they eventually settled on.

The three partial fingerprints were lifted from the inside of the door to the south bedroom, the room into which all the nurses had been forced at gunpoint. The first print, of Speck's right index finger, appeared above and to the right of the doorknob, and the second, of his right middle finger, directly to the right of the doorknob. The third print, of his left middle finger, appeared 16-1/2 inches' distance from the floor, 2-1/2 inches from the edge of the door.

Speck was six feet one inch tall. In order to leave a print so close to the floor he had to be sitting on the bed nearest the door. And that was what law enforcement posited – he had sat on the bed facing the door, and swung the door shut with the middle finger of his left hand, with the finger perpendicular to the door.

This was the same bed upon which he had placed Gloria Davy after tying her up. He had to have swung the door shut with his left hand and then removed Gloria's clothing before assaulting her on the bed. There are problems with this story as well.

In Corazon's second version of events, Gloria was the last victim. Everyone else in the house, except the hidden Corazon, already lay dead in the other bedrooms. Why the sudden need for privacy after indiscriminately stabbing, choking, and strangling seven women in the other rooms? Recall that this rape did not even take place in Corazon's first version of events.

Corazon heard Speck unzipping and removing Gloria's slacks. But he had tied her feet together, so I guess that he then removed the ankle ligatures, and he also had to remove the hand ligatures in order to take her blouse off. She was found nude, with her hands tied behind her with pieces of her white-and-purple blouse, so at some point, he had fully tied her up with the white cloth strips, then removed the cloth strips and her clothing, and then re-tied her hands behind her back with strips cut from the blouse.

And during all this degradation strong-willed Gloria never spoke up, fought with him, scratched him, or screamed? In its quest to portray the nurses as meek, passive, obedient victims who went silently to their deaths, the official story did them as great a disservice as the news media who reveled in salacious accounts of rape and molestation.

It's also worth noting that there were eighteen prints that did not match the inked impressions of anyone on record. Nothing became of these prints. The fingerprint search was focused only on matching the fingerprints of Richard Speck. Now it's time to take a closer look at them.

At that time fingerprints had to share between eight and twelve points of comparison to be considered a match. According to Lieutenant Emil Giese, the clearest print taken from the door shared ten identifying features with Speck's fingerprint of his left middle finger. Later on this rating would be bumped up to 17 and the print would be hailed as the best of the batch of three. The copy of this print appeared blurry and smudged.

Was someone expressing gallows humor by using the impression of Speck's middle finger as proof of guilt?

Saturday, July 16, PM

Under the guidance of senior fingerprint expert Burton Buhrke the south bedroom door was removed and brought to the crime lab for submission into evidence.

The door appears in a blurry photo (not shown) taken at the crime lab. On the floor in front of the door is the beer can that yielded Richard Speck's fingerprints. It was interesting to see these two items photographed together, like partners in crime. Did the beer can provide the prints so badly needed by the prosecution, and did police then transpose them onto the door? The prints became a hotly contested issue at trial and are discussed further in the next chapter.

The Black Jacket, or "Suit Coat"

Corazon described the killer as dressed in all black and wearing a black "suit coat." Gene Thornton had given Speck a black rayon-lined corduroy jacket on July 11[th,] two days before the murders. Law enforcement theorized that he wore the jacket to the townhouse to hide his telltale tattoos on both arms. This does not make sense for several reasons.

- Chicago was in the throes of a heat wave that week, with temperatures soaring into the nineties. On the afternoon of July 13th, the heat reached 87 degrees, dropping into the low seventies that evening – hardly weather calling for a rayon-lined corduroy jacket.
- Law enforcement believed that he intended to leave no witness behind who could identify him based on his tattoos. Why the need to hide the tattoos if he intended to eliminate all the witnesses? Ironically Corazon, the sole survivor, testified that she did not see any tattoos on the killer.

Years later, when Assistant State's Attorney Martin reviewed the evidence in storage, he observed that the black jacket contained no traces of blood, and Dennis L. Breo, co-author of Martin's book *The Crime of the Century: Richard Speck and the Murders That Shocked the Nation*, remarked how hot Speck must have felt wearing that jacket.[52] The prosecutor dared not make these same observations during the trial, while the defense either missed, or passed on, the chance to do so.

The Three T's

Three other items of clothing were entered into evidence: two BVD and one Hanes men's white t-shirts, size 38-40M, the size worn by Speck. Like the black jacket and the large Navy hunting knife, the t-shirts had been given to Speck by his helpful brother-in-law, Eugene Thornton.

The storyline of these t-shirts was developed by law enforcement, who theorized that Speck, a neat freak, had brought several t-shirts to the townhouse in his red-and-black plaid zipper bag so that he could change his shirt after each killing. "The fastidious Speck had brought plenty of extra t-shirts, anticipating the blood and sweat he would incur."[53]

The first was a sweaty and crumpled white BVD t-shirt found on the living room floor near Gloria's body. The second white BVD t-shirt was taken from Speck while he was in the hospital for the purpose of linking the first shirt to him. The third t-shirt had a dubious trajectory, and was not found until two weeks after the murders.

By July 16th police felt they had the direct evidence that all prosecutors dream of having: fingerprints linking Speck to the crime, clothing, and an eyewitness with the memory of a computer. Ten days later, Speck was indicted on eight counts of first-degree murder.

However, unable to find a murder weapon, law enforcement was still in search of the one magic bullet that would put their monster down. Despite previous memos to the effect that all relevant evidence had already been taken into custody, the dogged Detective Wallenda returned to the townhouse on July 29th to dig up one more piece of evidence that would put the final nail in Speck's coffin.

This time his search came up big. On the floor of the south bedroom, near one of the bunk beds, Wallenda found a man's white Hanes t-shirt, size 38-40M, wrapped around the purple-and-white striped slacks and white panties that Gloria Davy had worn the night of the murders. Police were convinced that this t-shirt belonged to Richard Speck, and that he had wrapped his shirt around Gloria's slacks and panties after undressing and assaulting her.

This shirt had three drops of blood in the chest area. Police believed that the drops of blood came from the scratch on Speck's chest, the result of his struggle with Valentina Pasion. The blood was Type A, Speck's blood type.[54] Police were now excited to have one more piece of incriminating evidence in their arsenal. But I found numerous issues with the t-shirt evidence:

- The State's observant star witness, so observant of every detail of the crime, never mentioned a zipper bag or t-shirts.
- Captain Dragel had confirmed the removal of all clothing evidence on the 14th. How was a bundle of slacks and t-shirt still on the south bedroom floor, in plain sight, two weeks later, next to the bed on which Gloria Davy was supposedly raped?
- The victims' families were in the townhouse on the 15th, which left another opportunity for these articles of clothing to be moved. It beggars belief that they simply remained on the floor, untouched, until Wallenda's final evidence-collecting visit two weeks later.
- Corazon had lay hidden near the bed upon which Gloria was allegedly raped. She would have been just inches from the bundled up shirt and slacks. She never mentioned the shirts, or a zipper bag, even though her recollections of Speck removing Gloria's clothing and the sexual assault were precise to an unnerving degree.
- Only two shirts were found, one containing no blood, the other with three bloodspots. The murder scene was a veritable bloodbath, yet no bloody t-shirts were found in the townhouse or in Speck's hotel room. If the purpose of the change of shirts was to avoid blood and sweat, where were all the bloody shirts? We were told that he had

brought "plenty of extra t-shirts" in the plaid zipper bag, (the bag that Corazon never saw), yet only two t-shirts were found in the townhouse.

- Speck awoke the next morning wearing his same clothes from the night before, which bore no traces of blood. He allegedly changed shirts but not his pants or shoes, neither of which bore any trace of blood even after stabbing six of eight nurses to death.

The spots of blood on the third t-shirt called to mind Sergeant Vrdolyak's misadventure with the t-shirt he found in Speck's room at the Raleigh Hotel – the one he had bled on and initially tried to pass off as bloody evidence. From what I can tell, though, they were not one and the same shirt – one was a Hanes shirt, while the one found wrapped in Gloria's slacks and panties was a BVD brand.

Two things are noteworthy: Vrdolyak almost got away with submitting falsified evidence, and prosecutor Martin actually considered submitting the t-shirt bloodied by Vrdolyak anyway, knowing it was tainted.[55] Ultimately he decided against it, but considering the fingerprint fiasco, the botched narrative, the strange controversy over the rape of Gloria Davy, the puzzling photographs, and other contradictions in the case, one has to wonder what else was going on behind closed doors.

There were other explanations for the t-shirts. It was a very hot summer; one of the nurses' boyfriends could have simply changed his t-shirt at the townhouse and left it there. The families of the victims stated that the men's t-shirts did not belong to the nurses. Of course not – they would have belonged to the boyfriends. But it's not unusual for young women to wear their boyfriends' shirts as casual wear.

One white t-shirt plus one purple-and-white pair of slacks equals another red flag. There are now enough red flags to outfit a Marxist parade.

The Gun

Contrary to many popular but untrue legends of the crime, no murder weapons were entered into evidence. We already know the fate of Ella Mae Hooper's .22 caliber revolver, the "unfounded" gun, which was eventually found but not admissible as evidence. Like the sketchy composite and the knives, the description of the gun underwent changes.

The prosecution consistently referred to Speck's gun as a pistol, once describing it as having "six live cartridges in its clip,"[56] but the Röhm .22 was actually a revolver, which houses bullets in a revolving chamber, not a clip.

In Corazon's initial statement to police she described how she answered the door and "found an unknown white man standing there and he was pointing a small black revolver at her." So she recognized that it was a revolver, but when shown the actual revolver (that had finally been restored from "unfounded" status) she could only state that it looked "similar" to Speck's gun.[57]

There were two other items that were not submitted into evidence, but their presence in the story served a darker purpose. One was already gone before the murders occurred; the other was dredged from the murky waters beneath the Calumet River Bridge.

The Knife in the Water

Richard Speck always carried a knife. It was his way of projecting a tough guy image, and he would brandish it when provoked or to impress others. The incessant tall tales of his imaginary exploits and the knife were his way of creating the macho image he longed to portray.

The investigative team was anxious to question Judy Laakaniemi, the nurse whom Speck had befriended and visited in Michigan. They were especially interested to know the type of knife Speck carried, which they believed was a black switchblade. Judy told them it was a folding knife - the kind that is manually opened by inserting a fingernail into a slot on the blade's edge and pulling the blade out from the handle.

A switchblade knife has a retractable blade encased in a thick handle with a small button on it. Pushing the button will cause the blade to automatically flip or shoot out from the handle, which is both provocative and threatening.

The difference between a switchblade and a folding knife may seem trivial, but the prosecution consistently described Speck's knife as a black switchblade. I believe their reasons were more about perception and less about accuracy. The notion of Speck carrying an ominous black switchblade lent an even more sinister element to the mass murder of the student nurses: Death at the push of a button. I can't think of one crime movie from the 1950s and 1960s where some crook didn't flash a switchblade.

Many people carry folding knives, or penknives, as they are compact tools for carving, whittling, or peeling fruit. But what evokes a more threatening image, a black switchblade used by violent street gangs, or a folding knife used for peeling fruit? The former was assigned the role of Speck's weapon of choice, although he actually owned the latter. Prosecutor Martin did a much better job of creating the brutish macho image of Speck than Speck, the bumbling burglar, did for himself.

The searches of Speck's rooms at the Shipyard Inn and the Raleigh Hotel failed to locate the knife, but Detective Wielosinski was determined to find it. Police retraced his steps from the townhouse back to the Shipyard Inn, and saw that this path led across the bridge over the Calumet River, a handy place to dispose of a weapon. They cordoned off an area of the river and commissioned several scuba divers to search the murky waters for the knife.

The first two dives proved fruitless. Nothing turned up – no switchblade, not even an ordinary pocket knife. Not to be deterred, Wielosinski searched the river again, this time with a powerful magnet. He and his team paddled out in a small boat and hoisted a large magnet, fitted onto the end of a pole like a giant fishing lure, into the center of the river just north of the bridge. They dipped the pole into the water several times, and on their final try, voila! Police had their weapon.

It was a pocket knife with two folding blades. The larger blade measured 2-3/4 inches and the smaller, 2-3/16. The tip of the larger blade was reportedly broken off, leaving a flat edge. Police surmised that this had occurred when Speck used the tip of the knife to jimmy the screen off the kitchen window. An inscription on the knife read, "Shrade Walden, New York, USA."[58] It bears reminding here that a pushy reporter was responsible for popping the screen off the window, not the blade of a knife. The official story tended to get in its own way at times.

On the following page is a photo of my own knife that I've had since childhood. The blade measures 2-3/4 inches, the same length as the one retrieved from the Calumet River, and it is nearly identical in appearance. A knife this size would have become slippery and hard to control once wet with blood. Speck had large hands and long fingers, and the knife could have easily folded over onto them, but as already noted, there were no cuts or injuries on his fingers or hands.

The 2016 edition of prosecutor Martin's book *The Crime of the Century: Richard Speck and the Murders That Shocked the Nation* shows a fascinating photograph of the actual knife that was fished out of the Calumet River. But there was one problem: The knife was intact. There were no broken tips on either blade. So it either wasn't the actual knife, or the actual knife didn't have its tip broken off as Martin had stated. Nonetheless, Martin still insisted that the knife was "a black-handled switchblade," whose tip was broken off, "possibly when Speck jimmied the screen off the window."[59] Apparently he forgot that he had already told us about the pushy reporter who popped the screen off the window in order to get a look inside.

And the knife was not a scary black switchblade; it was identical to my own simple folding knife. Mine was not a Shrade Walden New York, but instead bore the eerie engraving "Camillus – USA," in a bizarre reference to Saint Camillus, the patron saint of nurses and hospitals.

As we know, no one broke the window screen with the knife. In the end the whole tortuous, and tortured, trajectory of the Calumet River knife may as well have ended up in a river. It was not submitted into evidence, and the prosecution was better off without it anyway. Pamela Wilkening's fatal stab wound measured over four inches in depth, which could not have been made by even the larger of its two blades, tip broken off or not.

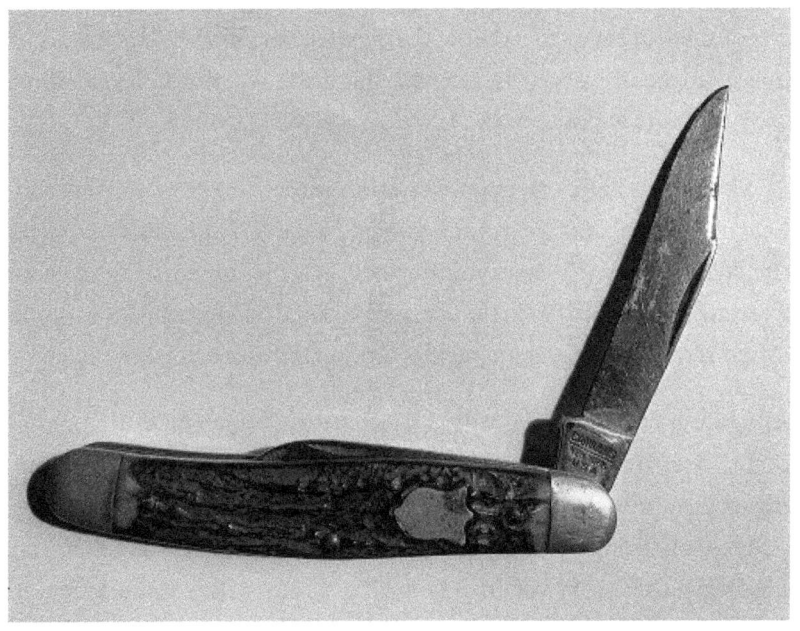

This is my own personal folding knife, or pen knife, very similar to the knife retrieved from the Calumet River by Detective Wielosinski and thought to be Speck's murder weapon.

A Weapon of Mass Distraction

Richard Speck was seen flashing another larger, more intimidating knife in the days preceding the murders. It was not submitted into evidence for reasons that will follow, but its brief association with Speck sprinkled seeds of doubt around the investigation.

Months prior to the murders, Gene Thornton had gifted his brother-in-law an imposing seven-and-a-half-inch hunting knife that he had gotten during his Navy days. Its thick, steely blade bore the inscription "Gene Thornton 727-80-94 U.S.N.R." It resembled today's Ka-Bar® Knife, complete with scabbard and a thick hilt between the blade and the handle. From the tip of its brown leather handle, with interspaced metal rings, to the tip of the blade, it measured nearly a foot in length. The blade was an inch and three quarters at its widest point.

The knife was the perfect conversation piece for Speck to show off. Legend had it that he would swagger through the seedy bars on the south side with this ominous accessory strapped to his belt in a juvenile ploy for attention. This misguided attempt to look tough raised more chuckles than hackles among the amused bar patrons.

According to the official story, Speck left this hunting knife behind in his room at the Shipyard Inn when he set out on his deadly mission to rob and murder the nurses, instead preferring to bring a much smaller pocket knife and the revolver stolen from Ella Mae Hooper. The story of this hunting knife raises a number of perplexing questions:

- A large hunting knife would have been his most efficient weapon, yet he did not bring it to the townhouse. Why?
- How did police know for certain that he did not bring the knife to the townhouse? Its use would have explained some of the deeper stab wounds and the enormous gashes found on some of the nurses.

Police proposed a few theories to explain away these questions: Speck did not bring the knife with him because he was afraid to be seen with it. This makes no sense; he had already flaunted the knife in public for all to see. And when he wore the black jacket to cover his tattoos – another theory - he could have concealed the large knife in his jacket. Or he could have stored the large knife in the alleged plaid zipper bag along with the alleged t-shirts. Was anyone thinking this through?

The story goes that Speck sold the large hunting knife on the 14th, the morning that the murders were discovered, and that he did so in order to unload a weapon that might, by association, connect him to the murders. However, based on the police and newspaper reports, and Dr. Ziporyn's account, it is certain that Speck sold the large hunting knife sometime in the late morning of Wednesday, July 13th, hours before the murders even took place.

Speck describes his movements on that morning: "I went off and got a room at the Shipyard Inn .... I had a big knife, really it was a dagger, like a bayonet. Anyway, I made another buck from that, sold it to some guy."[60]

Speck booked his room at the Shipyard Inn around 10:30 that morning. He drank and played pool, then walked a couple of blocks north to his favorite watering hole, Pete's Tap House, at 99th and Ewing.

At Pete's he met William Kirkland, a fellow heavy drinker, to whom he showed off the hunting knife, bragging that he had used it to kill several Viet Cong in Vietnam.

Speck offered to sell the knife to Kirkland, and then asked bartender Ray Crawford to hold the knife for him. Speck and Kirkland then walked over to the nearby Soko-Grad bar where Speck bought Kirkland a drink and agreed to sell him the knife for one dollar. Upon returning to Pete's, Crawford handed the knife over to Kirkland, who handed a dollar over to Speck – sale completed.

Like his other drinking companions, Kirkland found Speck's childish behavior annoying. By twelve noon, Speck headed for Eddie & Cooney's, and Kirkland was relieved to be rid of him. Thus the sale of the knife was completed by noon on the 13th.

When interviewed by detectives, Kirkland recalled that the sale was made on the 13th, but a second witness intervened and insisted that it happened on the 14th. A heavy drinker, Kirkland couldn't trust his slippery memory. He was convinced to change his statement. But the sale could not have happened on the 14th, as the following timeline, based on other reports, shows.

On the 14th, Speck did not awaken from a heavy, drug-induced slumber until 11:00 AM. He awoke with a gun in one hand and blood on the other, which befuddled him. He then washed up and went downstairs to the Shipyard bar where he drank beer and played pool. It was during this time that the policeman came into the bar and asked if the bartender had seen anyone matching the description of the suspect, while Speck stood just a few feet away.

By then it was around 11:45 AM. He then walked the few blocks north to Eddie & Cooney's, where he met up with Red Gerrald for a day of drinking and bar hopping. Gerrald stated that they met around noon. This left no time for Speck to have met Kirkland at Pete's in the late morning of the 14th and to have completed the knife sale at that same time.

This timeline explains how police knew for certain that the large knife was not used to commit the murders. But it was important to maintain the perception that Speck was trying to offload possibly incriminating evidence by selling the knife after the murders.

While the large hunting knife played no part in the crime, it served a useful role in portraying Speck as a violent, knife-wielding fiend. In this regard, a curious supplement was added to the original police report that outlined the sale of the knife to Kirkland.

In the first version of the sale, Speck and Kirkland discussed the sale of the knife, gave the knife to the bartender while they went to another bar, came back and completed the $1 transaction. The bartender then handed the knife over to Kirkland.

However, the supplemental report added that Speck then walked behind the bar, grabbed Crawford from behind and stuck the knife at his throat, play-acting how he would use the knife to kill someone. Crawford was left unnerved and shaken.[61] It is unclear why these events were not chronicled in the original report, but instead added as a supplement at the end.

However, when asked his impression of Richard Speck, bartender Crawford described him as "a very neat man, a very polite man, a very soft-spoken man."[62] This does not describe someone who had roughly grabbed him and made slashing motions at his throat with a large knife.

Police went to Kirkland's home and took possession of the knife. Predictably, it yielded both Speck's and Kirkland's prints, but no traces of blood. Films and photographs were made of the knife being processed in the crime lab, and these have surfaced in many documentaries and videos. These media incorrectly claimed that the knife was used in the murders and had Speck's bloody fingerprints all over them. Such were the false legends that multiplied in the wake of the mass murder, and they persist even today in podcasts, videos, and documentaries. The bad 'PR' intended by the story of the knife was very effective.

But the discrepancies regarding both knives made no difference. Law enforcement had brought in their man. Together with Corazon Amurao they were the toast of the city, and the media paid due homage. "Rarely has a police investigation been conducted more expertly than the one that led to the arrest of Richard Speck," hailed the *Chicago Tribune*.[63]

The final tally of evidence consists of a faulty description of the killer, an eyewitness who changed her story, false information regarding the manner of entry, FBI memos that contradict police reports, police reports that contradict sworn testimony, a lack of bloody fingerprints, three smudged fingerprints of sketchy origin, a compromised crime scene, two t-shirts of questionable origin, no murder weapons, no cuts or injuries on Speck's person, no blood on Speck's clothing, suggestions of evidence tampering, a timeline that tells the wrong time, photographs that contradict the narrative, and stories that don't make sense. The story of Fish Mouth, the murderous seaman, was bobbing in a sea of red flags.

CHAPTER FIFTEEN

THE TRIAL

Play It In Peoria

After Chief Wilson's public declaration of Speck's guilt, the defense felt a change of venue was the only chance to afford their client a fair trial. Little did they realize that this maneuver would play right into the hands of the prosecution.

The new site for the trial would be Peoria, a rural conservative community about 130 miles southwest of Chicago by way of Route 55. The Caterpillar Tractor Company, manufacturer of heavy machinery and equipment for construction, farming, and mining, was the lifeblood of the county, providing the majority of jobs.

Peoria is the largest city on the Illinois River, hence its name, "the River City." In 1966 the backbone of the city's economy was largely comprised of farmers and blue collar workers, no-nonsense, hard-working people who did not take lightly to lawbreakers and murderers. History shows that the citizenry of the past were not beyond taking the law into their own hands in the interests of justice.

The vigilante persona of the town took shape in 1851, when two men, Brown and Williams, were convicted of murder and sentenced to hang on December 30th. Aware that a third perpetrator was still in the wind, the judge called a delay of the execution. The delay so enraged the public that they stormed the jail and attacked the prisoners, anxious to mete out punishment on the spot. But in their haste to string up the scoundrels, no one remembered to bring a rope, and the two men were returned to jail. Fearful of more backlash, the sheriff abandoned plans to locate the third perpetrator and went ahead with the hangings two weeks later. Some 15,000 citizens were in attendance at the courthouse gallows - 9,000 more than the entire population of the town. Many more hangings plunged their way into the crime lore of Peoria, and it was thus christened the "hanging county" of Illinois.[64]

This reputation suited the prosecution team perfectly. They sought nothing less than a conviction and a death sentence for Richard Speck, and they would come by it more easily in conservative Peoria than in liberal Chicago.

Doing the Right Thing

In a move that initially raised eyebrows, First Assistant State's Attorney John J. Stamos named a team of his subordinates to prosecute the Speck case, handing the reins over to Assistant State's Attorney William J. Martin. Although a conviction of Chicago's most despised criminal would have added an attractive feather to his cap, Stamos declared that he could best serve his office in an administrative capacity. It wasn't about the power or the prestige, he claimed; he trusted his team to bring the murderous monster Speck to justice.

They would honor the office motto posted above his desk: "Do The Right Thing," a mantra that Stamos often repeated to his staff. It was a spin on the popular sixties slogan, "Do Your Own Thing," and it resonated in a hip way with the public and the media. Doing the right thing would secure a conviction and a death sentence through the good graces of the people of Peoria.

And so the lesser experienced prosecutorial team of William Martin, James Zagel, George Murtaugh, and John Glenville were charged with the task of securing a guilty conviction and a death sentence in an out-of-the-way venue. Both maneuvers went hand in hand. The strongest evidence against Speck - the eyewitness identification and the fingerprints - was problematic. I believe that the he prosecution, aware of this shortcoming, was doing damage control in advance; should Speck be acquitted, the blame would fall to the State's Attorney's underlings, and away from the glaring spotlight of Chicago.

The tactic of appointing a junior prosecutor to lead a major criminal prosecution calls to mind the O.J. Simpson trial, where Los Angeles District Attorney Gil Garcetti appointed Marcia Clark, an able but undistinguished trial attorney, as lead prosecutor in *The People of the State of California v. Orenthal James Simpson*. That trial, an embarrassing media spectacle, was christened "The Trial of the Century".

Jury selection began on February 20, 1967 and ended on March 30th, 1967, consuming far more time than the trial itself. It was a laborious process. Assistant State's Attorney Martin purposely selected only those jurors who supported the death penalty. Those who opposed the death penalty were immediately excused. After several weeks spent questioning 610 prospective jurors, seven men and five women were chosen, all supporters of capital punishment. This biased method of jury selection formed the basis of an unsuccessful post-conviction appeal.

Once selected, the names of the twelve jurors, their occupations, the names of their employers, and the employers' addresses, were publicized in the media. It is unthinkable by today's standards, but unremarkable back then. Other aspects of the trial, however, were sketchy by any standards.

The drawn-out jury selection process could not have concluded with a more unsettling and eerie tragedy. On that same day, March 30th, a small Delta jet crashed into a hotel, killing all nine passengers aboard and seventeen hotel guests. All seventeen – eight boys and nine girls – were high school seniors enjoying a graduation trip. The hotel was near the airport in, of all places, New Orleans.

The venue and jurors now set, all the prosecution needed was a verdict of guilty and a death sentence. Speck's one-way ticket to Stateville's "Old Sparky" was about to be punched.

Cast of Characters

Criminal investigations and prosecutions were handled through the Criminal Division of the Cook County State's Attorney's office, headed by chief Louis Garippo. The State's Attorney at the time was Daniel P. Ward, an alumnus of DePaul University School of Law, where he served as Dean before joining the State's Attorney's Office. In late 1966, after the indictment of Richard Speck, Ward received a seat on the bench of the Illinois Supreme Court, and his position was awarded to a fellow DePaul law school graduate, First Assistant State's Attorney John J. Stamos who, with Garippo, supervised the prosecution team.

First Assistant State's Attorney John J. Stamos, of Greek Orthodox parentage, grew up on the city's south side, near 92nd and Commercial, a stone's throw from some of Richard Speck's favorite watering holes. He was educated at DePaul University, the largest Catholic university in North America, and obtained his law degree from DePaul University College of Law. A tight confraternity of DePaul alumnae populated the Chicago judicial system, including its notorious mayor, Richard J. Daley, who served in office from 1955 until 1976 when his son, Richard M. Daley, took up the mantle.

A veteran of World War II, Stamos served in the U.S. Army Medical Corps in Belgium, where he performed clerical duties in the psychiatric unit of a hospital. His experience in the burgeoning field of psychiatry afforded him the perfect background for managing the Richard Speck case. Many psychiatrists were consulted in this case, and their assessments proved unfavorable to Speck's defense. With the exception of his psychiatrists, Speck hardly spoke to anyone; visits from his defense team were infrequent, and the police never questioned him.

The members of the prosecution team were George Murtaugh, John Glenville, James Zagel, and Assistant State's Attorney William J. Martin, who served as unofficial team leader. Martin had just five years of experience with the State's Attorney's office but was well regarded by his superiors. Born August 19, 1936, in Oak Park, Illinois, Martin, of Irish Catholic descent, attended Fenwick High, a college preparatory high school guided by a Dominican Catholic philosophy. He then attended Loyola University, a Jesuit institution, followed by Loyola School of Law, where he founded and served as editor of the *Loyola Law Times* newsletter.

After obtaining his law degree in 1961, Martin's goal was to serve as public defender. He set his sights on working with Chicago's best-known defense lawyer, Gerald W. Getty, whose claim to fame was his success in death penalty cases; Getty had never lost a case in over 400 trials. Martin interviewed with Getty himself, anticipating an offer to join the firm, but the job went to someone else, leaving Martin surprised and disappointed. He then reversed course and sought employment on the prosecutorial side of the aisle, receiving an appointment to Assistant State's Attorney.

In an ironic twist of fate, he would face off in court against his former idol five years later, in *Illinois v. Richard Speck*, where he secured not only a speedy conviction but a death sentence, ruining the perfect record of the man who had denied him his dream job.

Martin credited his success in the Speck case with his ability to laser focus on the task at hand, a quality finely honed through his many years of Jesuit training. He also had an affinity for religious mottos. When describing the shiftless Richard Speck, he quoted the Jewish Talmud: "If you don't know where you're going, any road will take you there."[65] Based on certain questionable actions undertaken by the prosecution, it seems he also ascribed to the Jesuit motto, "Any means to an end."[66]

Richard Speck's defense team was headed by Chief Defense Counsel, Gerald W. Getty, assisted by James Gramenos, James Doherty, and Jerome Wexler.

Born in 1911, Gerald Winkler Getty attended Mount Carmel High School in Mount Carmel, Illinois. He received his Bachelor's Degree from the University of Illinois and his law degree from DePaul University School of Law. After serving as a government attorney he was appointed as Cook County Assistant Public Defender in 1945, rising to the post of Chief Public Defender in 1954. His claim to fame as defense attorney was his successful defense of over 400 death penalty cases, until *Illinois v. Richard Speck* came along, dealing him his first loss.

Presiding over the Speck trial was sixty-one-year old Judge Herbert C. Paschen, a kindly, grandfatherly figure whose calm yet firm demeanor kept strict order in the courtroom. He was a contemporary of incumbent Mayor Richard J. Daley. Both men attended DePaul University and DePaul Law School at roughly the same time. Paschen rose to the position of judge during the time that Daley's Democratic political machine was making and breaking people in prominent positions. That same judgeship had eluded defense counsel Getty; he was an outlier, considered too independent in his approach to certain legal rulings to be part of the inner circle.

In an effort to prevent a media circus from overtaking the trial, Judge Paschen issued stern directives limiting the number of newsmen allowed in the courtroom, their access to the attorneys, and their ability to broadcast directly from the courtroom. This directive came under fire by the Illinois Supreme Court in response to complaints that the directives restricted the freedom of the press. Paschen relented by relaxing some requirements, but held firm that no recordings could be made and no photographs be taken inside the courtroom.

Witnesses for the Prosecution

Martin began the opening round of testimony with the two men who had given Speck a ride to East Chicago on July 12th for the job assignment on the Sinclair Great Lakes freighter that had fallen through. Dante Bargellini, ship steward, and George Mackey, ship's engineer, testified that Speck, angry about the cancellation, griped all the way back to Chicago, where he told them to drop him off at the National Maritime Union.

They had also seen him at the NMU the next day, which was just a block from the nurses' townhouse, thus establishing that Speck was in the area of the townhouse on the day of the murders. The prosecution theorized that he had been scoping out the townhouse for a possible robbery, and to this end he had spent the night of the 12th sleeping on a bench in Luella Park, directly behind the nurses' townhouse.

This part of the story was not true. In its desire to establish the official story the prosecution failed to take the weather into account.

A teeming thunderstorm on the night of the 12th had sent finicky Speck, not the outdoor type, sheltering in a vacant apartment building around 103rd Street. Yet they continued to build a narrative in which Speck slept in Luella Park in order to spy on the nurses with the intent to rob them.

"This Is The Man!"

The courtroom held its collective breath in anticipation of the testimony of the star State's witness, Corazon Amurao. Portrayed as a courageous heroine by the media, all she needed to do was convincingly relay the official story and withstand cross-examination by the defense. She had nothing to worry about; anyone who dared challenge her would be seen as an insensitive brute, further stirring the jury's sympathy toward her. Petite yet powerful, Corazon mesmerized the courtroom with her amazingly detailed and precise account of the vicious murders of her housemates.

The moment everyone was waiting for came early in Corazon's testimony when prosecutor Martin asked her to identify the man who had brazenly robbed, tied up, and brutally strangled and stabbed her housemates.

While prepping his witness for testimony, Martin had asked Corazon to identify Speck with a flourish, and she came through brilliantly. In a scene worthy of a made-for-TV movie, Corazon slowly descended from the witness stand, strode gallantly to the defense table and, pointing her finger just inches from Speck's blank face, declared "This is the man!" The courtroom, held spellbound by the testimony, exploded into excitement. Judge Getty had to pound his gavel to restrain the frenzied herd of reporters from stampeding their way to the pay phones outside the courtroom.

Cross-examination of the star witness began on the third day of the trial. Defense counsel Getty had his work cut out for him. He needed to attack the two items of direct evidence - Corazon's eyewitness description of Speck, and the fingerprints found on the south bedroom door.

He focused his efforts on the composite sketch, which showed a man with crew-cut dark hair, clear skin, and nondescript features. Following is an excerpt from the relevant portion of her cross-examination.

"GETTY: You never told the artist he had a crew cut?

CORAZON: I did not tell him.

GETTY: Well, did the police artist, did he ask you whether you noticed the man's teeth?

CORAZON: I can't recall if he asked me.

GETTY: So you never told him anything about the man's teeth?

CORAZON: I did not tell anything about the teeth.

GETTY: Did you tell the police artist that you noticed anything about the tattoos?

CORAZON: I did not tell him, I did not notice any tattoos.

GETTY: The man that was in your apartment had long sleeves, is that correct?

CORAZON: Yes, sir.

GETTY: He was not dressed in a black coat, or was he, or was it a black jacket?

CORAZON: All I know it was black clothes. I don't know whether it was a coat or a jacket.

GETTY: Did the police artist ask you if you noticed anything about his hands?

CORAZON: I can't recall, sir.

GETTY: Did he ask you if you noticed anything about his lips?

CORAZON: I can't recall.

GETTY: Did he ask you if you noticed anything about his nose?

CORAZON: I can't recall, sir.

GETTY: Did he ask you if you recalled anything about the color of his eyes?

CORAZON: I can't recall the color of his eyes.

GETTY: Did he ask you if you recalled – did he ask you anything about his eyes at all?

CORAZON: I can't recall, sir.

GETTY: Did he ask anything about his eyebrows?

CORAZON: I can't recall.

GETTY: Did he ask anything about his eyebrows?

CORAZON: I can't recall.

GETTY: Or the shape of his eyebrows?

CORAZON: I can't recall.

GETTY: Did he ask anything about his ears?

CORAZON: I can't recall, sir.

GETTY: Whether his ears were close to the head or far away from the head?

CORAZON: I can't recall, sir.

GETTY: When you say, "I can't recall," does that mean you can't recall telling the artist or you can't recall about the man?

CORAZON: I can't recall about the man, about his ears, about his nose, or about his eyes, I can't recall.

GETTY: You can't recall anything of that, about the man that was in the apartment, Miss Amurao, you can't recall anything about the man that was in the apartment relative to his eyes, size of his eyes, or eyebrows?

CORAZON: No.

GETTY: Or you can't recall the man that was in the apartment, anything about his lips?

CORAZON: No, sir.

GETTY: And you can't recall anything about the man that was in the apartment, as to the size or size of his ears or whether they were away from his head or close to his head?

CORAZON: I can't recall, sir."[67]

We will never know why the sketch turned out the way it did. Otis Rathel was not called to the witness stand.

Rathel, who passed away in 1989, was the first African-American employed as sketch artist for the Chicago police. Corazon had spent nearly an hour in conversation with him for the purpose of creating the composite sketch. Yet at trial she could not recall what Otis Rathel looked like. On cross-examination by Getty "...Miss Amurao admitted she could not tell him what the police artist looked like, whether he was Caucasian or Negro."[68] As mentioned before, she apparently had difficulty with cross-racial identification, having been in this country for only ten weeks when the murders occurred.

Corazon's memory lapse notwithstanding, M.W. Newman, reporter for the *Chicago Daily News,* summed up the print media's infatuation with the State's star witness: "Corazon Amurao was the greatest trial witness I have ever seen. Her memory for detail was astonishing and her sincerity couldn't be doubted."[69]

Two Knives?

The Walsh brothers and Sergeant Richard J. Oliva, who drank with Speck at the Shipyard Inn after a brief altercation with him, established Speck's whereabouts and demeanor on the night of the murders. They agreed that he did not seem intoxicated, which was corroborated by star witness Amurao.

Sergeant Oliva, a chief warrant officer (CW3) on leave from Vietnam, took the stand in full dress green military uniform to describe his confrontation with Speck at the Shipyard Inn bar in the hours preceding the murders. He saw Speck drop a knife on the floor and watched him pick it up. Speck snarled, "What are you looking at," and waved the knife menacingly in his direction.

In fact, he testified that Speck had waved not one, but two knives, one being a large hunting knife about four inches long, while the Walsh brothers saw Speck brandish one knife and a gun.[70] Oliva's mention of the large hunting knife is curious. We have already noted that the large hunting knife had been sold to William Kirkland on the 13th, hours before Oliva met Speck. And that knife was not four, but seven and a half inches in length. The prosecution had overdone it in coaching their witnesses.

Eye on the Prize

Next to testify for the prosecution was Claude Lunsford, a.k.a. B. Brian. Prosecutor Martin considered Lunsford a man of integrity, a veritable "knight-of-the-road."[34] He may as well have played Roger Miller's 1965 hit song "King of the Road" when Lunsford took the stand.

After Corazon, Claude Lunsford was one of the prosecution team's favorite witnesses. A curious connection between Martin, Lunsford, and Speck's brother-in-law Gene Thornton played itself out during their testimonies.

Lunsford had a wife and children, but according to Martin, nobly refused to dishonor them with his wayward lifestyle, so he stayed away, riding the rails and drinking himself to oblivion when he could afford it. He sometimes worked as a day laborer, sending money home to his family after paying off his bar tabs.

As Speck's last drinking buddy, Lunsford was instrumental in notifying the Starr Hotel that dangerous fugitive Richard Speck was laid up in cubicle 584, bleeding to death. He may have had his eye on the $10,000 reward for information leading to his capture.

Lunsford testified that Speck pestered him endlessly about learning how to ride the rails. When asked by the defense how one could hop a freight train, Lunsford explained, "… you go to the yard and see a switchman, and he will tell you what track it's on and what time and where it goes."[71]

At this point Getty interjected, "But the switchman always tells you when they're going to leave?" In an homage to the honest switchmen who helped him catch his trains Lunsford replied, "They always tell you, and they always tell you the truth."[72] This flattering remark seemed to be directed at a specific person in the courtroom. Could one of those honest switchmen have been Gene Thornton, Speck's brother-in-law, who worked as night switchman in the Chicago rail yards?

Next to testify was Fannie Jo Holland, an African-American resident of the Cabrini-Green housing project where Speck had taken a taxi after bringing Red Gerrald uptown. She testified that she saw Speck at 4:30 PM on the 14th, heading in the direction of N. Dearborn. It was unusual for a white male to take a taxi to this housing project, and fair-haired, pale-faced Speck, with his tan suitcase and black-and-red plaid bag, stuck out like a sore thumb.

The testimonies of Fannie Jo Holland, Red Gerrald, and Claude Lunsford supported the prosecution's theory that Speck's flight uptown showed consciousness of guilt. All the prosecution needed now was a knockout punch, and it would be delivered by the tips of three fingers.

The Fingerprints

The State was understandably concerned about the fingerprint testimony, so much so that prosecutor Martin decided not to rely on Burton Buhrke, senior fingerprint expert for the Chicago PD. Martin feared that Buhrke's scholarly demeanor and extensive knowledge on the subject would overwhelm the jury with details, so he chose Emil Giese, a handsome, youthful lieutenant on the police force, to deliver the fingerprint testimony.

But Martin was still worried. He decided to reach out to an objective third party in hopes of adding an additional fingerprint expert to his witness list. And so he approached the FBI.

An interoffice FBI memo from Agent N.E. McDaniel to Assistant Director Lester Trotter dated April 4, 1967 advised that the State's Attorney asked the FBI to provide a fingerprint expert to testify for the prosecution. The State wanted an unbiased, objective expert who was not affiliated with the Chicago police.

Director J. Edgar Hoover was annoyed with the manner in which this request was handled. In a handwritten response dated April 5th, scribbled and returned on the same memo, he advised: "I am not pleased with this turning to me as the last alternative particularly since it is Chicago Police Dept. If the Supt. Of Chicago Police Dept. makes the request I will consider it."

The Superintendent was not asked, and the FBI did not comply. With the trial already in progress, the prosecution was now in a mad rush to secure an objective fingerprint expert. They were especially motivated when, that very same day, they got wind of a rumor that Getty had contacted a well-known fingerprint expert. With lightning speed, the prosecution issued a subpoena for this expert to come to Peoria and testify on their behalf. Enter Dr. Andre Moenssens.

Belgian-born Dr. Moenssens began the study of fingerprint technique in the early 1950s and quickly developed an esteemed reputation in the field. By this time he had authored fifteen articles and two texts, and was head instructor at Chicago's Institute for Applied Sciences. The prosecution badly needed an objective voice without police connections to quell Getty's contention that the fingerprints had been transferred from the beer can to the door in an effort to frame Richard Speck.

Fingerprints can be made on two distinctly different types of surfaces: porous and non-porous. Porous surfaces, like paper and cloth, absorb oils from the skin and this absorbency maintains the integrity of the print. Non-porous surfaces, like glass or aluminum, also record fingerprint impressions, but are not absorbent, allowing for the print to remain flush on the surface and become smeared or smudged through touch or handling. Non-porous prints have one attribute: they are easily transferred from one non-porous surface to another by means of an adhesive substance.[73]

Crime lab technician Scanlon had removed Speck's prints from the beer can by means of an adhesive, which he brought back to the crime lab. The beer can was one shining example of a non-porous surface. Next to consider is the structure of the south bedroom door.

The door was a type commonly used in construction. It was a hollow door with a plywood base and a lacquered finish – a non-porous surface made to order. Getty needed to extract from Moenssens that it was possible for fingerprints to be transferred from one non-porous surface to another. Moenssens replied yes, it was.

Getty then followed up with the logical deduction that it was therefore possible for the prints to have been transferred from the beer can to the door. Moenssens quickly retorted that it wasn't possible, not in this instance. He was not pressed to explain why this particular instance was different from any other.[74]

Getty's next attempt to score points on cross-examination was to extract an admission that the fingerprints on the south bedroom door bore similarities to those of Suzanne Farris and Gloria Davy. On this point Moenssens agreed that they were similar in classification but not identical. He insisted that the print taken from near the base of the door was identical to Richard Speck's, and, adding insult to injury, he upgraded the rating of the print from a lowly 10 to a dazzling 17.

As his final Hail Mary, Getty asked Judge Paschen to allow the jurors to view the fingerprints with a magnifying glass – not only Speck's prints, but those of Suzanne Farris and Gloria Davy, whose prints bore certain similarities to Speck's. This request sent the cool and collected prosecution team into a frenzy of objections. The usually unflappable Martin exploded: "We want the truth in this case, and we are not going to play games and give the jury a magnifying glass and a bunch of these fingerprints and ask them to go back there and get confused."[75] Anxious to remain firmly in control of the narrative, Martin was not about to let the jury exercise any degree of independent thinking or analysis.

The Coroner's Contradiction

One of the glaring inconsistencies of this case was the prosecution's assertion that Gloria Jean Davy had been raped and sodomized. A police report claimed that her anus had been mutilated, evidence of a violent anal assault, but this finding was not confirmed by coroner Andrew Toman's testimony, and it is not mentioned in the pathologists' reports, which stated that the body cavities were "unremarkable."

According to law enforcement, semen evidence was found on Gloria's buttocks and a blanket on the living room sofa, but the prosecution was reluctant to fortify this with actual scientific testimony. Martin could have put crime lab technicians on the stand to explain this evidence, but he had concerns over the chain of custody of the samples.

He was also worried about confusing the jury with hours of testimony by lab technicians who would then be subjected to cross-examination. In a questionable move, Martin opted to rely only on Corazon's verbal description of the rape. He felt that the emotional impact of such horrendous testimony would be enough to convince the jury that Gloria Davy had indeed been raped.

It beggars belief that the prosecution did not use every bit of scientific evidence at its disposal to establish that Gloria had been raped and sodomized, especially after the kerfuffle with the coroner, who "did not submit testimony to verify the implied rape of Gloria Davy, which was described by Miss Amurao."[76] Martin chose to rely completely on Corazon's retelling of the rape rather than the testimony of forensic experts, which he considered "unnecessary."[77]

Why was he concerned about exposing his forensic witnesses to a lengthy cross-examination? Up to this point Getty had played paddy-cake with his courtroom adversaries. It is odd that Martin didn't present every available piece of evidence, but this particular evidence concerned the rape of Gloria Davy, which was suspect. Martin had also kept the senior fingerprint expert Burton Buhrke off the stand, instead choosing the younger, less qualified Lieutenant Giese. Martin's strategy clearly relied more on perception than reality.

But the decision to avoid long hours of additional testimony fell right into step with the warp speed at which all had taken place. The murders happened early on the 14th, the eight autopsies were completed that same afternoon, Gloria Davy was buried on the 16th, Speck was arrested early on the 17th, Speck was indicted on the 26th, Speck was tried and sentenced just ten months later. Like the questionable fingerprints, all was done and dusted very fast.

The Defense Opens, and Closes

Stages of the trial eerily coincided with disastrous events elsewhere. First came the plane crash in New Orleans. Then, the opening day of defense testimony was greeted with a bomb threat, requiring all trial participants to hurriedly evacuate the Peoria courthouse. Order was quickly restored after no bomb was found, and the trial resumed without incident. Perhaps someone was sending a message, and its intended recipient could have been on either side of the aisle.

First to testify for the defense was Michael Compateso, the factory worker who had shot pool with Speck between 8:40 and 8:57 PM at the Shipyard Inn on the night of July 13th. Compateso's main contribution was his description of Speck's brown work boots. Corazon had described the attacker as wearing black shoes, and Gene Thornton, even though testifying for the defense, offered his opinion that Speck was probably wearing black shoes that night.

Police searches of Speck's two hotel rooms had yielded no sign of blood on any of his clothing or possessions. It's hard to believe that he deftly managed not to get a single drop of blood on his clothing or shoes, regardless of whether they were black shoes or brown work boots.

Alibi-Bye

Speck's defense witnesses numbered only eleven to the State's forty-two: eight relatives, including his brother, sisters, brother-in-law Gene, and mother, Michael Compateso, with whom Speck shot pool on the night of the murders, and a waitress and a bartender from Kay's Pilot House. The bomb scare may have been a hoax, but a bombshell was about to explode inside the courtroom: Richard Speck had an airtight alibi.

Gerdena and husband Murrill Farmer handled the table service, bartending, and short order cooking at Kay's Pilot House, one of

Speck's frequent hangouts on East 100th Street, just a block north of the Shipyard Inn. They claimed that Richard Speck had visited Kay's twice on the night of the murders.

Factory shift workers were the backbone of their business and the Farmers could set a clock by their comings and goings. The second shift at the nearby Arco Door Company and Garvey Grain Elevator factories let out at midnight, when thirsty workers began pouring in for their nightcaps.

Murrill Farmer remembered that Speck had been at the bar twice on the evening of the 13th; once, between 8:00 and 8:30 PM, when he left for the Shipyard Inn and played pool with Michael Compateso between 8:40 and 8:57. He recalled that Speck was wearing a red shirt during his first visit. The two had conversed while Speck sat and drank at the counter.

He noticed when Speck returned a few hours later, around 11:30 PM, now clad in a black polo shirt. During the course of their conversation Speck explained that he had spilled a drink on the red shirt and changed into the black shirt before returning to Kay's. This is corroborated by Patrick Walsh's testimony that Speck spilled a drink on his red shirt while he sat with them at the Shipyard Inn between 9:00 and 10:00 PM.

Around 11:30 PM Speck sat at the bar and engaged in small talk with Murrill. He ordered a hamburger and a bag of potato chips around midnight. Gerdena placed the patty on the grill, but customers who had just gotten off their shift began to fill the place. She asked Murrill to finish cooking the hamburger while she waited tables.

Murrill Farmer provided a convincing description. At first glance, he thought Speck was "a German sailor" because of his looks and his tattoos. The prosecution took him to task; Speck did not have a German accent, and therefore, Farmer had to be mistaken.

What Martin disregarded was that Speck's appearance – blue eyes, sandy blond hair, aquiline nose, and fair complexion – were common traits of someone of German ancestry. Farmer also recalled the tattoo on Speck's right shoulder bearing the inscription "Rich and Shirley," a precise identifying feature that would eliminate practically everyone else. He recalled that on his second visit, around 11:30 PM, Speck was dressed in all black - shirts, pants, and shoes; he may have exchanged the brown work boots for his black shoes when he changed from the red to the black shirt.

This testimony fits the timeline of events. Agnes Budak Goze, the manager of the Inn, stated that she saw Speck leave the Shipyard Inn around 10:15 PM, which gave him time to go to his room, change his clothing, and walk a block north to Kay's Pilot House sometime between 11:00 and 11:30 PM.

The testimony of the Farmers was compelling, but everyone chose to ignore it. The premature condemnation of Speck in the media, the heinous nature of the crime, the prosecution's skillful handling of dubious evidence, and the heartbreaking loss of eight upstanding young women clouded the jury's perspective. Martin had masterfully struck an emotional chord in the jurors, while Speck sat looking dull and disaffected throughout the trial. The blurry fingerprints and Corazon's riveting testimony, flawed though they were, sealed the deal for the prosecution.

The Farmers' alibi so worried the prosecution that they sought to exclude the Farmers from the witness list. Only one thing prevented them from doing so – that pesky Brady law that had forced them to investigate the tip from Buenos Aires after letting the matter slide for five months. Rather than break the law, Martin had to break the Farmers' credibility in any way possible.

On cross-examination Assistant State's Attorney Glenville attacked the timeline: how could a busy bartender and waitress possibly keep track of all the comings and goings of the customers? Couldn't the Farmers have seen him at a different time, or on a different night, and gotten confused?

The Farmers held firm; their night shift customers were as reliable as the clock that punched their time cards. Much to the discomfort of the prosecution, Murrill Farmer would not budge in his testimony: "I noticed a crude tattoo on his right arm that contained the word 'Shirley'... I'd fixed the time as between 12:15 and 12:30 that morning...I'd stake my life on it."[78]

Glenville then sought to discredit Farmer's description of "a German sailor," because Speck did not have a German accent. But by "German" he was referring to Speck's appearance, not his speech.

The prosecution attempted to discredit the alibi by introducing a statement by the owner of Kay's Pilot House, who said that Speck was there on the 11th or 12th and not the 13th. However, key to the testimony of the Farmers was that Speck had shown up twice on the 13th, once clad in a red shirt, and then later in a black shirt.

The Farmers held fast to their claim that on the night of July 13th, during the exact time of the murders, Richard Speck sat eating a hamburger at Kay's Pilot House. Unable to discredit the worrisome alibi, Martin knew that he had to double down his attack on the Farmers. In his closing arguments he again attempted to shatter their timeline of the events, pontificating to the jury, "the human mind is not a stopwatch!"[79]

Some of Martin's remarks in this case raised irony to a high art form. It was his own star witness whose uncanny memory had served as efficient timekeeper for every traumatic incident that occurred on the night of the murders - "from one to two minutes," "about five minutes," "between twenty and twenty five minutes," "about twenty minutes," "about forty minutes," and so on. Corazon's human mind was an impeccable stopwatch for the prosecution, but for the defense, the Farmers' keen memory could not be trusted.

The alibi is compelling for many reasons. The Farmers had nothing to gain by stepping forward; they had no deals to make or rewards to collect. They did not know Richard Speck. They bravely came forward in a hostile climate that had already judged Speck guilty. They had described his features, his clothing, his manner of speech, one of his tattoos, what he ate, and at what time. As alibis go, this one is as ironclad as it gets, but in the end, nothing would nullify the emotional impact of the crime and the power of the prosecution.

Speck, who had sat glassy-eyed and listless throughout the trial, showed little interest in the proceedings, but bristled when his former friends took the stand for the prosecution. It was the only time he showed any visible reaction, aside from when his mother blew him a kiss.

Richard Speck was resigned to the fact that he had killed the eight nurses; who was he, a low-life loser, to contradict the people's star witness, the prosecution, the police, and the psychiatrists? He still could not remember the night of the crime, and so assumed the mantle of guilt. When the unanimous verdict of guilty came down after only 47 minutes of deliberation, he barely blinked.

The Right Stuff

The trial concluded on April 30, 1967. Five weeks later, on June 5, 1967, Richard Speck was sentenced to death by electrocution. One year later to the day, Senator Robert F. Kennedy would be gunned down in the Ambassador Hotel in Los Angeles by Sirhan B. Sirhan, another questionable suspect who remains imprisoned today for a shooting earmarked by suspicious evidence.

Another milestone occurred during the trial: Incumbent Mayor Richard J. Daley, now 64, won a landslide reelection in the Chicago mayoral race. His popularity was at an all-time high, aided by his decisive putdown of the race riots and the quick apprehension of Richard Speck. These catastrophic events had served to grease the well-oiled Democratic political machine, and it kept on rolling right along.

Court Fees and Spending Sprees

Just three days into the trial, Cook County Controller Charles R. Hodgman expressed concerns about the rapidly ballooning trial expenses, which were already threatening to burst the allotted budget of $100,000, worth almost a million dollars today. A member of the city board, Charles Chaplin, was not joking when he decried the expenses as "ridiculously high. No individual could afford to pay the costs that the taxpayers are paying in this case."[80]

Part of the runaway expenses were due to the change of venue, requiring all attorneys and witnesses to lodge at local Peoria hotels, with members of law enforcement frequently hopping the Ozark Airlines puddle-jumper from Chicago to Peoria when needed.

Speck's former drinking buddies, Claude Lunsford and Red Gerrald, ran a tab for their daily six packs and pints of whisky, deemed a necessary expense by the prosecution. The Ramada Inn was like a palace for the two barflies; for ten days they got to sleep in real beds with clean sheets, complete with bathrooms, fresh towels, hot meals, and most importantly, free booze to keep their spirits buoyant and their tongues lubricated.

For her part in the trial, witness Fannie Jo Holland, who placed Speck at the Cabrini-Green housing project on the 15th, substantiating evidence of flight, demanded that her mandatory pints of whiskey be nothing less than 100 proof.[81] Even with costs ballooning way over budget, the prosecution signed off on this expense.

The defense team stayed at a Voyager Inn for a nightly cost of $10 per room, while the more upscale prosecution team favored the $12-a-night Ramada Inn. Other necessities, like meals, carfare, airfare, taxis, and other incidentals, ran up a tab faster than Imelda Marcos at a Manolo Blahnik shoe sale. But the State felt it was worth it; the prosecution strategies and the change of venue worked to perfection. It all played very well in Peoria.

And it paid well too. State's Attorney Stamos invited the victorious prosecution team into his office for a celebration. Each team member was handed an envelope containing a bonus check in the amount of $1,000. With the trial budget overblown in the tens of thousands, why quibble over a few thousand more? Stamos offhandedly explained, "Shit, it's the least we can do for you, after all you have done for us."[82] You and us? Weren't the prosecution team and the State's Attorney's office one and the same? Or were there other entities lurking in the shadows behind the prosecution with vested interests in the case?

In the State's eyes, the prosecution team had skillfully managed all aspects of the trial; they fortified a shaky identification; they elevated blurry fingerprints to an art form; they cracked a rock-solid alibi, and they dealt Chief Public Defender Getty his first defeat in a death penalty case. They convicted the hapless, hopeless Richard Speck. They did the right thing.

Assistant State's Attorney Martin, now free from the grueling demands of the past nine months, returned home to celebrate with his family. The handsome $1,000 bonus was equal to ten percent of his $10,000 salary, cause alone for celebration. But lavish as he was with the runaway trial budget, the spending spree was now over. On his first night home he treated the family out to dinner at McDonald's.[83]

NOTES
PART II: THE EVIDENCE
Chapter Nine: "Dragnet"

1 John P. Quinlan to J. Edgar Hoover, "Memorandum," Federal Bureau of Investigation, Washington, D.C., July 14, 1966.

2 John P. Quinlan to J. Edgar Hoover, "Memorandum: Richard Franklin Speck," Federal Bureau of Investigation, Washington, D.C., July 21, 1966.

3 Quinlan, "Memorandum: Richard Franklin Speck," July 21, 1966.

4 Breo and Martin, *Crime of the Century*, 65.

5 Altman and Ziporyn, *Born to Raise Hell*, 40.

6 Altman and Ziporyn, 41.

7 https://academic.udayton.edu/race/03justice03.htm

8 Robert Wiedrich and William Jones, "Speck's Kin Take Stand in His Trial," *Chicago Tribune*, April 13, 1967.

9 Breo and Martin, *Crime of the Century*, 98.

10 https://www.domu.com/blog/chicago-coordinates-chicago-grid-system

11 Jack Lerner, "Investigation of Possible Murder Suspect," [section name illegible], Chicago Police Department, July 15, 1966.

This memo described how police lifted prints from the hotel room of another person of interest to see if they matched up to prints taken from the crime scene; apparently it was a method then in use by Chicago PD.

12 George Murtaugh and Byron Carlile, "Supplementary Report," Area 2 Homicide, Chicago Police Department, July 16, 1966.

13 "Hunt Ex-Convict As Killer," *Sunday Star,* (Washington, D.C.), July 17, 1966.

14 Breo and Martin, 118.

15 Breo and Martin, 396.

16 John Quinlan to J. Edgar Hoover, "Memorandum," Federal Bureau of Investigation, Washington, D.C., July 17, 1966.

17 https://www.ccbhs.org/pages/CermakHealthServicesofCookCounty.html

18 https://www.findlaw.com/criminal/criminal-rights/lineups-and-other-identification-situations.html

19 Breo and Martin, *Crime of the Century,* 118.

20 "Money Granted in Speck Suit," *Denton Record-Chronicle,* (Denton, Texas), October 19, 1972.

Chapter Ten: "Doctor Dad"

21 Breo and Martin, 374.

22 Altman and Ziporyn, 32.

23 Altman and Ziporyn, 14.

24 Altman and Ziporyn, 48.

25 Altman and Ziporyn, 14.

26 Altman and Ziporyn, 209.

27 Altman and Ziporyn, 82.

Chapter Eleven: "The Six Faces of the Panel"

28 Altman and Ziporyn, 60.

29 Breo and Martin, *Crime of the Century,* 195.

30 Namanja Radojevic, Bojana Radnic, Stojan Petkovic et al, "Multiple stabbing in sex-related homicides," July 2013, *Journal of Forensic and Legal Medicine,* 20(5): 502-7. DOI: 10.1016/j.jflm.2013.03.005 pub med.

31 https://www.practicalhomicide.com/articles/sexrelatedhomicides.htm

32 Adam Higginbotham, "The Long, Long Life of the Lipstick Killer," April 30, 2008, https://www.gq.com/story/william-heirens-lipstick-killer-chicago

33 Linze Rice, "70 Years After 'Lipstick Murders,' Doubt Over Killer's Guilt Still Lingers," January 7, 2016, https://www.dnainfo.com/chicago/20160107/edgewater/70-years-after-lipstick-murders-doubt-over-kill

34 Altman and Ziporyn, *Born to Raise Hell,* 68.

35 https://m.facebook.com/TheHollywoodOccult/posts/900909116690701?locale=h._IN8_rdr

36 Breo and Martin, *Crime of the Century,* 378.

37 Breo and Martin, 379.

38 https://my.clevelandclinic.org/health/diseases/8874-traumatic-brain-injury

Chapter Twelve: "Cry for Me, Argentina"

39 A.B. Eddy to Mr. Gale, "Richard Franklin Speck – Unlawful Flight to Avoid Prosecution – Murder," FBI Headquarters, Washington, D.C., January 10, 1967.

40 Memorandum to S.A.C. Chicago from Director, FBI, "Richard Franklin Speck, aka UFAP – Murder," February 2, 1967.

Chapter Thirteen: "Untying the Knots"

41 "Pathological Report and Protocol," Institute of Forensic Pathology, Cook County, Illinois, July 1966, nos. 146-148, 151-153.

These are the pathology reports for Pamela Wilkening, Suzanne Farris, Nina Jo Schmale, Valentina Pasion, Patricia Matusek and Gloria Davy. Various direct quotes from these reports have been made in this and other chapters and are so indicated.

42 S.F. Ely and C.S. Hirsch, "Asphyxial deaths and petechaie: a review," *J Forensic Sci 2000;* 45(6): 1274-177.

43 Jack Claridge, "Rigor Mortis and Lividity," https://www.exploreforensics.co.uk/rigor-mortis-and-lividity.html

44 "Nurse's Story of Death Night: Tells Jurors of Mass Murder," *Chicago Tribune,* April 6, 1967.

The *Chicago Tribune* published an excerpt from the trial testimony of Corazon Amurao and all quotations from Amurao's testimony are taken from this excerpt. The transcript was complete except for the testimony regarding the rape of Gloria Davy, which was excluded.

45 http://www.vivo.colostate.edu/hbooks/pathphys/digestion/basics/transit.html

46 Jack Claridge, "Rigor Mortis and Lividity."

47 "Protein Digestion, Absorption, and Metabolism," *LibreTexts Medicine,* August 14, 2020, https://med.libretexts.org/Courses

48 Altman and Ziporyn, *Born to Raise Hell,* 20.

49 Breo and Martin, *The Crime of the Century,* 304.

Chapter Fourteen: "The Evidence"

50 Breo and Martin, 66.

51 Breo and Martin, 100.

52 Breo and Martin, 408.

53 Breo and Martin, 66.

54 Breo and Martin, 331.

55 Breo and Martin, 331.

56 Breo and Martin, 177.

57 Breo and Martin, 136.

58 Breo and Martin, 177.

59 Breo and Martin, 177.

60 Altman and Ziporyn, 40.

61 [name redacted], "Supplementary Report," Chicago Police Department, Area 2 Homicide, July 17, 1966.

62 Breo and Martin, 25.

Chapter Fifteen: "The Trial"

63 "Police Had Line on Speck Only Hours After Slayings," *Evening Star,* (Washington, D.C.), July 18, 1966.

64 https://peoriapubliclibrary.org/about-ppl/local-history-genealogy/early-peoria-killers-williams-brown/

65 Breo and Martin, 210.

66 Burke McCarty, *The Suppressed Truth About the Assassination of Abraham Lincoln,* 1924, http://jmgainor.homestead.com/files/111/02.htm

67 Robert Wiedrich and William Jones, "Survivor Accuses Speck," *Chicago Tribune,*

April 6, 1967.

68 Ray Manahan, "Can't Recall Killer's Face, Massacre Survivor Admits," *Pantagraph,* (Bloomington, Illinois), April 6, 1967.

69 Breo and Martin, 329.

70 Breo and Martin, 318

71 Breo and Martin, 338.

72 Breo and Martin, 338.

73 https://dps.mn.gov/divisions/bca/bca-divisions/forensic-science/Pages/evidence-processing.aspx

74 Breo and Martin, 350.

75 Breo and Martin, 354.

76 Ray Manahan, "State to End Testimony Against Speck This Week," *Pantagraph,* (Bloomington, Illinois), April 10, 1967.

77 Breo and Martin, 305.

78 Robert Wiedrich and William Jones, "2 Witnesses Give Alibi On Death Night," *Chicago Tribune,* April 14, 1967.

79 Breo and Martin, 419.

80 "Speck Trial May Exceed $150,000," *Chicago Tribune,* April 7, 1967.

81 "Speck Trial May Exceed $150,000."

82 Breo and Martin, 376.

83 Breo and Martin, 239.

PART III

THEORIES

CHAPTER SIXTEEN

RECAP

This was a complex crime with many moving parts. Part I focused on the backstories of Richard Speck, the nurses, and the events leading up to and including the night of the crime. Part II covered the apprehension and arrest of Speck, the evidence, and the trial. Part III focused on possible motives for the crime based on extensive research into related events. Some of it is my own speculation, based on verifiable facts.

Before diving into Part III, the following review may prove helpful.

- There was no break-in; the intruder either walked in or was let in.
- The description of the killer's movements made no sense.
- It was supposedly a robbery, but jewelry was left on the bodies.
- The intruder rounded up the nurses, cut ligatures from a bedsheet and tied several of them up, all in the dark.
- Nurses who were reportedly tied up were not tied up.
- Injuries on the nurses suggested more than one attacker.
- The coroner would not confirm the alleged rape of Gloria Davy and her body showed no sign of injury, other than evidence of ligature strangulation.
- Gloria Davy had fixed lividity in her back, but was found face down.
- Valentina Pasion, said to be asleep in bed, was still dressed in day clothes.
- Corazon Amurao stated that she and her roommate were in bed when the intruder came, but their beds, cluttered with items, had not been not slept in.

- Partially digested or undigested food in Gloria Davy and Valentina Pasion suggests a different timeline of their killings.
- The composite sketch of the killer omitted vital facial features of Richard Speck but included a crew cut with dark hair, which he did not have.
- A short black hair was found in the fingers of Valentina Pasion, consistent with a crew cut and dark hair, but was not taken into consideration. Particles of skin were also found under her fingernails.
- The FBI files conflict with police statements and witness testimony.
- No weapons were entered into evidence, but the knife thought to be the murder weapon was not long enough to have inflicted the four-inch stab wound on Pamela Wilkening.

These findings have led me to conclude the following:

There was more than one killer, at least two and possibly three.

Three nurses were stabbed, three were strangled, and two suffered a combination of both. This suggests the participation of at least two individuals, and perhaps a third. There was possibly also a third man who kept Corazon Amurao away from the bloodshed.

The killings were done in a blitz-style attack.

The blitz-style attacks explain why no one had time to scream or escape. The nurses were ambushed by one attacker from behind and immediately incapacitated, either by ligature, choke hold, or neck compression, while a second and possibly a third attacker wielded the knife. The autopsy reports provide ample clues in this connection.

The murders were premeditated.

It is no coincidence that unit 2317, next door to the townhouse, was vacant. This eliminated any possibility of witnesses who might see or hear something coming from the nurses' quarters. There may have been accomplices who watched the townhouse and knew when all of the nurses were finally inside, and who may have been noticed by eyewitnesses. This was not a random mass murder.

Richard Speck did not commit the murders.

- His fingerprints were suspicious. Even after two days of searching they did not turn up in the townhouse until prints had been lifted from a beer can in his hotel room.
- Speck had no injuries on his fingers or hands after allegedly delivering 40 stab wounds with a 2-3/4 inch folding knife.
- A scratch on his chest was attributed to a struggle with Valentina Pasion, but he was said to be wearing a black jacket during the murders (later changed to a white t-shirt, an element introduced into the story after one, then two, men's white t-shirts, Speck's size, were found in the townhouse).
- He reportedly manhandled the nurses, but left no bloody fingerprints or hand prints anywhere. Washing up after each killing was not enough to explain away the lack of bloody prints.
- There was no blood on his clothing, shoes, or in his hotel room.
- The large hunting knife, an ideal weapon, was sold hours before the murders.
- He awoke fully clothed after the murders wearing a clean black shirt and slacks, the same clothing worn the night before.

- Speck had an airtight alibi. Murrill Farmer recalled details of his appearance, what he said, and what he was wearing during both his visits to Kay's Pilot House, the last visit taking place at the same time as the murders.

Richard Speck had been pre-selected to take the fall because of his habits, his criminal background, and his proximity to the townhouse in early July. No one would believe a criminal's excuse of a blackout, and no one believed his alibi, ironclad as it was. His own immaturity, low intelligence, poor memory, and weakness of character enabled him to be convinced of his own guilt.

One or more killers had military or professional training.

The two centimeter sized bruises on Suzanne and Valentina are significant; two centimeters is the exact width of a signet ring, such as those issued by the military, universities, or professional institutions. Military members are required to wear their hair in short or crew-cut style, like the short black hair clutched between Valentina's fingers. No wonder there was such a kerfuffle about the killer not having a crew cut! That is exactly what he had. If not military experience – where soldiers are trained to ambush and kill – one or more killers had a professional education and wore a signet ring from the institution.

It's also worth recalling that two bloody (and complete) shoeprints were found on the floor of the west bedroom. One had straight-across grid lines, as found in footwear worn by medical professionals, and one bore a grid pattern similar to those found on combat and military-issue boots. These detailed shoeprints were made when the blood was still fresh.

Law enforcement would have been well advised to be on the lookout for a man with black hair, worn in a crew cut, wearing a large ring and professional shoes or boots, who had a scratch on his head, face, arms, or neck, and blood on his shoes.

These observations are based on evidence found at the crime scene.

<u>One or more killers knew the nurses.</u>

I believe the murders were motivated by anger and revenge toward one or more nurses in the townhouse, and that the rest sadly were killed to eliminate witnesses and to send a message. This explains how the killers easily gained entry to the townhouse without raising anyone's concern; they entered as friendly visitors known to the nurses, and then enacted their deadly plan.

Certain influential individuals known to the nurses visited the townhouse on the very day of the murders. I'll circle back to that later.

<u>The killers knew the layout of the townhouse.</u>

They did not commit any murders in the south bedroom. That room was most visible from the picture window that overlooked the rear parking lot, which had frequent traffic from other student nurses and townhouse occupants.

They also knew that four of the nurses slept in the south bedroom, while only two each slept in the east and west bedrooms. It was easier to invite someone into one of these smaller, out of the way rooms, attack her, cover her body, and then shut the door. I believe that is the reason that six nurses were killed in these rooms, while Gloria was killed downstairs and Patricia was ambushed on her way out of the bathroom.

These two front rooms also afforded more privacy within which to commit the killings. The killers couldn't kill everyone at once, so throughout the evening they ushered the nurses into the rooms where they were immediately subdued. They then covered the bodies and kept the doors closed. Not everyone was in the house at the same time, so the killings had to take place over a period of hours – but not the hours given us by the official story.

<u>Were the nurses really tied with cloth strips cut from a bedsheet?</u>

There were too many discrepancies in the official story concerning who was tied up and who wasn't. The fact that Suzanne Farris, Mary Ann Jordan and Valentina Pasion had cloth strips simply draped across their bodies invites the thought that the cloth strips were staged. Hours passed between the last murder and Corazon's cry for help, which left time for crime scene manipulation.

A few crime scene photos of the bodies showed that the white cloth strips tied around the nurses' ankles were still pristine white and not saturated with blood. Blood from the stab wounds would certainly have dripped down on these, unless the women were already down, as I suggested before, and the cloth strips were tied post mortem.

It is worth noting that Corazon, who allegedly spent agonizing hours hiding underneath a bed with her hands and feet tightly bound, had no ligature marks on her arms or legs when examined by doctors. Of all the nurses only Pat Matusek had "impression bands" on her wrists. Not everyone was tied up.

<u>Evidence was suppressed or manufactured.</u>

Detective Wallenda's improbable find of the t-shirt wrapped around Gloria Davy's slacks, and Sgt. Vrdolyak's plan to submit a t-shirt containing his own blood, signal that law enforcement was not beyond manipulating evidence in their favor. Same can be said of the manner in which Speck's fingerprints appeared on the south bedroom door and of the dubious t-shirt wrapped around Gloria Davy's slacks.

The sole surviving witness was unreliable.

There were too many inconsistencies between Corazon's initial police statement and her trial testimony. The excessive number of details that she recalled from the murder night stands in stark contrast to her inability to accurately describe Richard Speck without the aid of law enforcement, or Otis Rathel. Her account of the crime contradicts information in the police reports as well as the FBI files, and her own trial testimony conflicts with information given in her first police statement.

The witnesses introduced other possibilities.

The report of the witness who saw two people exit a dark grey 1963 Pontiac and enter the townhouse around 12:30 did not fit the narrative. Suzanne and Mary Ann returned to the townhouse just in time to meet the 12:30 AM curfew but they were on foot. Did the two parties just miss each other by minutes?

The behavior of the driver of the Pontiac is also suspicious; he circled the townhouses twice, then stopped and waited a moment before driving off. Was he waiting for a signal? Was someone conducting surveillance on the townhouse to make sure everyone had returned?

Witness Bill McCarthy found the parking lot full, and circled the neighborhood until a space became available at 1:30 AM. The sightings by both witnesses leave room for speculation regarding the comings and goings of persons other than the nurses. A nurse in 2315 also reported seeing a man park his car at 3:00 AM. Bill McCarthy stated that he took the last open space at 1:30, which means that someone else left a vacant space after 1:30 and before 3:00 AM.

The same questions that have haunted this crime over the decades - why didn't they scream, why didn't they fight back – could not be answered until the false official narrative was completely dismantled. The answers now come into sharper focus.

They didn't scream because they were taken off guard and ambushed like prey; their predators either overcame them by neck compressions or ligatures from behind, stifling any noise. One killer stood on one side while one attacked from the other.

The alternate scenario invites a huge elephant into the room. What was Corazon Amurao doing while the atrocities were being committed on her housemates? She was not physically harmed; the killers, and their sponsor, needed a live witness to perpetuate the frame-up of Richard Speck.

I believe Corazon acted under coercion or threat to herself and her family. Any persons powerful enough to orchestrate such a heinous mass murder also had the power to deport her back to the Philippines, harm her family, prevent her from ever working again, or worse. A closer look at Corazon will follow.

If this alternate scenario represents what really happened, it offers some small modicum of relief in the knowledge that the nurses were not subjected to long, drawn-out hours of terror and trauma. It debunks the foolish notion that the nurses, exuberant young women with everything to live and fight for, simply went passively to their brutal deaths because of their training. And it dispels the ghost of those haunting unanswered questions, why didn't they scream, why didn't they fight?

But there was still no relief in store. If Richard Speck was truly set up to take the fall, who was behind such a nefarious scheme? It wasn't my intent to try to solve the murders, but I had a hunch where to look for a possible motive. What I discovered proved to be more shocking and disturbing than the official story itself.

CHAPTER SEVENTEEN
HYPOCRITICAL OATH

It was July 1967, the first anniversary of the murders, when a young African-American woman found herself in a dilemma. She was eighteen years old, pregnant, and suffering from sickle cell anemia. Fearing complications for herself and her baby, she consulted her physician. At that time abortions were illegal in Illinois but were permitted in cases involving serious medical conditions. The patient's doctor granted her medical permission to terminate her pregnancy on this basis.

After the abortion the young woman expressed concern about her ability to have children in the future. It was no problem, her doctor assured her; she would be able to have children whenever she chose. At his direction, a student nurse provided her with a contraceptive device to allow for her to better plan her next pregnancy.

Some years later the young woman, now ready to start a family, had trouble conceiving a child, and once again sought the advice of her doctor. Much to her shock and dismay, he informed her that she would never be able to bear children; a pelvic examination revealed that her tubes had been tied.

The procedure was supervised by Dr. John P. Harrod, Jr. Harrod was a well-known and influential figure in Chicago medical circles. He was also chief of OB/GYN at South Chicago Community Hospital.

Barbour v. South Chicago Community Hospital

It had taken the young woman thirteen years to discover that doctors at SCCH, including Harrod, had deliberately sterilized her, lied to her, and given her contraceptive devices that they knew were unnecessary. Stunned by this betrayal, she filed a malpractice suit against SCCH in 1980. Those thirteen years worked against her in a cruel way. The lawsuit, and subsequent appeal, were decided in defendant's favor on the ground that the statute of limitations for bringing legal action had expired.[1]

The implications of this are staggering. Was this just the odd exception, a one-off, or was South Chicago Community Hospital engaged in the covert sterilization of its indigent and minority patient population?

SCCH was sued numerous times over the years for all manner of malpractice. The list was long enough to scare off an entire patient population, had they only known. But a one-off it wasn't. Another suit, *Green v. Heron,* was brought against SCCH by a young woman who learned that a tubal ligation had been performed on her by Dr. Patrick Heron. Heron's boss was Dr. John P. Harrod, Jr., also named in the lawsuit.[2]

Dr. Harrod was chief of OB/GYN at SCCH during the time that both illegal tubal ligations were performed. The hospital's associate director, Dr. Harlan Newkirk, was also aware that such procedures were taking place; he had been deposed in *Green v. Heron*. The suit was dismissed on appeal.[3] Dr. Harrod, 58, died in March 1983 while this case was being adjudicated, and ultimately no one at the hospital was held accountable.

SCCH, no stranger to lawsuits, was sued for malpractice in 1977 concerning the treatment of an unborn fetus. In *Mennes v. South Chicago Community Hospital* the hospital was charged with negligence in the deaths of Asuncion Villoso, a young Hispanic woman, and her unborn fetus of eight months.[4] Once again, the worrisome Dr. Harrod was the attending physician. Decision was again rendered on behalf of the hospital.

The lawsuits did nothing to diminish the reputation of Dr. Harrod, who held an esteemed position among the medical fraternity of Chicago. In addition to being head of OB/GYN at SCCH, he was also chairman of the medical advisory board of Planned Parenthood Foundation of America and a member of the Illinois Citizens for the Medical Control of Abortion. In 1978 he appointed a board of five members to study abuse at abortion clinics in the city. Abuse was the operative word:

"A five-month investigation by the Better Government Association revealed that many women were subjected to substandard care and that some abortions were being performed on women who were not pregnant."[5]

Abortions on women who were not pregnant? One wonders what on earth was being done during these procedures, but we already have a good idea. The title of the source article, "Stricter Clinic Control Urged," was a dazzling understatement.

It seems ironic that Harrod, who was performing illegal tubal ligations, would be waging war on illegal abortions, but it makes sense. Legalized abortions would fall under the control of the medical establishment, and we have already seen what happened to Ms. Barbour and Green while under Harrod's care.

Harrod was involved with population control well before the Sixties. In 1961 he was elected Chairman of the Chicago branch of Planned Parenthood's medical committee. The *Daily Calumet* summed up the goal of the organization in this broad statement: "... the association concerns itself with a plan to control the size of families and the eventual population of the world."[6]

These lofty goals were reminiscent of the ideology of the then thought-to-be-defunct Third Reich - minority races, considered inferior, needed to be subordinated or eliminated. As in Ms. Barbour's and Green's cases, I imagine the families or the population would not be in on the plan. Harrod's idea of population control was direct and drastic: why fuss over the fate of an unborn fetus when you can just prevent its conception altogether? For him and his colleagues sterilization, although illegal in Illinois, was their final solution.

One only wonders how many tubal ligations were performed on minority women that went undetected. Ms. Barbour and Green were made aware of their infertility only because they sought treatment for it, which was rare for minority women at that time. Even now, "white women, women with higher education levels, and women with higher incomes are at least twice as likely to seek treatment as other groups of women."[7] And this is due to technological advances in infertility treatment today; it was an entirely different situation back in the Sixties.

How many other sterilized women simply assumed that either they or their partners were infertile? And if they had discovered that their infertility was due to an illegal tubal ligation, how many had the means or the desire to pursue legal redress? Ms. Barbour and Green represent the tip of the iceberg.

The lawsuits establish that SCCH, a nurse training hospital, was willfully engaged in the unauthorized, unethical, and immoral sterilization of minority female patients without their knowledge or consent. I wondered how the nurses in townhouse 2319 must have felt about that.

The nurses' biographical information yielded important clues regarding their character. Several of them were idealistic, outspoken young women. Pat, Suzanne, and Mary Ann wanted to specialize in pediatrics. How would they have felt about depriving women of their reproductive rights? About violating the trust between practitioner and patient? About breaking the law?

One of Gloria Davy's dreams was to serve in the Peace Corps. Created in 1961 by President John F. Kennedy, the Peace Corps was a volunteer organization for American youth would spend one year in Third World Countries to provide assistance to the victims of starvation, disease and war. Several thousand signed up for the Peace Corps during the Sixties. By 1966, the Peace Corps was active in fifty-five countries, most of which were in Africa.[8] Would someone who wanted to help the starving, sick people of Africa willingly assist in the illegal sterilization of African-American women in this country?

Suzanne, Mary Ann, Pat, and Nina Jo had strong personalities and Merlita and Valentina were deeply religious. It would take only one of them to voice displeasure over what was happening in the OB/GYN ward at SCCH, perhaps to threaten disclosure. I believe the murders were intended to silence one or more potential whistleblowers among the group, with the rest eliminated as witnesses. Only one, Corazon Amurao, had to be spared in order to finger Richard Speck. She was kept sequestered not just for her own protection, but to learn and safeguard the official story that she was charged with promoting.

If exposed, the consequences of the sterilizations extended beyond the livelihood of the doctors and the hospital. Chicago could ill afford more race riots and violence in the streets. The revelation that illegal sterilizations were being performed on African-American women in a Chicago hospital could have catastrophic results. And there would be economic consequences as well.

The Nurse Training Act of 1964, Public Law 88-581, HR 11241, had paved the way for Filipino nurses to work in U.S. hospitals, but its reach extended much farther. The Act authorized $283 million dollars in grants for the development of four and five year nursing programs, student loans, and the building and expansion of nursing schools on regional, state and local levels.[9] The revelation that the hospital was committing illegal sterilizations on its minority patient population presented a serious threat to the financial well-being of the hospital. This provided a powerful motive; something had to be done to silence any well-meaning whistleblowers.

I believe that certain doctors at SCCH were directly involved with the mass murder of the eight student nurses, and that they were powerful and prestigious enough to arrange a cover-up and a frame-up to protect their secret. If one or more nurses threatened to blow the whistle, all had to be silenced, as witnesses to the misdeeds or the murders themselves.

Footprints left at the crime scene included patterns commonly used on medical personnel footwear, and also, military footwear. Military combat experience would have been extremely helpful in dispatching so many victims within a short period of time. In my opinion the killers included a doctor and/or accomplices, some of whom had military training.

Doctors and veterans are accustomed to death, they don't shy away from the sight of blood or gore, and they know the vulnerable parts of the human body. Doctors have access to sharp instruments, surgical scrubs, and gloves which, when bloodied, are easily disposed of in the hospital with no one the wiser. The same applies to bloody clothing. Military personnel are trained in tactical combat and would know how to employ chokeholds or carotid compressions in order to subdue a person.

Two possible links come to mind: that Suzanne Farris was having a problem with an instructor at the hospital, and the mystery note from Argentina that named a doctor as the real perpetrator. Unfortunately I found no further information about Suzanne's problem, but the hospital misdeeds gave credence to the Argentine tip and brought it into much clearer focus.

The Argentine tip provides a possible personal motive for the murders, but I believe there was something more crucial at stake – something of far greater consequence than a doctor having illicit relations with a student nurse. Preventing the exposure of an illicit affair – or avenging an affair gone wrong - is always a possibility, but the doctor also had to have a tremendous amount of clout and connections to pull off a frame-up of Richard Speck. I believe that something potentially more consequential than an illicit affair was involved. Perhaps the student nurse threatened to reveal not only the affair, but other illegal activities that were taking place at the hospital.

Good in Birth

The ramifications of the illegal sterilization procedures also run deeper than medical misdeeds; they are evidence that doctors at South Chicago Community Hospital were engaged in the practice of eugenics – what was then called the "new science" of population control. And many powerful and influential people supported this practice.

Eugenics is derived from the Greek word meaning "good in birth" or "strong in birth."[10] It is based on the belief that the human race can be improved by culling inferior or undesirable genetic traits from the population. This is accomplished in several ways: the sterilization of specific groups, enforced segregation by gender, or encouraging selective breeding among specific types of people.

During the reign of the Third Reich in Nazi Germany it was accomplished by mass murder – the murder of Jews, homosexuals, Communists, the mentally ill, and others. After the world was exposed to the horrors of ethnic cleansing and human experimentation the doctrine of eugenics faded into the background, but in appearance only.

Eugenics became popular in the nineteenth century, receiving strong support from the wealthy upper class who unfavorably viewed the exploding growth of the "bottom-feeding" middle and lower classes and sought to restrict their growth. Support for eugenics was strong among captains of industry like the Rockefellers, Morgans, Carnegies, and all those who considered themselves superior to ordinary humans.

These captains of industry created their own cottage industries intent on furthering their elitist plans of selective breeding and population control, which involved a range of experiments on humans and animals. The Carnegie Institute, founded by billionaire industrialist Andrew Carnegie, ran an experimental eugenics department at Cold Spring Harbor in New York. John D. Rockefeller also invested heavily in eugenics experimentation; the University of Chicago was founded on a grant from his Foundation.

The growing practice of eugenics in the United States was not a renegade phenomenon. The 1927 decision of the U.S. Supreme Court in the landmark case of *Buck v. Bell, 274 U.S. 200, 47 S. Ct. 584 (1927)* ruled that the state-enforced sterilization of certain undesirable individuals did not violate their constitutional rights.[11] Many states quickly fell into lockstep with this ruling and established their own eugenics boards. Staffed by doctors, psychiatrists, legislators and social workers, these boards would determine if a prisoner or a social miscreant, deemed "unfit," should be allowed to bear children who, in their view, would be just as big a burden on society as their parents.

The early 1930s saw a sharp rise in the popularity of eugenics, in parallel with the expansion of the National Socialist Party in Germany, where Hitler was elected Chancellor in 1933. That same year the prestigious Journal of the American Medical Association (JAMA) published an article promoting the practice of eugenics as a good way to ensure the preservation of the German race and culture.[12]

The 3rd National Congress on Eugenics was held in New York during August 21-23, 1932, attended by eminent scientists, psychiatrists, doctors, business leaders, judges, and politicians. Notable attendees included Leonard Darwin and R. Ruggles Gates, two names strongly linked to eugenics.

Several prominent Nazi eugenicists also attended this Congress, courtesy of the Bush/Walker family, who prepaid their passage aboard the Hamburg/Amerika shipping line.[13] It is no coincidence that this congregation met at the American Museum of National History amid the fossils of species doomed to extinction because they were no longer the fittest to survive.

Thirty-three states established their own eugenics boards, whose staff routinely ordered the legal sterilization of criminals and the physically or mentally unfit. Illinois was not one of these 33 states, although many supporters had tried mightily to pass bills through the General Assembly in 1925, 1929 and 1933. The prevailing sentiment in Illinois was that forced sterilization was too inhumane a method of dealing with the population problem.[14] Unfortunately, South Chicago Community Hospital didn't get that memo.

Population Crisis

Following the end of World War II the ruling ranks grew steadily concerned over population expansion. The arrival of the "baby boomers" heralded an era of unprecedented growth in the economy and the population. The government was worried - what to do about the staggering growth rate among the poor and underprivileged, the mentally feeble, and the criminal elements of society?

One solution was birth control, but that went against the grain of many religious leaders, including the Pope. A more radical approach, the legislation of abortion, stirred as much heated controversy then as it does today. Both methods had inherent drawbacks, causing the need for serious consideration about what to do and how to go about it. The problem of the growing population led to a series of congressional hearings known as the Population Crisis Hearings of the 89th Congress. The second session of the series were held in Washington, D.C. in January 1966.[15]

I believe that some doctors at SCCH literally took matters into their own hands, acting as their own self-appointed eugenics boards, except that the victims were not the feeble-minded or physically disadvantaged; they were the black female population of Chicago. "In America, eugenics was a code word for the subjugation, sterilization, and eventual elimination of the black race."[16]

The unethical and immoral practices at SCCH stayed under the radar until *Barbour v. South Chicago Community Hospital* exposed one case of covert sterilization thirteen years after it had actually happened. Statistics show that these procedures successfully remained secret because of the unlikelihood of their discovery. By 1965, there was only one sterilization on record for the entire state of

Illinois. It was performed in 1916 on a sex offender who voluntarily chose to be sterilized rather than face a lengthy prison sentence.[17]

Yet sterilization was being practiced in at least one Chicago hospital in the Sixties that we now know of. Influential members of the medical profession, like Dr. Harrod, were quite adept at keeping their dirty secret, and their patients were completely unaware of what had been done to them under cover of routine gynecological procedures.

But the covert practice of eugenics wasn't contained just within the walls of the operating room at SCCH. Professor Paul Lombardo of the College of Law at Georgia State University, an expert on eugenics in America, states that the 1960s and 1970s:

"... probably generated more sterilizations than any of the eugenics laws and they weren't called eugenic sterilization. That is just women going into county hospitals, being pregnant and being told either after the fact or just before it happened that they were going to be sterilized, because they were on welfare or they had too many babies, according to someone's opinion....It was told to me by people who practiced in those hospitals."[18]

Professor Lombardo, who studied eugenics in America for over thirty years, was not told of the abuses until many years after they had occurred.

One wonders whether those who assisted in the procedures were intimidated or coerced into doing so under threat of losing their jobs. What about those who refused to take part in the procedures for moral reasons, or worse, threatened to blow the whistle? How far were the doctors willing to go to protect their dirty secret? I believe that the horrific murder of eight innocent nurses offers one shocking answer to that question.

Lombardo's research showed that those who had been sterilized were informed either just before or just after the procedure. As if the illegal procedure wasn't bad enough, the doctors at SCCH took matters to another level. They did not even bother to inform their patients, making their actions all the more nefarious.

Any nurses who were aware of the procedures, or who participated in them, faced stiff challenges if they dared speak up or object. As one nurse, who began practicing in 1964, explained to a journalist:

"In the early 1960s, 'nurses were treated as handmaidens of physicians... the doctors gave orders and nurses carried them out,' with no questions .... With no formal avenues to report a physician's behavior, nurses who spoke up often faced reprisal."[19]

Another nurse who practiced in the Sixties related:

"Doctors were gods. We had to get up when they came into the nurses' station. Everyone waited for the doctor to come to see what he had to say. He was the final word on everything. And if the doctor made a mistake or prescribed something wrong? You would absolutely not be able to tell a doctor what he was doing was wrong ... if I had done that in nursing school, I wouldn't be a nurse today."[20]

The power wielded by the doctors over the fate of the nurses' jobs, and future livelihood, was threatening and intimidating. These testimonies illustrate that any misstep outside of the doctors' directives, no matter how well-intentioned, could bear severe consequences. And these accounts were told by nurses who practiced at the same time as the eight nurses.

In my opinion the possible exposure of the illegal practice of sterilization, or other illegal activities, set the stage for the tragic mass murder of the eight nurses. Toxic emotions were also in the mix. The killing was fueled by resentment and anger at the potential whistleblower for threatening to come forward.

The very thought that that influential members of a hospital would destroy anyone threatening its livelihood was shocking to the citizens of the Sixties. The belief in our institutions, our law enforcement, and our judicial system was still intact. Sadly, it was that blind faith in our institutions that made the false narrative and the subsequent cover-up of the nurses' murders possible.

A statement made by Joseph Matusek, father of Patricia Ann, could not make this point more clear: "All I want to say is to thank the hospitals for what they are doing to protect nurses."[21] If he only knew.

CHAPTER EIGHTEEN

DO THESE DOTS CONNECT?

<u>Better Living Through Chemistry</u>

Nothing is known about the sailors who gave Speck the mystery injection on the night of the murders. We only know what Speck told his psychiatrist: "One was a little Puerto-Rican looking guy. Then there was a chubby guy. But I don't know their names."[22] He also was not sure whether there were two or three sailors.

It was widely reported that the substance injected was heroin, but Speck, no stranger to street drugs, disagreed. "I don't know what it was exactly but it wasn't heroin. It was something in a blue bottle, I think. I don't remember a thing after that."[23] Street heroin comes in powder form in a packet, not a blue bottle. The substance in the blue bottle sounds like a pharmaceutical preparation, such as one obtained from a pharmacy – or a hospital.

Speck's memory loss spanned about fifteen hours. He finally remembered waking up the next day at 11:00 AM, and he was surprised to wake up fully clothed: "I had on black Ivy Leagues and a new black shirt with white buttons. Everything was clean."[24] He had a revolver in one hand and blood on the other hand but no injury. A meticulous killer who had deftly, and improbably, avoided all spillage of blood, and who neatly washed up after each killing, left the crime scene with blood on his hand and failed to rinse it off before going to bed?

It's difficult to evaluate the role played by the mystery injection. It invites interest because of Speck's prolonged memory loss on the most important night of his life. But Speck occasionally suffered blackouts and memory lapses and he took street drugs indiscriminately. The injection could have been just another careless blunder in another drink and drug-filled binge. For all he knew or cared, it could have contained rat poison.

If the injection was deliberate and the memory loss intentional, then another scenario is possible. Speck's mental make-up was weak, self-loathing, and easily impressionable. He trusted the judgment of the psychiatrists and law enforcement above his own. After spending only a few weeks in the company of numerous psychiatrists and doctors he came to believe that he had committed the murders but blacked out any memory of them. If this theory is correct, the masterminds of the plot were successful.

Drugs may play yet another role in the nurses' murders. All types of drugs were readily available through the hospital – drugs powerful enough to render an individual helpless. If the nurses were administered drugs through food, drink, or injection, they may have passed out before any violence took place. This would explain the lack of blood spatter, screams, or resistance.

Toxicological analyses were done on all of the nurses, but only for the presence of alcohol or barbiturates. If any drugs were used to sedate the nurses they were outside the range of those included in the tox screen.

There is one more possibility. The mass murder supposedly began late on the night of July 13th, continuing into the 14th. According to records located in the website ancestry.com, July 13th was Gloria Davy's 22nd birthday. We were told that she celebrated the return of her fiance's mother from the hospital that day, but a birthday is even more cause for celebration. Surprisingly, none of my other resources mentioned that it was Gloria's birthday.

Gloria had close friends in the townhouse; she, Suzanne, Pat, and Nina Jo planned to attend each other's weddings. Some small party or celebration may have taken place, presenting an opportunity for someone to plant a sleep-inducing drug into food or beverage. The nurses would then grow suddenly sleepy and lie down or pass out, presenting an easy target for their killers. This too would explain the lack of screaming, fighting, or defensive wounds.

My speculations may seem far-fetched, but no more so than the idea that an impaired lone gunman easily restrained, tied up, and methodically stabbed and strangled eight vibrant young women over a period of four and a half hours without any noise or resistance, getting no blood on himself and suffering no injuries.

More Dots and Question Marks

If I could ask Eugene Thornton one question, it would be, why did you give a 7-1/2 inch Navy-issue hunting knife to a convicted felon who was known to pull knives on people? He may as well have given a blow torch to an arsonist. Although this knife was not used in the crime, its association with Speck helped fuel the frightening image of a knife-wielding maniac.

And the legend of this massive knife had legs. Some video documentaries relate that this large knife, covered with Speck's bloody fingerprints, was the murder weapon. Nothing could be further from the truth. Speck sold the hunting knife to William Kirkland prior to the murders. Police knew that it was not the knife used in the crime.

Other dots that surround Thornton are the black jacket that he loaned to Speck days before the murders, his Navy affiliations, and his awareness of Speck's habits and hangouts. It was Gene Thornton's idea to bring Speck to the NMU to apply for seafaring work, which placed him in the vicinity of the nurses' townhouse.

There is also the possible connection between Thornton, a night switchman for the railroad, and Claude Lunsford, a rider of the rails. Lunsford had gone out of his way to praise the night switchmen in his trial testimony, and both men were instrumental in tracking Speck down. And at the end of the line, an innocent man was railroaded, and many lingering questions remain, the main one being, were these just coincidences?

Dr. Harlan Newkirk

Dr. Harlan Newkirk was an associate director of SCCH in the mid-1960s and later became CEO of the hospital. In 1986, twenty years after the mass murder of the nurses, the hospital held a small memorial. Newkirk had spoken infrequently about the murders, but what he revealed on this day was another bombshell:

"Newkirk, in a rare interview about the tragedy, said that on July 13, 1966, he had personally been in the townhouse at 2319 E. 100th Street 'checking on the security arrangements. We had double locks on all doors, and the back window was screened in. I believe that Speck walked in an unlocked front door.'[25]

Why would the associate director of a hospital visit a nurses' dormitory to check the door locks just hours before a violent home invasion? As it turned out, his strangely timed security check made no difference. He apparently was not aware that Corazon had testified that the front door was locked. Was Newkirk's visit on the murder day a coincidence, like the absence of the next-door neighbors who happened to be away on vacation?

The Elephant in the Room

"You are surprised that I survived? But I come from the place where they make *balisong* (long knives). Why should you be surprised?"[26]

Thus spoke Corazon Amurao when asked about her remarkable escape from death at the hands of Richard Speck. She was referring to a unique style of knife made only in her home province of Batangas, Philippines.

Also known as a "butterfly knife," the *balisong* has two long, sharp blades that slide out from inside the handle. When both blades are extended the knife resembles the shape of a butterfly. Today the knife is considered extremely dangerous, and is illegal in many countries, as well as some U.S. states. In the wake of the butchering of her friends and roommates by knife-wielding murderers, I found the *balisong* brag peculiar.

Corazon was concerned about her image. One day she saw a man looking through the living room window and stuck her tongue out at him. This odd story made its way into the newspapers after the murders, and she feared that word of it might get back to a potential love interest of hers in the Philippines. She entreated prosecutor Martin to quash the story to avoid embarrassment, and he gladly did so. Corazon's cooperation was crucial to the prosecution, and no effort was spared to accommodate her desires.

No effort, and no expense. The State's Attorney's office went to extraordinary lengths to keep Corazon and family sheltered and well cared for. Martin marveled that she never asked him for anything, except to quash that embarrassing tongue incident. However, the amenities provided by law enforcement tell a different story.

Corazon did not want to return to work and was excused from hospital duty. She asked to be housed in an off-site apartment, and that her mother Macario and cousin Roger (Rogelio) be brought from the Philippines to stay with her. They arrived at the end of July 1966 and remained until the end of April 1967.

She requested an apartment large enough for the three of them. For the first several weeks they stayed at the Moraine on the Lake, a once posh resort that had seen better days, but still provided a swimming pool and tennis courts, which the family enjoyed.

After one month they moved to a two-bedroom apartment at the Sheridan-Surf apartments in the New Town section of the city. Round-the-clock detectives shared a separate one-bedroom apartment next door. Four detectives shared the bodyguard duties: two during the day, and two overnight, providing protection 24/7.

Cousin Roger, an engineer by trade, wanted to work, and the State's Attorney's office found him a job. Corazon's father, Ignacio Amurao, remained in the Philippines due to ill health. Law enforcement saw to it that Mr. Amurao's medical bills were all paid, as well as all family debts. It is not known whether Roger or Corazon contributed to these expenses.

Early in her visit, mother Macario experienced a medical emergency. She spent one month in the hospital, where she stayed under an assumed name. She also needed dental work, approved and paid for along with all hospital expenses.

During the nine months of sequestration, the detectives kept the family entertained, taking them on elaborate shopping trips to Marshall Field, sightseeing tours of the Brookfield Zoo and Shedd Aquarium, brunches, picnics, and movies. When indoors they would play ping pong and cards. The detectives taught Corazon how to play penny poker, her favorite game.

On one shopping expedition to an upscale department store, mother Macario had her eye on a luxurious Rolex watch, but a conscientious detective convinced her that a Timex would work just as well. Guarding the Amurao family was a dream job for the detectives on duty but a nightmare for the taxpayer.

The decision to shelter Corazon for those long pre-trial months had not gone unchallenged. Nursing supervisor Josephine Chan insisted that returning to work would be the best therapy. But Corazon wasn't just afraid of Speck, being alone, or the dark – she was very afraid to return to the hospital. She claimed that she was afraid to make mistakes on the job. Was she afraid of something more?

Corazon was brazenly approached by Amelito Mutec, former Ambassador to the United States, to give paid interviews with the major media networks, who were lining up to hear her story. According to Mutec's offer, she would fork over a gluttonous 25% of her earnings to the Philippines government. Aware of the bad optics of exploiting her situation for financial gain, she staunchly refused all offers. When the Philippine diplomats continued to apply the pressure, she hired a U.S. attorney to help her fend off their mercenary requests.

With the strain of her trial testimony behind her, Corazon, her family, and her round-the-clock bodyguards returned to the Sheridan-Surf Apartments in time to celebrate the Easter holiday. And celebrate they did, as prosecutor Martin retold in his book:

"Corazon enjoyed a sumptuous Easter brunch at Chicago's Conrad Hilton Hotel with her family and bodyguards. Oblivious to the proceedings in Peoria, Cora and Mama continued to regularly get out of the Sheridan-Surf for shopping expeditions ... she would go bowling on Saturday, have Sunday brunch at Henrici's Restaurant...."[27]

"Oblivious to the proceedings in Peoria" showed a detached side of Corazon who seemed to recover quickly from her ordeal. She appeared content to move on from Chicago and focus on her return home to the Philippines.

On April 28, 1967, nearly one year to the day that she first arrived in Chicago, Corazon returned home to her native San Luis a heroine. It marked the end of a hellacious year, but a new beginning for her. She had received $5,000 - half of the $10,000 reward - for information leading to the capture of Richard Speck, equivalent to almost $50,000 today. The money would serve her well for her new start in life.

The remaining $5,000 of the reward was split between Dennis Ryan, the gas station attendant who had held Speck's luggage overnight, and the police. This was the only time I ever heard of the police sharing a cash reward with civilians for the apprehension of a suspect, and it wasn't the only such cash reward handed out to law enforcement, as previously noted.

Corazon campaigned for a seat on the city council in San Luis and won. On January 5, 1969, she married her sweetheart, Albert Atienza, a local attorney. She sent a wedding invitation to her friend and mentor, Assistant State's Attorney William Martin, with whom she had formed a strong bond. He was unable to attend. Also invited were President and Mrs. Ferdinand Marcos; it is not known whether they attended.[28]

The day before her wedding Corazon informed a reporter from the *Chicago Tribune* that she and her husband wanted to move to the U.S. and live in Washington, D.C. The Philippines was rife with crime, and she felt that the U.S. was a much "safer" place to live. It's ironic that she would feel safer in a country where she had experienced the traumatic murder of eight colleagues. When asked about the murders in 1969, she remarked, "It seems so long ago. I've forgotten."²⁹ Her capacity to forget was apparently as strong as her ability to remember.

There are so many mysteries about the petite Filipina heroine. What - or who – was at SCCH that had so frightened her? Was she afraid of individuals with inside knowledge of the murders? Or was she afraid because she *had* inside knowledge of the murders?

What was she doing while the massacre was taking place? Why did she spend so much time in the townhouse afterward? Why was she singled out for the role of sole survivor? Was she coerced into promoting a false narrative, under threat of deportation, harm to the family, or worse? Or was she a willing participant in a cover-up?

Unless the real story behind the murders comes to light, these questions are not likely to be answered. Corazon, now eighty years old, no longer gives interviews. This much is certain – as sole survivor, her capacity for self-preservation was much stronger than anyone might have imagined.

Ratlines?

Another theory again involves drugs. What if one or more of the nurses had discovered some other illicit activity at the hospital, such as drug dealing, theft, or trafficking? This idea is not so far-fetched as it may sound.

Ferdinand Marcos was elected President of the Philippines in early 1965; he had campaigned on a platform opposing any intervention in the Vietnam war. However, once in office he pivoted a full 180 and agreed to an alliance with the United States, on the basis that the Philippines would provide only humanitarian aid to Vietnam. The Philippines began sending contingents of medical professionals and advisors west to Vietnam in 1964. Psychological operations, or "psywars," were also conducted by the Philippines contingent.[30]

The first contingent of Philippine aid to Vietnam was successful. Coincidentally or not, it took place in August 1964, the month before LBJ's Nurse Training Act was signed into law. An agreement approving a second wave of assistance was signed on July 14, 1966, the very date of the murders. By the second wave, military aid and soldiers were also joining in the effort, raising the Philippine presence in Vietnam from 16 persons to over 2,000.[31]

Coincidentally or not, the opening of borders from Vietnam to the Philippines was notable because it paralleled the opening of the border east to the United States by way of the Nurse Training Act. The timing is interesting; aid began flowing west to Vietnam and nurses began emigrating east to the United States within the same time period in 1964.

This is not to besmirch any of the Philippine nurses who came here to work in our hospitals; they were dedicated caregivers who provided much needed assistance during a time of great need. My point is that under the right circumstances, open borders facilitate the trafficking of drugs, contraband, or people.

It is documented that heroin was smuggled to the States from Asia during the Vietnam war, and the passage via the Philippines would have offered a tempting ratline to exploit. It's another theory of mine, but merits consideration. Any unexpected witnesses to such trafficking, such as well-intentioned whistleblowers, would certainly have to be eliminated.

Re-paving Memory Lane

The most fascinating aspect of this crime was memory: Corazon remembered everything, and Speck remembered nothing. I have often wondered whether either of them had undergone any sort of mental manipulation aided by hypnosis, drugs, or mind control. This is not so far-flung an idea as it sounds.

After World War II the United States government began conducting covert experiments on the human mind - how it could be manipulated, controlled, and influenced, often without the human's permission or knowledge. This operation was first known as Project Bluebird, then Project Artichoke, and finally, MK-ULTRA.[32] By now some readers may have already wondered whether Richard Speck or Corazon Amurao were exposed to hypnosis or MK-ULTRA programming. It can't be proven, but it can't be ruled out.

Research and experimentation with MK-ULTRA programming began in the early 1950s and possibly earlier. It has been well documented that such experiments took place in many major cities, including Chicago, and were not limited to laboratories; clinics, hospitals and certain places of employment engaged in human experimentation, not always with favorable results.[33]

Hospitals? South Chicago Community Hospital was already engaged in illegal and unethical sterilizations - what else were they up to? The hospital's purpose was to service a low-income community of minorities, an ideal group of test subjects for those who considered themselves far superior to the ordinary populace in every respect. If they had no qualms about covertly sterilizing the minority population, who knows who else was fair game.

This is not science fiction or conspiracy theory. In a 1994 report the United States Government Accounting Office admitted as much:

"During World War II and the Cold War era, the Army and the Navy conducted two major chemical research experiments in which thousands of service members were used as test subjects. An unknown number of other chemical tests and experiments were conducted under contracts with universities, hospitals, and medical research facilities. In some of the tests and experiments, healthy adults, psychiatric patients, and prison inmates were used without their knowledge or consent or their full knowledge of the risks involved."[34]

Experiments in mind control also sought a way to enhance, erase, or implant memories. One government-sponsored experiment proved that a potent mixture of hypnosis and drugs could in fact cause memory loss of specific events. In this experiment a suspected Russian double agent was given a mix of chemicals reminiscent of the strange substance injected by Speck. Team Artichoke, as the group was called:

"... plied him with a mixture of drugs and hypnosis under the cover of a 'psychiatric-medical' exam....Afterward, the team reported that [code name] had revealed 'extremely valuable' information and that he had been made to forget his interrogation through a hypnotically induced amnesia."[35]

Richard Speck spent at least 22 hours in interviews with the panel of six psychiatrists, and was also interviewed by other doctors. It is unknown whether he was hypnotized or given truth serum, as Ziporyn had feared. However, had Speck confessed while under hypnosis or truth serum the doctors would no doubt have made this known to law enforcement.

If Speck's memory had been tampered with, the same could apply to Corazon Amurao. If she saw anything other than what she related, that memory could pose a threat to the real movers behind the crime. In my opinion, it's possible that she, too, underwent some form of hypnosis or mental alteration in order to convincingly promote the official story. Her capacity to recall extremely detailed aspects of the night of the crime was exceptional, while her memory was otherwise undistinguished.

She seemed to recover from the trauma of the crime quickly. In 1969, just three years later, she stated that she had forgotten it. Some have accused her of complicity, and that is one more mysterious legacy of the crime. Unless she comes forward, I doubt we will get the full picture. For all we know, her real memory may have gone the way of Richard Speck's that night, in her case replaced by a tightly scripted narrative. In any case, she knows what really happened on that night.

My thoughts about Corazon Amurao match up about the same as those for Richard Speck. Despite their appearance on opposing sides of the crime, both were useful tools with which to construct a false, but extremely effective, narrative. And in their own way both made the best of extremely stressful situations.

Messages in Blood

Many elements of the crime point to a targeted assassination that delivered strong messages. Mary Ann Jordan was the only one to be stabbed in the eye (the left one), suggesting that this horrific wound carried a message: She saw too much.

Valentina Pasion was the only nurse to have her throat slashed viciously enough to expose her larynx: Don't talk. Pamela Wilkening had a cloth gag in her mouth – again, don't talk.

The rumored rape and sodomizing of Gloria Davy served up humiliation and desecration; this is what happens to girls who get too big for their britches. The criss-crossing of the bodies of the

Filipina nurses may also be symbolic; in occult symbolism the shape of the 'x' symbolizes the cross of Saint Andrew, a martyr sacrificed for his beliefs.

The nurses were murdered on the anniversary of the death of Saint Camillus de Lellis, patron saint of nurses and hospitals, and many of them were laid to rest on the day of the Feast of Saint Camillus. Once unearthed, this saintly rabbit hole bored down so deeply that I could practically glimpse the earth's core. The symbolic aspects of this crime are plentiful, but they involve a very different perspective. A second book on this subject, *Desperate Rites: Astrology and the Occult in the Richard Speck Murders,* is now available in ebook and print format.

Aside from the nursing profession, the murders made an indelible wound on the collective psyche of women in general. Empowered by the growing feminist movement of the Sixties, women desirous of careers were growing a voice in the workforce and wanted this voice to be heard: equal pay, equal treatment, and equal opportunities for employment. It was a very tall and threatening order for the male-dominated power structure. Women, once easily dominated, were now growing in power, presenting a threat to the old world status quo.

And all had not been well in the nursing establishment of the Sixties; across America, nurses were staging strikes and voicing their complaints over poor pay, long hours, and subpar treatment by their superiors. During the week of the murders over a thousand nurses threatened to walk off the job in California, and the impetus spread like wildfire to nurses in other states. That same week the *Chicago Tribune* reported that hundreds of nurses in New York City had walked off the job, and 22 nurses in Idaho were set to follow in their colleagues' footsteps.[36]

The nursing protests mirrored the anti-war movement; both challenged the establishment while inspiring others to take up the cause. While the steady influx of Filipino nurses had helped offset the decline in the nursing population, it did not remedy the core of the problem. The growing unrest among the nurse population and its desire to change the status quo continued to upset the old guard.

The savage murder of eight nurses was a symbolic slap in the face to women striving for independence in the workforce. Nurses, beware! These eight independent young women wanted their own careers, and look what happened to them. Better stay in your place and keep your mouth shut. The message of this crime reverberated throughout the female population of America, regardless of age or career.

The murders sent out other subliminal suggestions to the public. The official narrative placed heavy emphasis on passivity; the nurses had been trained to remain passive in the face of threats. The anti-war protesters were pacifists, demanding an immediate end to the Vietnam war. The subliminal message: pacifism is bad, fighting is good. The murders served as a vehicle for anti-war propaganda as much as the Manson murders served to take down the anti-war pacifist hippie movement.

CHAPTER NINETEEN
THE AFTERMATH

The nation breathed a collective sigh of relief after Richard Speck was captured and indicted for the brutal slayings of the eight nurses, but it was short-lived. The phenomenon of the motiveless mass murder was here to stay.

On August 1, 1966, less than one week after Speck's indictment, a former Marine named Charles Whitman, fully armed with assault rifles, climbed the Tower Building of the University of Texas in Austin and fired down upon innocent students and passersby on campus.

The "Texas Tower Sniper" killed and wounded 45 people and continued his rampage until shot and killed by police. The siege lasted 90 minutes, after which police discovered that Whitman had begun the carnage by first killing his wife and mother. He left behind a bizarre suicide note describing how he was driven by persistent and destructive thoughts that he was unable to control.

His suddenly violent, unpredictable behavior was attributed to a small tumor in his brain. Whitman added a new face to the growing phenomenon of the motiveless mass murderer, and the Manson Family would follow on his heels just three years later in August 1969. From week to week the public was being pummeled by reports of seemingly irrational, random acts of violence.

The mass murder of the eight Chicago nurses had already left lasting emotional and psychological scars on nurses everywhere. Some were haunted by fear for years afterward – fear of going out in the daytime, of turning out the lights at night, of being alone, of seeing Richard Speck again. In a strange turn of events, the possibility of ever seeing Speck again was not as unlikely as it seemed.

Speck, whose parole releases had time and again defied logic, ended up cheating the hangman as well. He was scheduled to die in the electric chair on September 1, 1967, but the death sentence was set aside while defense counsel appealed the biased method of jury selection.

Their request for a new trial was denied, but they obtained a re-sentencing hearing. Timing was on Speck's side; in 1972 the State of Illinois repealed the death penalty. On September 20th Speck was re-sentenced to serve from 400 to 1200 years in prison, or, as one might reasonably assume, life without parole?

Not by a long shot. Even with this long sentence hanging over his head he came up for parole not once, but seven times between 1976 and 1991. The thought of Speck being let loose from prison was abhorrent to the public, and especially the families of the slain nurses, who religiously attended each parole hearing to voice their objections.

After the first few denials Speck did not even bother to attend the hearings. He had settled into prison life very well, enjoying his newfound notoriety and, as the horrified public would someday learn, plenty of sex, drugs, and an unsightly and unprecedented transformation.

Transformations

The mass murder left countless lives permanently changed, and over time, once-tranquil Jeffery Manor changed as well. The National Maritime Union on E. 100th Street became the Greater Morning

View Church. The Raleigh Hotel, where Richard Speck spent one night, is now an office complex. The Moraine on the Lake, once a posh resort for the privileged, and which once housed Corazon and her family, closed in 1971. It went the way of Paradise in Joni Mitchell's hit song of that same year, "Big Yellow Taxi" – they paved it and put in a parking lot. The inimitable Pink Twist was also razed and reduced to rubble, also converted to a parking lot.

The squalid Starr Hotel instead reversed course and rose from the ashes. Demolished in 1982, the site was resurrected and remade into three high-rise luxury rentals named the Presidential Towers. In just sixteen years Chicago's sleazy Skid Row rose from the effete to the elite.

Business as usual went on at South Chicago Community Hospital. Still located at E. 93rd Street, it is now named Advocate Trinity Hospital. Dr. Harlan Newkirk proudly accomplished a merger of the hospital with Evangelical Health Care Systems. Besides being an executive and leader in the health care field, Dr. Newkirk was a prominent member of various religious organizations and charities for kids, including the Son Shine Boys' and Men's Christian group. As CEO of South Chicago Community Hospital, he was certainly aware of the physical and ethical violations being committed on minority women patients, and I also suspect he had inside knowledge of the crime.

The stars of many principal characters rose after Speck was put away. Detective Jack Wallenda went on to serve as investigator for the Cook County State's Attorney and chief investigator for the Attorney General. In 1977 he was appointed executive director of the Illinois Liquor Control Commission.

First State's Attorney John Stamos became Dean of DePaul Law School and was appointed to the Illinois Supreme Court, following in the footsteps of his predecessor, Patrick J. Ward. Stamos served as judge on the Appellate Court from 1968 until 1988, when he, too, was appointed to the Illinois Supreme Court, where he served until 1990.

Other State's Attorneys also climbed the proverbial ladder. In 1968 William J. Martin advanced to the Office of Chief of Special Prosecutions for the Cook County State's Attorney, and tried many cases before the Illinois Supreme Court.

After several years with the State's Attorney's office, Martin fulfilled his longtime ambition to serve as defense counsel. In 1970 he founded the criminal defense firm of Martin, Breen & Merrick, and in 1993 co-authored *The Crime of the Century,* a useful but slanted reference for the official narrative that has been deconstructed in these pages. The book was reprinted in 2016 under the title *The Crime of the Century: Richard Speck and the Murder of Eight Student Nurses,* to commemorate the fiftieth anniversary of the crime.

Also an aspiring journalist, Martin tried his hand as a true crime writer in his retirement; when he died in 2017 he left behind an incomplete manuscript for a detective novel. But the prosecution team and law enforcement had already left one completed work of fiction behind: the official story of the mass murder of eight student nurses.

Doctor Dad's Downfall

It seems everyone's careers skyrocketed in the wake of the Speck conviction. Everyone, except for Speck's father figure and confidante, Dr. Marvin Ziporyn, who co-authored the best-selling book *Born to Raise Hell* about his private sessions with Richard Speck. While hugely profitable, the bestseller came at quite a cost. In the wake of the scandal about the book, Ziporyn was fired from his lucrative part-time job with the Cook County justice system.

For a time he continued to make a name for himself as a criminal forensic psychiatrist. In 1980 he was called upon to profile Chicago's serial killer, John Wayne Gacy, by analyzing several passionate letters that Gacy had written to a female love interest.[37]

Law enforcement was not especially fond of the psychiatrist, whose support of the temporary insanity defense often complicated the prosecution of violent offenders. At one trial in 1985 Ziporyn came under harsh cross-examination by the prosecutor in a manner he found disrespectful and demeaning. He cursed the prosecutor and was charged with contempt of court. A series of motions sent the courtroom kerfuffle snowballing all the way to the Illinois Supreme Court. Ziporyn won on appeal.[38]

He continued to work in the medico-legal field until 1992, when the Illinois Psychiatric Society and American Psychiatric Association expelled him for ethical violations and the Illinois Department of Professional Regulation revoked his license to practice medicine.

Wrongful Deaths, Righteous Suits

In 1970 the families of the slain nurses sued South Chicago Community Hospital for breach of security, claiming that the hospital did not do enough to ensure the safety of the nurses in their townhouse. It was even more bizarre that the associate director of SCCH, Harlan Newkirk, was in the townhouse checking the door locks on the very day of the murders. Apparently he found no fault with the locks at that time, yet his hospital was still sued.

At this time Corazon and her husband decided to return to the United States to join as plaintiffs in the suit. The lawsuit against

SCCH was settled out of court for an undisclosed sum shared by Corazon and the families.

Corazon and the families also filed a civil suit against Richard Speck under the Illinois Wrongful Death Act to block him from receiving any and all proceeds from the sale of the paintings and drawings he had created while in prison. The suit awarded 1.5 million dollars to Corazon and 250,000 to each family, but on paper only. Speck paid nothing toward the judgment; its main purpose, to prevent him from profiting from any creative work, was achieved.

There was one more lawsuit to go, and, like much of this case, its premise was truly mind-boggling. Under the dramshop act, tavern owners can be held responsible for serving an intoxicated customer if the customer then goes on to commit a felony. The families and Corazon filed suit against both the Shipyard Inn and Kay's Pilot House on the basis that on the 13th of July they had served an intoxicated Richard Speck, who then went on to commit mass murder. Both Kay's and the Shipyard Inn quietly settled out of court for an undisclosed sum.

Numerous witnesses on that night had testified that Speck did not appear intoxicated. Corazon herself had firmly insisted that Speck was not under the influence of alcohol or drugs. As she told police:

"He was not drunk. His conversation was done in a normal manner. He didn't stagger. He didn't slur his words. I know he was not under the influence of any narcotics or barbiturates.... I have given drugs and I have seen people under the influence of drugs. Speck was not."[39]

In her initial statement to police, the intruder "had been drinking." (That was the same report where she forgot to mention the knife.)

Speck was not immediately arrested after the murders, so there was no blood alcohol test to substantiate the claim of intoxication. But it could be proven that he had been drinking in both establishments on that night, and regardless of his degree of intoxication, that was enough to bring the parties to settle out of court.

The dramshop lawsuit illustrates how certain facts in the case were played both ways. Corazon had stated that she smelled alcohol on Speck's breath when he tied her up, suggesting that he was impaired. But the prosecution feared that any impairment might assist an insanity defense. After her original statement, Corazon firmly insisted that he was not intoxicated.

However, once the trial ended, attorney Casimir Wachowski, who handled the other lawsuits, filed a dramshop lawsuit against both Kay's and the Shipyard Inn. This is not to criticize the families of the nurses for filing the lawsuits, but to show how easily the facts of the case were manipulated. Before the trial, Speck was not in any way intoxicated, but after the trial, he was. Keeping track of the discrepancies and contradictions was sometimes laughable, but other times, infuriating. I could have modeled for the famous Edward Munch painting "The Scream."

Following the legal victories, Corazon's dream request was fulfilled. She and her husband moved to Washington, D.C., where she restarted her career as nursing administrator for the Veterans Administration of Georgetown University Hospital. Georgetown was an institution founded in 1789 by the Jesuit order. Prosecutor Martin, of Jesuit background and training at Loyola University and Law School, must have been proud.

The Jesuit-Catholic connection was strong everywhere one looked - DePaul, the *alma mater* of most of the State's Attorneys, defense counsel, and judge, was the largest Catholic institution in North

America, while Georgetown was the America's oldest Catholic and Jesuit university. DePaul University and Law School had educated practically everyone involved in the case, from the State's Attorney's office to the office of the Mayor of Chicago to the Illinois Supreme Court. Even defense counsel Getty, who lost the case, gained in reputation and status. In 1970 DePaul University, his *alma mater,* conferred upon him the Honorary Degree of Doctor of Humane Letters.

Corazon quietly raised her family in the Virginia suburbs of Washington, D.C. She attended the reunions held on the twentieth and fiftieth anniversaries of the murders of the eight nurses in 1986 and 2016, which was the last time she agreed to be interviewed. She made few public appearances, but one was of particular interest. Naturally, it took place in Chicago.

Chicago Revisited

In April 1993 Corazon appeared as a guest on the *Oprah Winfrey Show*.[40] While on stage she shared a tearful reunion with Jack Wallenda and Renaldo Cozzi, her former detective and bodyguards, and her mentor, former Assistant State's Attorney William J. Martin. The show celebrated her heroic survival of Chicago's worst mass murder, while reinforcing the random and senseless nature of the crime and exploring its long-term effects on the public. Included as guests were Judy Dykton Radzik and Betty Jo Purvis, sister of Patricia Ann Matusek.

Throughout the interview Oprah continued to harp on the senseless, random nature of the crime and its paralyzing effect on the American public, and hammered home the idea that people were no longer safe in their homes – typical mass media treatment of a horrific mass murder. She pressed Corazon for answers to the persistent questions that have plagued us over the years – why didn't they scream, why didn't they fight back? Corazon's responses threw another slant on the official narrative.

When discussing the generic composite sketch, Oprah asked:

"OPRAH: Is it based on your description that they were able to catch him?

CORAZON: I think so, yeah.

OPRAH: And you remembered the tattoo?

CORAZON: Uh-huh (nodding yes)."

This is another contradiction to add to the list. In Corazon's trial testimony she stated, "I did not notice any tattoo." Corazon appeared to be taking her cues from Oprah, who completed some of her sentences for her throughout the interview.

"OPRAH: And then what, he tied you up one at a time?

CORAZON: Uh-huh (nodding yes).

OPRAH: What we're trying to understand is, it's one man, he has to tie everybody up, one at a time, so in my mind I've always thought, "Why didn't, you know, the other seven of you, why didn't six or five or three people say, all right, let's get him?"

CORAZON: I was also thinking about that after the incident. I said, how come we did not even fight him, you know, and he was doing it. I really just, you know, I do not know why, how, because every time some one moved, he has the gun pointed at you. So I was just scared, just seeing that gun pointing at me every time I moved. So I didn't, you know, that's why I was not able to do anything about it and probably some of my friends was not able."

I'm not a certified statement analyst, but I have studied the subject. The frequency of "you know, I really just, you know, I do not know, you know" indicates sensitivity to the question and suggests the speaker is trying to be convincing. It makes sense in view of the fact that her story underwent many changes.

This time Corazon completely left out her heroic account of hiding in the closet with Valentina and Merlita, from which came the legend that she rallied them to resist the intruder. Over the years she has presented four iterations of the closet scenario. I believe all of them were pure invention.

In Scenario 1, after Speck marched them into the south bedroom, gun at their backs, she, Merlita, and Valentina made a mad dash and hid in the closet at the far end of the room, pulling the door tight to prevent the intruder from opening it. In this scenario there was no fear of the gun, even though the intruder could have shot them in the back or fired into the closet.

According to a popular story, she rallied her friends to fight the intruder, but she did not testify to this at trial. Instead, the three of them spent about five minutes in the closet. The scenario ended when one of the other nurses coaxed them to come out, saying, "He won't hurt us." This story changed three more times after the trial.

In Scenario 2, there wasn't enough time to figure something out, even though five minutes would have been enough time to say, "Let's rush down the stairs and get help."

In Scenario 3, they didn't fight back because their hands were tied. But they were not tied up when they ran and hid in the closet – that happened afterward.

In Scenario 4, she was too afraid to move because the intruder kept his gun pointed at her. This is a stark departure from Scenarios 1 and

2, when she and her Filipina housemates ran into the closet at the risk of being shot in the back.

So no one ever ran into the closet? Probably not; like many other stories within the story, this was an embellishment that came later, like the discovery of the white t-shirt twisted around the slacks of Gloria Davy that supposedly lay in plain sight for two weeks until Detective Wallenda magically retrieved it at the eleventh hour.

Oprah also posed the same questions to former prosecutor William Martin, with similar results:

"OPRAH: Perhaps you can give us some kind of insight into the question, I know, and even in the book, is about why the nurses didn't fight.

MARTIN: The girls were in a physical location in which being in the end townhouse and on all four sides they had no opportunity whatsoever, if they had screamed to get help. There was a park behind them, a school across the street. The one common wall they had, the next door neighbors were on vacation, which the girls knew. And the other wall was solid brick, where they were, and even though in a residential neighborhood they were really an island with no opportunity to call help if screams would cause this man to turn violent."

Here hard logic was used to explain the nurses' lack of reaction to the crime, like the theme of passivity justified their lack of resistance. While being viciously attacked, would anyone refrain from screaming just because they thought no one would hear them?

Residents and nurses routinely drove or walked through the parking lot every evening and might have heard screams. Tammy Sioukoff heard one scream between 12:30 and 12:45. The notion that no one screamed because they didn't think the screams would be heard is ridiculous.

What better explains the lack of screaming is that the nurses were quickly blindsided by more than one killer, rendered unconscious or drugged, and had no chance to scream.

"OPRAH: But do you uh, do you think that they, as what Cora has said here, they didn't know that that was going on, they didn't know that he was, you know, being violent, was committing murder in the next room? .... Even until his death he never confessed to the crime. Do we know why he did it?

MARTIN: We don't know why he did it.

OPRAH: Did he go there to kill them, do we know that?

MARTIN: ...he may have killed previously. And when he went there, he went to a place where he had known from being in that neighborhood earlier in the week, that there were young women living in that townhouse. He picked the end townhouse and pried open the back door, went in, and with his gun subdued them and what was in his mind initially, I'm afraid we'll never know."

The simple answer was yes, he went there expecting to kill them. The State always contended that the murders were premeditated. They relied heavily on the questionable t-shirt evidence to illustrate that Speck had brought changes of shirts with him in order to avoid blood spatter, and that went to premeditation.

Martin again let slip that "he pried open the back door," forgetting that the window screen had been pried open by a nosy reporter (according to his own book!) and that no sign of forced entry could be found. He was still sticking fast to the narrative.

Rather than explore any real facts surrounding the murders Oprah continued to emphasize its aftereffects: that women are no longer safe in their homes, that women are unable to protect themselves, that mass murders happen at random for no explainable reason, that there is no real strength in numbers.

Oprah addressed the everlasting questions that reverberate to this day in the wake of the horrific slayings:

"OPRAH: And why didn't they scream? Because I'm thinking if somebody had screamed then the other women would've known, this is really serious, he's not just taking them out having a conversation.

MARTIN: Well, the first girl he took out, he placed a gag in her mouth after he removed her from the south bedroom and it would appear the girls never really had a chance to scream...."

The "first girl" was Pamela Lee Wilkening, who was found with a cloth loosely placed in her mouth and another cloth strip tied around her face. He did not answer the question in regard to the other nurses, who were not gagged. But here I agree with him - no one had a chance to scream.

Another interesting fact came to light during the interviews. One of Corazon's bodyguards, Renaldo Cozzi, revealed how Corazon was coached while kept under wraps for the nine months between the murders and the trial:

"We had to prepare for the trial. That was another big hurdle for her to jump, only being in this country three months at the time, uh, she was curious about how our political system and judicial system worked, she was worried about testifying, so we had to keep her at ease, and tell her just what to say and what she couldn't say, how to answer the questions. That was about it."

Earlier in his interview, Cozzi described how his job was to keep Corazon distracted, to keep her mind off the murders, which begs the question, which was it? Did they coach her on what and what not to say, or keep her mind off the murders?

Everyone was given to believe that Corazon was kept sequestered for her personal protection, but there was more to it. Speck was locked up, posing no threat to her. The police telling her "just what to say and what she couldn't say" is key to why she was kept in seclusion for so many months. Corazon was heavily coached, mistakes, missteps and all.

I believe she was kept sheltered so that she could memorize the official story inside and out. And there were still plenty of distractions, like shopping trips to luxury stores, dinners, brunches, poker games, visits to arboretums and aquariums and the like.

Another reason was to avoid contact with the media, who craved access to the courageous survivor and her blockbuster story. Law enforcement could ill afford to allow access to her; too much exposure and too many questions would have revealed obvious flaws in the narrative. And in the years following the murders that is exactly what happened - Corazon's handle on the narrative began to slip. Had the story of the closet caper been true, she would not have changed it so many times.

During the Oprah interview Corazon admitted that she had suffered some survivor's guilt after the murders, but had never sought counseling or therapy. She was reluctant to discuss the murders, but had gotten over them and now felt "okay".

When asked about Speck's death in 1991, she felt relieved that he was dead, but also made a strange admission. She wondered whether he was really dead or not. A fake death? Given that she herself had participated in spreading a fake narrative, her skepticism is hardly surprising.

The Defense Speaks

Another documentary about the crime issued in the 1990s entitled *Richard Speck*.[41] It featured Assistant State's Attorney Martin, who frequently gave interviews about the crime, and defense attorney James Gramenos, who did not.

Prior to becoming a defense attorney, Gramenos was an FBI agent and a skilled interrogator. He recounted the following about his 1966 interview with Corazon:

"It was a lengthy interview, using the skills that I had developed over the years of interviewing subjects that ranged from homicide individuals, bank robbers. It was an interview where those of us that have read it, and the prosecution having read it, if it was just a common, non-notorious case or a bench trial, it would have been a finding of not guilty."

He concluded that "the woman had been coached at great length." The extent of her coaching was evident when she testified at trial about first seeing Richard Speck: "I noticed that ... the clothes were dark from the shoulder to the foot."[42] In his book *The Crime of the Century* prosecutor Martin states, "Cora stared at him for a few moments and saw that he was dressed in black from shoulder to shoes."[43]

When describing Gloria Davy's discovery of the intruder in the south bedroom, she testified that "Miss Davy was surprised and she screamed in a low voice." Martin described the incident, "When Gloria put her hand on the knob, Speck opened the door for her. Surprised, she screamed in a low voice."[44] The words were practically the same, although how one screams "in a low voice" is perplexing.

Coaching Corazon was a complex matter. She was expected to retell a highly detailed account in English, a second language that she did not have full command of, while maintaining a calm and credible demeanor. She would have to be in full control of her own emotions – fear, guilt, or anger – in order to deliver the narrative and defend it on cross-examination. It was a task that required extensive preparation.

It is noteworthy that Corazon testified at the trial in English without the aid of an interpreter. Just nine months earlier, she had struggled to convey her description of Richard Speck to sketch artist Otis Rathel even with an interpreter present. Prior to trial she was kept away from the public; her only exposure to English came from her bodyguards and the prosecution team. In order to give such a command performance she had to have received extensive preparation in English on every facet of the official story.

Speck, Lies, and Videotape

Having cheated the hangman, Speck was moved off death row in 1972 to join the lifers who would be his cellmates and neighbors for the next 400 to 1200 years. By all accounts he adapted well to prison life, working only when required, spending the rest of his time eating, sleeping, and loafing.

His brief artistic period was over; Paint By Number kits were replaced by buckets, overalls, paint rollers, and trays. He appeared content to shuffle through his days. Gone was the neat, meticulous, carefully groomed Speck; in his place was a bloated, fatuous figure with long greasy hair and a ghoulish countenance. Folds of skin drooped down his pock-marked face like melting wax dripping from a candle.

Richard Speck was actually happy in jail, but no one would know just why until he was out of the picture. Death came for Speck on December 5, 1991, just a day shy of his fiftieth birthday. The cause was a sudden heart attack, which had also claimed his biological father 44 years earlier.

Besides the mass murder of the eight nurses, he left a bombshell legacy that would not be discovered for five more years. It caused a scandal that rocked the entire Illinois prison system like a 9-magnitude earthquake, showering shame and disgrace on prison officials and law enforcement.

Bill Kurtis was a news anchor for WBBM-Ch 2 in Chicago and a producer of true crime documentaries for the A&E and PBS television stations. In May 1996 Kurtis came across an unbelievable find: a grainy VHS videotape of two Illinois prisoners engaging in oral sex, snorting cocaine, and joking about the horrible crimes that one of them had committed. One prisoner stripped down to his underwear, exposing floppy, grotesque breasts and skimpy undies. Egged on by an inmate off-screen, he joked about having killed eight nurses in Chicago.

The video had been filmed by another inmate who had somehow managed to smuggle large, clumsy videotape recording equipment into the prison for the purpose of filming a mock interview of mass murderer Richard Speck. In full display were money and cocaine, which Speck snorted off the leg of Ronzelle "Honey Bun" Larimore, one of his prison lovers, or "main rides". A third inmate, posing as an interviewer, filmed the video and gave it to his attorney in hopes of selling it to raise money.

It did raise money, but not the way he hoped. The video sat in someone's drawer from December 18, 1988 when it was filmed, until May 1996, when Kurtis became aware of it. Kurtis bought the video for $5,000, with the proceeds going to a victims' rights foundation. He then produced a documentary based on the video, which aired on the A&E television network. It was the ghost of fall guy Richard Speck coming back to haunt, and humiliate, the entire Illinois Department of Corrections and the city of Chicago.

The video was a mock interview, with one inmate acting as interviewer and Speck as interviewee. The vulgar, offensive interview was a thumb in the eye of the prison system, the justice system, the nurses, their families, and ultimately, the entire viewing audience. Everybody. Below is an excerpt:[45]

> "INMATE: Did you kill 'em?
>
> SPECK: Sure I did.
>
> INMATE: Why?
>
> SPECK: It just wasn't their night.
>
> INMATE: How do you feel about killing those ladies?
>
> SPECK: Like I always felt, had no feeling. If you're asking if I felt sorry, no."

The video went on in great length about Speck's predilection for black male lovers, his lack of remorse for the slain nurses, and his huge appetite for daily sex. It was beyond repulsive. To add insult to injury Speck laughed, "If they knew how much fun I was having they'd-a turn me loose."

Speck was indeed having fun, but the only thing turned loose was the wrath of the public and the embarassment of prison officials. The backlash from the scandal forced a two-year internal investigation into the corrupt practices that had been taking place inside prison walls for years: the sale and distribution of cocaine and other drugs, the brewing of homemade "hooch," guards having sex with inmates, inmates bribing guards, and so on. The video was someone's bizarre idea of exposing and shaming the prison system, and it worked.

The video also raised a number of other issues. How did an inmate manage to smuggle a bulky, heavy VHS recording camera into the prison? It was probably done through a bribe, proving its point before the video was even filmed. The setting of the video was odd; there were chairs and a table in an area that doesn't resemble a prison cell. There was a pile of money on top of the table in plain view. The whole setup was suspicious.

The other issue was Speck's obvious transformation. He now sported chemically-induced breasts that he was proud to display. Apparently the flow of drugs was such that anything could be had for the right price, including female hormone preparations.

Some felt that Speck chose to develop female traits in order to survive his time in prison; if he had something that other inmates desired, the better things would be for him. If that was his strategy, it worked. In addition to his notoriety as America's first mass murderer, he would also become America's first transgender prisoner. It is not known whether the drugs were surreptitiously given to Speck or he requested them on his own. Once again, drugs cast their ominous shadow on the story.

But the other, more troubling issues posed by the video were his callous responses to the questions about the murdered nurses. Many have taken this as an outright confession. In my opinion he was playing a sick joke on everyone. After 25 years of incarceration, he was right that he "had no feeling."

Early on in his incarceration even Speck came to believe that he had committed the murders. Mentally he was no match for the pressure of the psychiatrists, the police, the prosecutors, or Corazon Amurao, so he just gave up trying. "Everybody says I did it. Must be so. If they say I did it, I did it."[46]

Speck told other wild stories to a reporter ten years prior to the video. In a 1978 interview he bragged that it was indeed heroin that he injected prior to the murders, contradicting his earlier statement that it wasn't heroin. He also said he was accompanied by a "black dude" when he killed the nurses[47] and an "effeminate homosexual," whom he later murdered.[48] There was no evidence to support these bizarre claims.

In prison Speck was still the loudmouthed loser who bragged about his murderous military exploits, his wild drug-running escapades and his conquest of every barmaid in sight. He enjoyed the title of America's first mass murderer; it gave him automatic street cred among his fellow inmates. The moniker of mass murderer finally gave him the respect and approval that he had always desired from his peers.

The videotape caper left me with one last insight regarding the frame-up of Richard Speck. Here was an aimless perpetual offender who could not hold down a job, who wiled away his days drinking and drugging, whose future prospects were bleak. What if he had been offered the stability of three hots and a cot, all the sex and drugs he wanted, in exchange for taking the fall for the murder of the eight nurses? He would never again have to search for work, pay bills, or seek out a sex partner. Behind bars he would achieve the tough guy cred that he always longed for, the stability of a structured life, and all the sex, booze and drugs he could handle. Was a lifetime stint in Stateville, the prison palace of perversion, Speck's reward for playing the fall guy?

Martin's Wish List

Armed with direct evidence – an eyewitness and fingerprints – Assistant State's Attorney Martin had everything he needed to secure a conviction for Richard Speck, and he got it after only 47 minutes of jury deliberation. But Martin remained dissatisfied. He was missing one final item of direct evidence, a confession, and this bothered him in the years following the trial. He was therefore quick to jump on the crass comments made by Speck in the Stateville video. At long last, here was his confession.

But there's an interesting thing about Speck's supposed confessions. Law enforcement, especially Martin, had always portrayed Speck as a cunning, lying piece of excrement whose word couldn't be trusted. When Speck couldn't remember the murders he was lying, when he fled the police because of his warrants in Texas he was lying, when he said practically anything else he was lying, but when he joked about committing the murders, they suddenly chose to believe him?

In my view this insistence on having the confession that had eluded police suggests that Martin was harboring some guilt over the whole affair. He had won the case by a landslide – why did he need the assurance of the one thing he couldn't have? By all accounts, the trial was a slam dunk, Speck was guilty, case closed. This is the nagging of a guilty conscience, one that knew all along how weak the direct evidence really was, how contrived the narrative really was, what a sham the trial really was.

Unlike the others, whose careers catapulted on the strength of the Speck conviction, Martin did not choose the brass ring. He could have followed in the footsteps of First State's Attorney Ward and Stamos all the way to the Illinois Supreme Court, but he instead chose to open his own law firm, Martin, Breen & Merrick, a criminal defense firm.

Like his former idol, Gerald Getty, William J. Martin became counsel for the defense. Ironically, his specialty was defending other attorneys who had been accused of misconduct. Had Destiny turned in another direction, had Getty hired Martin years before, it could well have been Martin who defended Richard Speck. Imagine how different the official story might have been.

Spinning the Narrative

At one point in the video Speck referred to two verbal exchanges that he had with Pam Wilkening after he took her to the east bedroom. In this scenario Pam threatened to pick him out of a lineup and spat in his face. He became enraged and lost control, plunging the knife into her chest. At that point he realized that he would have to kill all the nurses to avoid leaving witnesses.

This was one of the many Speck murder stories that circulated after the murders, but it had no basis in fact. Once again, the narrative strayed from its initial course; if Speck was triggered into a murderous rage by Pam's defiance, the murders were spontaneous rather than premeditated. This was yet another turn on the narrative merry-go-round. I could have made good use of the head-spinning technique featured by Linda Blair in "The Exorcist" movie.

The origin of the story of Pam's defiance has never been explained, but it did not come from Corazon, who heard only sighs of "Ah!" from down the hall as the killings took place. Corazon was not in the room with Pam, so she couldn't know if Pam spat on Speck, and Speck never spoke of the murders until years afterward. I believe the story was created and given traction in the media. It played well, like the Peoria trial, but it made no sense.

The story of Pam's defiance trips up the passivity theme – the nurses didn't resist – the nurses didn't try to fight back. This theme was heavily emphasized in the narrative, but here it is contradicted by Pam's bold words and actions. The spin masters didn't know when to leave well enough alone.

Speck also made a curious remark concerning his suicide attempt at the Starr Hotel. He claimed that defense counsel Getty invented the suicide story in an effort to stir sympathy for his client. This is another fantastical remark. Getty was not appointed to represent Speck until three days after Speck was hospitalized; he could not have reverse-engineered the suicide attempt.

In the infamous prison video Speck was blowing smoke, and all these years later, law enforcement was inhaling.

CHAPTER TWENTY
MYTH-INFORMATION

The tragic story of the mass murder of eight student nurses is legendary in the annals of true crime. Legendary is a good word; the legend of the crime was based entirely on a false narrative.

So effective was this false narrative that we need only search on "Richard Speck" or "Richard Speck nurse murders" to pull up a whole plethora of stories which simply parrot the same things. Three years of intensive research show that we have been lied to for over five decades.

It's time to draw the curtain on this charade. The eight innocent nurses did not receive their due justice, and deserve much better. And the perverse, and persistent, rumors of rape, torture, and sodomy caused unspeakable anguish for their heartbroken families.

Here are some of the myths surrounding the case that the evidence does not support.

<u>Speck killed and raped women in other states.</u>

There was no evidence to support this rumor. He was a person of interest in a murder and a burglary/rape that took place in Monmouth, Illinois in April 1966, but no charges were brought against him. His brother-in-law, Gene Thornton, was a close friend of the Monmouth Chief of Police and could have brought Speck in if necessary.

<u>Speck shot heroin into his arm hours before the murders took place.</u>

He recalled that the substance was in a blue bottle. Street heroin comes in small packets; pharmacy preparations or medications come in blue bottles.

Speck slept in Luella Park the night before the murders in order to spy on the nurses.

There was an intense thunderstorm that night accompanied by heavy downpours of rain. Speck was finicky about his clothing and his appearance, not the type to sleep outdoors, especially in bad weather. He dropped his bags off at the Manor Shell gas station on S. Torrence Avenue and sheltered inside a vacant apartment building until early the next morning.

Speck left his fingerprints all over the townhouse.

Police found three blurry partial prints on the inside of the south bedroom door, all of questionable origin. One was only sixteen and a half inches from the floor, an awkward placement considering the configuration of the room. Police found no bloody fingerprints or palm prints, and they did not focus at all on bloody footprints, which should have been plentiful considering the killers' movements between the bedrooms.

This rumor falls squarely at the feet of Chief O.W. Wilson, who told reporters that Speck had left 32 fingerprints all over the townhouse, when in reality, police had found a total of 32 or 33 fingerprints after processing the crime scene, 18 of which went "unidentified". Only three partial prints thought to belong to Speck were found, and these were similar in classification to the prints of Gloria Davy and Suzanne Farris.

Crime lab techs had no success finding Speck's fingerprints inside the townhouse until they took latent prints from a beer can found in Speck's hotel room. After that, all systems were "go!"

Speck's knife contained bloody fingerprints.

No knife was found at the crime scene and no knife was admitted into evidence. Police confiscated and examined the large Navy-issue hunting knife that Speck sold to William Kirkland but ruled it out as the murder weapon.

Rumors of that knife persist to this day. A few Youtube documentaries show film footage of the knife, accompanied by narration that it was this knife, filled with Speck's bloody prints, that helped convict him. They got it all wrong. No gun or knife was submitted into evidence at the trial. The only murder weapons in evidence were the white cloth ligatures.

All of the nurses were raped or molested.

This is one of the more outlandish, and disrespectful, rumors about the murders that the media took off and ran with. Many reports circulated that all of the nurses were nude, or raped, giving rise to hideous headlines like STUDENT BUILDING INVADED BY SEX MANIAC and REPORT HOSPITAL AIDES RAPED.

The medical examiner would not confirm that any rape or sodomy had taken place, and the autopsy reports did not substantiate this rumor. But the exaggerated stories of bloody rape and mutilation sold newspapers, with no consideration for the families of the victims. The media violated the nurses in their own callous way.

Gloria Davy was raped and sodomized.

This has been extensively discussed in a previous chapter. Prosecutor Martin's book mentions that semen was found on Gloria's buttocks. The autopsy report does not describe the presence of semen or evidence of sodomy. While semen could have been deposited by the killer(s) without evidence of actual physical violence, this was not corroborated by the pathology report.

Although a police report stated that Gloria Davy's anus was "mutilated,"[49] the pathology report confirmed that her genitalia was normal and unremarkable. Of the hundreds of pages of police reports that I received in response to my FOIA request, none referred to a mutilated anus. The pathologist, Dr. E.H. Tapia, noted that all body cavities were "unremarkable." A mutilated organ is anything but unremarkable.

The nurses were found nude.

Only Gloria Davy was found nude.

Blood-soaked men's t-shirts were found at the crime scene.

One sweaty shirt was found near Gloria Davy's body, and another shirt was found wrapped up in Gloria's slacks. The first shirt could have belonged to one of the nurses' boyfriends; the other was discovered under suspicious circumstances and admitted into evidence. Both shirts were men's size 38-40M, the same size Speck wore. They were not blood-soaked, calling into question the prosecution's theory that Speck had brought shirts with him in a tote bag in order to change out of bloody shirts between killings.

Richard Speck confessed to Dr. Leroy Smith, the physician who identified him at the hospital after seeing his tattoo in the newspaper.

There was a $10,000 reward for the apprehension of Richard Speck. After Smith called the police, Speck asked Smith if he would receive the $10,000 reward for turning him in. A question about the reward does not constitute a confession.

Smith also said that Speck admitted to killing the nurses, but law enforcement discounted this, as Speck was still under the influence of anesthesia. It is odd, then, that they may have later subjected him to sodium pentothal; is a confession given under the influence of that drug better than a confession given under the influence of anesthesia?

I have problems with Smith's statement. He claimed that he only noticed the tattoo on Speck's left arm after scraping away blood that had congealed on his skin from his elbow wound. But Dr. Norcross had just performed surgery on his elbow. Did no one clean up the congealed blood on Speck's left arm either before or after he went into surgery?

Corazon Amurao identified Speck by his "Born to Raise Hell" tattoo.

This was another misconception about the tattoo on his left arm. Corazon Amurao testified at trial, "I did not notice any tattoo." This makes sense, because she said that he was wearing a black jacket. Later on, the t-shirts came into play – something that she also did not mention.

Speck was drunk and high on amphetamines on the night of the murders.

Yet in a period of four and a half hours he managed to subdue, tie up, and kill eight healthy young women in an extremely organized and efficient manner, in almost complete silence, avoiding blood on his clothing and leaving no bloody fingerprints anywhere in the townhouse? This is another example of the official story bordering on the preposterous. Let's review what he did ingest according to the records.

Throughout the course of the day Speck took six red birds, (sodium seconal, a depressant), drank a few beers, some wine, and at least ten whisky and cokes. He was also injected with an unknown substance. This toxic chemical cocktail was more likely to cause an overdose than incite the slaughter of eight young women.

Corazon firmly insisted that he was not under the influence of alcohol or drugs, until much later, when she and others sued the taverns for serving an intoxicated customer. The official story was as fluid as the whisky and cokes.

CHAPTER TWENTY-ONE
THERE'S SOMETHING ABOUT GLORIA

<u>G-L-O-R-I-A</u>

All the dizzying twists and turns of my research kept circling back to Gloria. Why did the night allegedly begin with her murder, only to then reverse course and end with it? Why was she the only one found in the nude, the only one found on the first floor, the only one rumored to have been viciously raped and sodomized? What was it about Gloria that set her apart from the rest?

The circumstances surrounding Gloria's death alone uncover serious inconsistencies and flaws in the official story.

Gloria had spent the evening of the murders at the apartment of her fiancé, Rob Stern, on South Shore Drive. The couple celebrated the release of Rob's mother from the hospital and, I believe, Gloria's 22nd birthday. They dined on steak and champagne. At the end of the evening Rob drove Gloria back to the townhouse, and they arrived in the parking lot around 11:30 PM.

Stern shared a bittersweet recollection of his last moments with her. As she was about to exit his car, one of her favorite songs, "You'll Never Walk Alone," played on the radio. Released in 1965 by British rock group Gerry and the Pacemakers, the song rose quickly to the top of the charts. Gloria listened to it, bid Rob goodnight, and walked to the back door for the last time.

Rob recalled that the back door was unlocked; Gloria did not use her keys to open it. He did not notice whether the window was open or its screen was off. Once inside the townhouse, she phoned in to the housemother, Mrs. Bisone, and then called her mother, as she always did after a night out. "I'm home, I'm safe," she reported, and then bid her mother goodnight for the last time.

Some eerie correspondences in the circumstances surrounding Gloria's death dragged me down a fascinating rabbit hole. "You'll Never Walk Alone" was a big hit from the 1945 musical "Carousel," by Rodgers and Hammerstein. The immensely popular musical was later made into a movie in 1956. I was very familiar with both songs. The vinyl LP soundtrack to "Carousel" shared space in my record rack with LPs by Gerry and the Pacemakers.

In the story of "Carousel" the main character, Julie Jordan, mourns the death of her husband, Billy Bigelow, who has met his demise by falling on a knife and dying of a stab wound during a botched robbery attempt – shades of what would befall Gloria and her fellow nurses. The lead character, Julie Jordan, shares the same last name as Mary Ann Jordan, the unfortunate young nurse who was spending that night as a guest.

Death by stabbing during a robbery gone amok. The tragic story of "You'll Never Walk Alone," Gloria's favorite song, served as an eerie testament to her final moments.

And that was not Gloria's only connection to the music of the times. In December 1965 a rock band called The Shadows of Knight released a hit single, "Gloria," ("G-L-O-R-I-A") which rose to number one in the band's home city, which happened to be, of all places, Chicago. The song was a hit throughout 1966. In a sinister, almost otherworldly reference to the events that transpired in the shadows of Gloria's last night, The Shadow of Knight's recording company was Dunwich Records 666.

Odds and Fellows

As if that weren't spooky enough, Assistant State's Attorney Martin, adept at sowing the seeds of incredulity even in his own work, made a quizzical reference to an arcane secret society when he told the story of when Speck met up with Claude Lunsford and another friend for the first time. He referred to the trio as "the odd fellows."[50]

Gloria's father, Charles E. "Chuck" Davy, was a member of the Odd Fellows, a secret society under the umbrella of Freemasonry, the oldest such group of its kind in the United States. As trustee of the West Pullman Odd Fellows, Davy held a respectable position within the group.[51] Was Martin dropping a breadcrumb?

Charles Davy was not the only secret society member on the periphery of the crime – one that I could discern, as there were probably others that I couldn't. Sergeant Richard J. Oliva, who testified that Speck had confronted him at the Shipyard Inn on the night of the murders, was a member of the Loyal Order of Moose, headquartered in Mooseheart, Illinois.

Membership requirements at that time were to be male, Caucasian, and have a military background. Like the Freemasons, joining the group required an elaborate ritual initiation. The Order of Moose command enormous wealth and political power in Illinois, including the ownership of schools, hospitals, office buildings, and even a crime scene cleaning business!

Sergeant Oliva piqued my interest only because he testified to seeing Speck brandish both a small folding knife and the large hunting knife at the Shipyard Inn. But Speck sold the large hunting knife earlier that same day. Patrick Walsh, friend of Oliva and another witness from the Shipyard Inn, testified that Speck brandished a gun and one knife.

Apparently Oliva was coached to introduce the large Navy-issue knife. Even though it played no role in the murders, the large knife, the biggest piece of non-evidence in this case, sent another red flag waving in my viewfinder.

This fact may lead nowhere, but the dots form an interesting cluster. Before entering the military, Oliva worked for a time at Republic Steel, where Charles Davy was a manager. They may, or may not, have known each other; thousands of men worked at Republic Steel in those days. This is probably one of those rare times that I can use the word coincidence, but it's worth noting.

I believe that Gloria's body was deliberately placed to give clues as to the real reason behind the murders:

- She was placed on the living room sofa on the first floor, where she would be found first.
- She was found nude, while no one else was.
- Corazon Amurao initially stated that Gloria was killed first, but that later changed. Someone wanted to place Gloria first. Then, she was supposedly killed last, as if to bookend her significance in the story.
- She was reportedly raped and sodomized, while no one else was. Someone had an ax to grind with Gloria, a strong-willed woman with a sassy mouth. The organizers of the murders wanted to humiliate and desecrate her.
- It was Gloria's birthday, another breadcrumb. I did not find one single reference stating that July 13th was her birthday, which is astounding considering the amount of attention that this crime has received over the years. And that leads me to my final point:
- Her birthday presented an opportunity for a celebration during that afternoon or early evening. A drink laced with

a powerful sedative could have quickly subdued some of the nurses, leaving them vulnerable to attack.

CHAPTER TWENTY-TWO

CRIMES OF THE CENTURY

"Crime of the Century" is an interesting label when you think about it. Like "Man of the Week," "Person of the Year," or "Most Valuable Player," our media loves to confer great honor to a heinous crime instead of judging it for the horror that it is. This fact intrigued me, and so I took a few trips down an enticing rabbit hole to dig further into crimes of the century.

What makes a good candidate for the designation of crimes of the century? It has nothing to do with the enormity of the crime or the number of victims. Instead, it promotes a sinister and fearful theme, often emphasizing a particular group or ideology.

Crimes of the century also share a flair for the dramatic, as we have seen time and again in the present case – "All my friends are dead!" "It's the crime of the century!" "The greatest single sex crime in history!" and "This is the man!" I also discovered a number of odd correspondences between named crimes of the century. Some of these may seem coincidental, but a curious pattern emerges as they are exposed. No matter their number or depth, those pesky rabbit holes often end up exposing the same dark matter over and over again.

May 1889 – The Murder of Dr. P.H. Cronin

Dr. Patrick Henry Cronin emigrated from Ireland to Chicago, bringing his strong political leanings with him. He was a member of the secret societies of Clan na Gael and the Royal Arcanum and Chosen Friends, groups who supported the liberation of Ireland from British rule.

Cronin was murdered by political enemies and became an Irish-American hero and martyr for his cause. His murder was highly publicized abroad, and many thousands attended his funeral, thus earning the title of "crime of the century." It is strangely noteworthy that Cronin was a physician at Cook County Hospital in Chicago. Chicago was the birthplace of the first "crime of the century," and deservedly so. There would be more.

This was a politically-motivated crime involving a Chicago doctor who belonged to a private society. Dr. Cronin's dream of independence for Ireland flew in the face of stalwart supporters of the British Crown, and a message had to be sent to the multitudes that such independence would not be tolerated. His supporters got the message as well.

May 1924 – The Murder of Bobby Franks by Nathan Leopold and Richard Loeb

The setting for this vicious murder of fourteen-year-old Bobby Franks was again Chicago. Franks was the son of a wealthy neighbor of Nathan Leopold, 19, and Richard Loeb, 18, also of respectable, well-heeled families. Both young men were highly intelligent. Leopold had already graduated from the University of Chicago and Loeb from the University of Michigan. But they were bored and disaffected with their lives, and began to commit petty crimes to see what they could get away with.

Gradually the risk-taking escalated to murder, and on May 21, 1924, they lured young Bobby Franks to a park where they strangled him and left his body in a culvert. A pair of eyeglasses found near the crime scene connected them to the killing, and they were convicted and sentenced to life in prison.

The notorious pair introduced the concept of the motiveless "thrill kill" murder to American society, and broke the stereotype of the common murderer as a lower-class, poorly educated, socially disadvantaged individual. It was widely rumored that Leopold and Loeb were homosexual lovers, a serious taboo in the 1920s that introduced another shocking element to the crime. Leopold and Loeb also considered themselves as intellectual supermen, an ideal lead-in to the fascist movement that was gathering traction at that time.

The idea that young, handsome, intelligent men of upper class breeding could callously murder a child no doubt set society on alert that killers could be anyone and lurk anywhere. Children were no longer safe at the hands of those who should have known better.

March 1932 – The Kidnap/Murder of Charles Lindbergh, Jr.

This crime occurred at the country home of famous aviator Charles Lindbergh in rural New Jersey. His two-and-a-half year-old firstborn son was taken from his crib in a second floor bedroom and found dead in a wooded area some months later. German immigrant Bruno Richard Hauptmann was later convicted in a sensational "trial of the century" and executed in the electric chair.

Many investigations have since supported Hauptmann's innocence, implicating a high-level conspiracy and cover-up. They contend that Hauptmann was framed and that Charles Lindbergh, whose sadistic behavior has been revealed only in recent literature, had a hand in staging the crime.[52] An avowed Nazi sympathizer, he was also a staunch supporter of selective breeding, or eugenics.

Bruno Richard Hauptmann was German, as was Richard Speck. For part of his life, Speck's last name was Lindbergh, taken from his stepfather, Carl Augustus Rudolph Lindbergh (whose initials oddly spell out his first name).

This crime involved a German immigrant named Richard, the name Lindbergh, the suspicious narrative of a kidnapping gone wrong, and an American hero who was a staunch supporter of the Nazi party and eugenics. The German immigrant with the middle name of Richard had a criminal record in Germany, making him an ideal patsy.

And again, your child is not safe in his crib even if you're a national hero.

November 22, 1963 – Assassination of President John F. Kennedy

Richard Speck drove a truck for the 7Up Company that delivered beverages to Jack Ruby's Carousel Club in Dallas. We can't ignore the significance of New Orleans, where Lee Harvey Oswald was active in his Fair Play for Cuba movement; also active in New Orleans was mob boss Carlos Marcello, suspected of helping to arrange the assassination. The trial of suspected assassination conspirator Clay Shaw, headed by New Orleans prosecutor Jim Garrison, took place in New Orleans, and prior to November 1963, an assassination of JFK had been planned to take place in, of all places, Chicago.

The assassination ultimately took place in Dallas, where Speck grew up, and was blamed entirely on Lee Harvey Oswald, although there were too many moving parts to attribute a crime of this enormity to one man. The "lone gunman" trope was born of the JFK assassination, and passed on to Speck, then James Earl Ray and Sirhan B. Sirhan, to round out the assassinations and patsies of the Sixties.

So was the term "conspiracy theory," which was slapped onto those seeking to discover the truth behind the assassination. Today it is still a derogatory term. In truth, many historical incidents do not involve a lone gunman but a group of people, which equals conspiracy, and in the absence of trustworthy media sources, one sometimes has to investigate independently to learn the truth. Two cases in point are the JFK assassination and the mass murder of the eight nurses.

JFK was supposed to be assassinated in Chicago first; Dallas, Speck's old haunting grounds, and New Orleans, both play prominent roles in this drama. And 7Up deliveryman Richard Speck knew Jack Ruby. JFK's assassination was likely motivated by a pro-war, right-leaning group. Lee Harvey Oswald was the patsy.

August 8, 1969 – The Sharon Tate Murders

The crime of the century tag traveled west to Hollywood, land of illusion. Five individuals, including actress Sharon Tate, hairdresser Jay Sebring, coffee heiress Abigail Folger, Wojtech Frykowski, and Steven Parent, were brutally stabbed and shot at the home shared by Tate and her director husband, Roman Polanski, who was filming in London at the time.

Charles Manson and his ragged band of followers, known as the Family, were convicted of the murders. Although Manson was not present, he became the country's first mass murderer by proxy. Subsequent investigations have shown that the evidence was flimsy at best, and that the murders were possibly the result of a drug deal gone haywire. The only direct evidence was a confession by Family member Susan Atkins, a known grifter and liar. The murders had profound sociological impact, discrediting and bringing down the so-called "hippie movement" practically overnight, which was thought to be one of the prevailing motives.

Both crimes had powerful social ramifications that changed the thinking of American society; both involved sham trials with little concrete evidence but plenty of narrative shaped by powerful prosecutors and their media lackies. And both may have been influenced by right-wing supporters who wanted America to adopt a more hawkish attitude toward law, order, and war, thus bringing an end to the peace-loving, pacifist flower children.

The theme of passivity so strongly emphasized in the nurses' murders, a clumsy way to explain why eight women with everything to fight for chose not to fight, also shows another important feature of so-called crimes of the century - they do not support pacifism. They also introduce or feature some extreme ideology, like the fascist notions of a superior race, as shown in the Leopold/Loeb and Lindbergh cases, and possibly, the mass murder of the eight nurses.

The Manson narrative previewed a dystopian future that included a violent race war named after the Beatles' eponymous hit song "Helter Skelter". The Helter Skelter was actually a carnival ride, a spiral slide around a tower at a British amusement park. The song referenced confusion and disorientation, the type of feeling you might experience after careening down a spiral slide.

Manson's race war never took place, but the Manson affair inflicted damage on the American psyche, creating fear, panic, and the ever-increasing need for assurances of law and order, safety, and security in the face of a growing social chaos. All the crimes of the century served this purpose, greasing the slide of a communal helter skelter, leading us farther into a land of confusion, disorientation, and fear.

I suggest we beware when the moniker "crime of the century" is applied to a modern-day crime. So far, so-called crimes of the century have been tailor-made for high drama, and nothing invokes high drama like a fake narrative replete with hyped-up misinformation and a fall guy who takes the rap.

Sadly, what is real and true are the unfortunate victims. The rest is born of hyperbole and illusion. It's like a magic show, where we sit mesmerized by what the magician's one hand is doing, totally oblivious to what the other hidden hand is really up to.

The Rabbit Hole of Names

A cursory review of the label "crimes of the century" has already revealed uncanny interconnections between the names of those involved.

The name of Charles Lindbergh's father was Carl August Mansson. He changed his name to Lindbergh after he emigrated to the United States.

Richard Franklin Speck's name was Richard Franklin Lindbergh for a time.

Baby Lindbergh's convicted kidnapper/murderer was Bruno Richard Hauptmann, a German like Speck, and a fall guy, also like Speck, with the middle name Richard.

Just a few years later came Charles Manson, also linking by the Manson name to the Lindbergh and Speck cases. Coincidence, or correspondence? These three crimes of the century are strangely intertwined by names, but the seeming coincidences don't stop there.

Speck's biological father was Benjamin Franklin Speck. To honor him Speck adopted Franklin as his middle name, and for some years he went by the name Richard Franklin Lindbergh. When he married in 1962 he changed his name to Richard Benjamin Speck. Benjamin Franklin was an important name in the Speck generations, and as strange history bears it out, Richard was also an important name to the famous American statesman Benjamin Franklin.

Franklin made his fortune as a printer in Philadelphia. One of his earliest publications was "Poor Richard's Almanac". Apparently he liked the name Richard; he also wrote under the pen name Richard Saunders. To honor him the U.S. Navy commissioned a freighter called the "Bonhomme Richard."

More correspondences abound between the two men. Benjamin Franklin established the first school of nursing in the colonies, and he was an active member of the Lodge of the Nine Sisters. On the murder night there were nine student nurses in a townhouse that served as a dormitory for a nursing school.

For all we know, Hans Adam Spach, Speck's first ancestor to set foot in this country, crossed paths with Ben Franklin in colonial Philadelphia. Ben Franklin's mother was Abiah Folger, making him a cousin to wealthy coffee heiress Abigail Folger, victim of the infamous Manson murders. Richard/Benjamin/Franklin/Lindbergh/Manson/Folger!

If one digs deep enough, repeating connections are found to exist between famous crimes and nefarious incidents. Author Peter Levenda explained this phenomenon well: "Events are related by invisible threads of connection that link them in ways too subtle to be measured by the normal cause and effect paradigm with which we are all familiar."[53]

So many invisible threads of connection are finally coming to light. If the arrival of Hans Adams Spach to the New World of Benjamin Franklin helped to spin this complex fabric, it is no wonder that by trade Hans Adam was a weaver of tapestries.

CHAPTER TWENTY-THREE

STRANGER THINGS

My Long, Strange Trip

If anything sums up my experiences exploring the deeply entangled web of this crime, it is that iconic song by the Grateful Dead, "What A Long Strange Trip It's Been." Led by curiosity, I had embarked on a simple quest to learn more about the eight nurses whose murders had upset me so badly as a young girl. Understatement of the decade: I got way more than I bargained for.

As overwhelming as the project felt at times, circumstances seemed to constantly guide me in the right direction. I would open a book or a file, and instantly find the data I was seeking. Names and places that I was researching would pop up in seemingly unrelated television programs or books. I experienced a synchronicity with certain events that Carl Jung himself would have envied. Having made some startling discoveries, I chose to write this book, but in an odd way it also chose me.

Strange confirmations of this came from unexpected sources. While drafting the section on the Lindbergh baby kidnapping, I noted that it was the 90th anniversary of that "crime of the century."

It was the Lindbergh case that had inspired me to write my first book back in 2012, which included a chapter on the kidnapping. My research pointed strongly to the conclusion that Bruno Richard Hauptmann, the convicted kidnapper/killer, was framed. Little did I know that I would come to the same conclusion about Richard Lindbergh/Speck, who had once headlined my adolescent "Most Hated" list.

I researched the musical "Carousel" and its iconic song "You'll Never Walk Alone" on January 3, 2021, and later heard that Gerry Marsden, lead singer of the British band Gerry and the Pacemakers, passed away that very day.

During the same week in July 2021 that I was researching her Planned Parenthood Foundation, I learned that the name of its founder, Margaret Sanger, was unceremoniously expunged from the signage at its headquarters due to her racist views.

Sergeant Richard J. Oliva, witness for the prosecution, was born on the day my parents got married, and other connections to him exist via certain personal numbers.

Assistant State's Attorney William J. Martin, co-author of the book that I have referenced, passed away in 2017. His funeral service was held at Salerno's Galewood Chapel in Chicago (no relation).

The Moraine-on-the-Lake resort where Corazon Amurao stayed was located in Highland Park, Illinois, the name of my town. There is also a hospital named after St. Camillus in Batangas, Philippines, Corazon's home province.

My old pen knife, shown in a photograph, closely resembles the knife dredged up from the Calumet River and thought to be the murder weapon. I've had the knife since childhood, but only recently discovered that it bears the inscription "Camillus" – an eerie homage to the patron saint of nurses and hospitals.

But my favorite woo-woo moment was when a friend called the day that I verified that Gene and Martha Thornton's Chicago address was 3966 N. Avondale Avenue. My friend left a message with her phone number. Her extension was 3966.

Reading the Hidden Hand

In crime investigations we concern ourselves with physical evidence. Our boundaries are defined by tangibles: fingerprints, blood spatter, weapons, witnesses, and metadata. Modern crime investigations have been greatly assisted by new developments in DNA analysis and the digital age has contributed with cell phone metadata and CCTV surveillance. The universe of crime analysis has expanded into dimensions beyond sight and sound. We have evolved from evaluating data to analyzing metadata. In my view, why not expand our search from the physical to the metaphysical?

Events are linked in weird ways that defy human understanding, especially events involving major crimes. My research consistently uncovered unusual and unexpected relationships between various parties, and eerily, myself. These oddities occurred more times than I can comfortably pass off as simple coincidence or not getting enough sleep. Often these connections were separated by both time and space, but were still too numerous to be ignored. Twentieth Century psychologist Carl Jung called such events synchronicities or meaningful coincidences - events that lack any causal connection, but which all the same appear to be related.

While criminology embraces the nuts and bolts of physical evidence, timelines, logistics and the like, crimes also have components that connect on multiple levels beyond the measurable. However, these levels do not meet the hard definitions of tangible proof that most true crime fans and investigators expect, so for those who do not wish to explore the supernatural and occult aspects of this crime, here is a good stopping point. Thank you for taking the time to read this book.

A second book about the occult aspects of the crime is currently in progress for those readers who wish to continue exploring along these lines (and dropping into a few rabbit holes along the way!)

Please check my author pages or Twitter/X account (@starsleuth) to stay informed. I'll see you in the next volume.

EPILOGUE

My coming of age began with the death of JFK and the uneasy uncertainty that followed – Vietnam, the Cold War, the prospect of an atomic apocalypse. Another gut punch, at least for me, was the massacre of the eight nurses. Over the course of the past five decades the awful truth behind these historic catastrophes has slowly leaked out, and it was not what we were told. Sadly, the same applies to the narrative of the nurses' mass murder, which was a fabrication to protect the real evildoers. In my view, this massive lie, propagated by the media and law enforcement, qualifies as one more "crime of the century."

The mass murder of the nurses was made doubly heinous by the manipulation and deception that sent an innocent man to prison and allowed the guilty to remain free. Eight lovely young nurses were brutally murdered for vengeful reasons and the authorities spun a twisted and dangerous web of lies. An unsavory but innocent man was convicted, and justice was denied the eight nurses and their families.

If you repeat a lie over and over again, people will come to believe it. This was the motto of Josef Goebbels who, as Nazi minister of propaganda for the Third Reich, understood the power of words. The oft-repeated but inaccurate story of the nurses' mass murder is just one case in point. Many of us still believe the false narrative. It is my hope that web sleuths or professionals alike will now take a deep dive into this crime, and others that have seemed suspicious, and continue to expose their sordid stories for what they really are.

In the early Sixties we still trusted our authorities. We should have been able to trust them. But after the murders of JFK, MLK, and RFK, and for me, the eight student nurses, the bonds began to fray.

Even so, there are still wistful times when I wonder what might have been. If only we could have believed them. If only we could believe them now.

In the wake of her sister Suzanne's death, Marilyn Farris McNulty sadly reminisced, "I wish that we all could have stayed the way we were on July 13, 1966."[54]

Sometimes I do too.

NOTES

PART III: THEORIES

Chapter Seventeen: "Hypocritical Oath"

1 *Barbour v. South Chicago Community Hospital*, 156 *Ill. App* 3d 324.

2 *Green v. Heron*, 635 *N.E.* 2d 837 (*Ill. App. Ct.* 1994).

3 https://case-law.vlex.com/vid/green-v-heron-no-889440153.

4 *Mennes v. South Chicago Community Hospital*, 100 *Ill. App.* 3d 1029 427 *N.E.* 2d 952, https://casetext.com/case/mennes-v-south-chicago-community-hospital

5 Ronald Kotulak, "Stricter Clinic Control Urged," *Chicago Tribune*, December 28, 1978.

6 "Elected Head of Medical Committee," *Daily Calumet*, (Chicago, Illinois), January 31, 1961.

7 Beata Mostafavi, "Low Income, Less Education Women Least Likely to Access Infertility Care," July 1, 2019, M Health Lab, http://labblog.uofmhealth.org.

8 https://www.peacecorps.gov/about/history

9 https://library.cqpress.com/cqalmanac/document.php?id=cqal64-1304273

10 https://www.genome.gov/about-genomics/educational-resources/timelines/eugenics

11 https://www.lexisnexis.com/community/casebrief/p/casebrief-buck-v-bell-1244374495

12 Walter Herbst, *It Did Not Start With JFK*, vol. I, (Mechanicsburg: Sunbury Press, 2021), 121.

13 Peter Levenda, *Sinister Forces: A Grimoire of American Political Witchcraft, Book Two: A Warm Gun*, (Waterville: Trine Day, 2006), 313.

14 https://www.uvm.edu/~lkaelber/eugenics/IL/IL.html

15 89th Congress, "Population Crisis: Hearings by the Subcommittee on Foreign Aid Expenditures of the Committee on Government Operations," US Govt Printing Office, Washington DC, Second session on S.1676 1-2/1966.

16 Peter Levenda, *Sinister Forces, Book Two*, 313.

17 https://www.uvm.edu/~lkaelber/eugenics/IL/IL.html

18 Kevin Begos, "The American Eugenics Movement After World War II, part 3," June 1, 2011, https://indyweek.com/news/american-eugenics-movement-world-war-ii-part-3-3

19 Dan Diamond, "What Health Care Has Lost and Gained Since the 1960s," March 22, 2012, https://www.advisory.com/daily-briefing/2012/03/22/after-mad-men-what-healthcare-has-gained-and-lost-since-1960s

20 Lynd Lampert, "Nursing in the 1960s," March 29, 2018, https://scrubsmag.com/nursing-in-the-1960s

21 "Jury Finds Speck Guilty, Recommends Electric Chair," *Wisconsin Journal*, (Madison, Wisconsin), April 16, 1967.

Chapter Eighteen: "Do These Dots Connect?"

22 Altman and Ziporyn, *Born to Raise Hell,* 200.

23 Altman and Ziporyn, 14.

24 Altman and Ziporyn, 41.

25 Dennis L. Breo, "Oh God, I'm the Only One Alive!" *Chicago Tribune,* July 6, 1986.

26 Loudon Wainwright, "Who the Gentle Nurses Were," *Life,* July 29, 1966.

27 Breo and Martin, *Crime of the Century,* 300.

28 "Attorney Is Invited," *Chicago Tribune,* January 3, 1969.

29 "Miss Amurao Plans to Live in 'Safer' U.S.," *Chicago Tribune,* January 4, 1969.

30 Matthew Jagel, "Showing Its Flag," Northern Illinois University, 2013, 21.

31 Jagel, 21.

32 John Marks, *The Search for the Manchurian Candidate: The CIA and Mind Control,* (New York: Times Books, 1977), 21-23.

33 Marks, 31.

34 Statement of Frank C. Conahan, "Human Experimentation: An Overview of Cold War Era Programs," Testimony before the legislation and National Security Subcommittee, Committee on

Government Operations, U.S. Government Accounting Office, Washington, D.C., September 28, 1994.

Readers interested in specific descriptions of experiments are invited to research the cases of Ebb Cade, Arthur Hubbard, and Billings Hospital, a clinical branch of the University of Chicago.

35 Statement of Frank C. Conahan, "Human Experimentation."

36 "Warns 1,000 Nurses Set to Quit," *Chicago Tribune,* July 12, 1966; "Walkout in NYC," *Chicago Tribune,* July 12, 1966; "22 Nurses Say They Will Quit Hospital Duty," *Chicago Tribune,* July 16, 1966.

Chapter Nineteen: "The Aftermath"

37 Mario Fox, "Chicago Paper to Publish Mass Murderer's Love Letters," *Chicago Tribune,* February 27, 1988, https://apnews.com/94c040055bda5cf94e4417874f84471

38 https://law.justia.com/cases/illinois/supreme-court/1985/59864-7.html

39 Breo and Martin, 238.

40 All quoted dialogue from the *Oprah Winfrey Show* in this section appears courtesy of the Youtube channel Programmed to Kill: "Programmed to Kill//Satanic Cover-up Part 205 (Richard Speck)," www.youtube.com/watch?v-W9-FPFXPTTig&t=599s[1]

41 All quoted dialogue in this section is taken from the video "Richard Speck," www.youtube.com/watch?v=slm_YDzx4vl

42 Breo and Martin, 325.

43 Breo and Martin, 45

44 Breo and Martin, 49.

45 "Crime Stories – Richard Speck: Born to Raise Hell," www.youtube.com/watch?v=H3s72mf1qA.

46 Altman and Ziporyn, 14.

47 Bob Greene, "Parents Should Watch Kids, Speck Tells Interviewer," *Rock Island Argus,* (Moline, Illinois), March 8, 1978.

48 "Speck Says He Killed Accomplice," *Journal Gazette,* (Mattoon, Illinois), March 3, 1978.

---

1. http://www.youtube.com/watch?v-W9-FPFXPTTig&t=599s

Chapter Twenty: "Myth-Information"

49 Altman and Ziporyn, *Born to Raise Hell,* 20.

Chapter Twenty-One: "There's Something About Gloria"

50 Breo and Martin, *Crime of the Century*, 98.

51 "Father and Son Named to Head Odd Fellows," *Suburbanite Economist*, (Chicago, Illinois), December 16, 1953.

Chapter Twenty-Two: "Crimes of the Century"

52 Lise Pearlman, *The Lindbergh Kidnapping Suspect No. 1: The Man Who Got Away,* (Berkeley: Regent Press, 2020), 421.

53 Peter Levenda, *Sinister Forces: A Grimoire of American Political Witchcraft: Book One: The Nine,* (Chicago: Independent Publishers Group, 2005), 260.

Epilogue

54 Breo and Martin, 408.

BIBLIOGRAPHY

"22 Nurses Say They Will Quit Hospital Duty." *Chicago Tribune.* July 16, 1966.

89th Congress, "Population Crisis: Hearings by the Subcommittee on Foreign Aid Expenditures of the Committee on Government Operations," US Govt Printing Office, Washington DC, Second session on S.1676 1-2/1966.

"Agreement on Panel to Examine Speck." *Chicago Tribune.* September 9, 1966.

Altman, Jack, and Marvin Ziporyn. *Born to Raise Hell: The Untold Story of Richard Speck.* (New York: Grove Press, Inc., 1967).

"Atienza's Lawsuit." *Central New Jersey Home News,* (New Brunswick, New Jersey), May 20, 1970.

"Attorney Is Invited." *Chicago Tribune.* January 3, 1969.

Begos, Kevin. "The American Eugenics Movement After World War II, part 3," June 1, 2011, https://indyweek.com/news/american-eugenics-movement-world-war-ii-part-3-3

Bernstein, Adam. "Chris Sizemore, whose many personalities were the real 'Three Faces of Eve,' dies at 89." *Washington Post,* July 29, 2016.

Breo, Dennis L., and William J. Martin. *The Crime of the Century: Richard Speck and the Murders That Shocked the Nation.* (New York: Skyhorse Publishing, 2017).

Breo, Dennis L. "Oh God, I'm the Only One Alive!" *Chicago Tribune,* July 6, 1986.

Carlile, Byron, and Jack Wallenda. "Supplementary Report." Area 2 Homicide, Chicago Police Department, July 14, 1966.

Chicago Police Department, "Reports on Murder of Gloria Davy and 7 others." July 14, 1966, Homicide File RD E208706, FOIA P592042.

"Crime of Century Three Years Old." *Daily Calumet,* (Chicago, Illinois), July 12, 1969.

"Crime Stories," A&E Television, episode: "Richard Speck: Born to Raise Hell," a Globalvision and Pacific Street Films Production, 1999, total run time (TRT) 59:59.

"Crime Stories – Richard Speck: Born to Raise Hell." www.youtube.com/watch?v=H3s72mf1qA[1].

Diamond, Dan. "What Health Care Has Lost and Gained Since the 1960s." March 22, 2012, https://www.advisory.com/daily-briefing/2012/03/22/after-mad-men-what-healthcare-has-gained-and-lost-since-1960s

Eddy, A.B., to Robert Gale. Memorandum: "Richard Franklin Speck – Unlawful Flight to Avoid Prosecution – Murder." FBI Headquarters, Washington, D.C., January 10, 1967.

"Eight Student Nurses Slain." *Chicago Tribune.* July 14, 1966.

"Elected Head of Medical Committee." *Daily Calumet,* (Chicago, Illinois), January 31, 1961.

---

1. http://www.youtube.com/watch?v=H3s72mf1qA

Ely, S.F., and C.S. Hirsch, "Asphyxial deaths and petechiae: a review." *J Forensic Sci 2000;* 45(6): 1274-1277.

"Father and Son Named to Head Odd Fellows." *Suburbanite Economist.* (Chicago, Illinois), December 16, 1953.

Fox, Mario. "Chicago Paper to Publish Mass Murderer's Love Letters." *Chicago Tribune,* February 27, 1988, https://apnews.com/94c040055bda5cf94e4417874f84471

Gavin, John. "Police Tell How Riot Started on West Side." *Chicago Tribune,* July 16, 1966.

Greene, Bob. "Parents Should Watch Kids, Speck Tells Interviewer." *Rock Island Argus,* (Moline, Illinois), March 8, 1978.

Greene, Bob. "The Voice of Richard Speck." *Chicago Tribune,* December 8, 1991.

Herbst, Walter. *It Did Not Start With JFK, vol. I.* (Mechanicsburg: Sunbury Press, 2021).

Higginbotham, Adam. "The Long, Long Life of the Lipstick Killer." April 30, 2008, https://www.gq.com/story/william-heirens-lipstick-killer-chicago

"Hunt Ex-Convict As Killer." *Sunday Star.* (Washington, D.C.), July 17, 1966.

Jagel, Matthew. "Showing Its Flag." Northern Illinois University, 2013, 21.

"Jury Finds Speck Guilty, Recommends Electric Chair." *Wisconsin Journal,* (Madison, Wisconsin), April 16, 1967.

"Kinsmen of Speck Testify for Defense, State Rests." *Pantagraph*, (Bloomington, Illinois), April 13, 1967.

Kinzer, Stephen. "The Secret History of Fort Detrick, the CIA's Base for Mind Control Experiments," September 15, 2019, https://www.politico.com/magazine/story/2019/09/15/cia-fort-detrick-stephen-kinzer-228109

Kotulak, Ronald. "Stricter Clinic Control Urged." *Chicago Tribune*, December 28, 1978.

Krassner, Philip. *The Essential Mae Brussell: Investigations of Fascism in America.* (Port Townsend: Feral Books, 2014).

Lampert, Lynd. "Nursing in the 1960s," March 29, 2018, https://scrubsmag,com/nursing-in-the-1960s

Lerner, Jack. "Investigation of Possible Murder Suspect." Chicago Police Department, [section name illegible], July 15, 1966.

Levenda, Peter. *Sinister Forces: A Grimoire of American Political Witchcraft, Book One: The Nine.* (Chicago: Independent Publishers Group, 2005).

Levenda, Peter. *Sinister Forces: A Grimoire of American Political Witchcraft, Book Two: A Warm Gun.* (Waterville: Trine Day, 2006).

Manahan, Ray. "Can't Recall Killer's Face, Massacre Survivor Admits." *Pantagraph*, (Bloomington, Illinois), April 6, 1967.

Manahan, Ray. "State to End Testimony Against Speck This Week." *Pantagraph*, (Bloomington, Illinois), April 10, 1967.

Marks, John. *The Search for the Manchurian Candidate: The CIA and Mind Control.* (New York: Times Books, 1979).

McCarty, Burke. *The Suppressed Truth About the Assassination of Abraham Lincoln. 1924,* http://jmgainor.homestead.com/files/////02.htm

McGowan, David. *Programmed to Kill: The Politics of Serial Murder.* iUniverse, 2004.

"Miss Amurao Plans to Live in 'Safer' U.S." *Chicago Tribune,* January 4, 1969.

"Money Granted in Speck Suit." *Denton Record-Chronicle,* (Denton, Texas), October 19, 1972.

Mostafavi, Beata. "Low Income, Less Education Women Least Likely to Access Infertility Care." July 1, 2019, M Health Lab, http://labblog.uofmhealth.org.

Murtaugh, George and Byron Carlile. "Supplementary Report." Area 2 Homicide, Chicago Police Department, July 16, 1966.

[name redacted], "Supplementary Report." Chicago Police Department, Area 2 Homicide, July 17, 1966.

"Nurse's Story of Death Night: Tells Jurors of Mass Murder." *Chicago Tribune,* April 6, 1967.

O'Neill, Tom, with Dan Piepenbring. *Chaos: Charles Manson, the CIA, and the Secret History of the Sixties.* (New York: Little, Brown and Company, 2019).

"Pathological Report and Protocol." Institute of Forensic Pathology, Cook County, Illinois, dated July 14, 1966, nos. 146-148, 151-153.

Pearlman, Lise. *The Lindbergh Kidnapping Suspect No. 1: The Man Who Got Away.* (Berkeley: Regent Press, 2020).

"Precedent Raises Other Questions." *Chicago Tribune*, September 15, 1987.

"Programmed to Kill//Satanic Cover-up Part 205 (Richard Speck)," www.youtube.com/watch?v-W9-FPFXPTTig&t=599s[2]

"Protein Digestion, Absorption, and Metabolism." *LibreTexts Medicine,* August 14, 2020, https://med.libretexts.org/Courses/American_Public_University/APUS%3A_An_Introduction_to_Nutrition_(Byerley)/APUS%3A

Quinlan, John P. to J. Edgar Hoover. "Memorandum." Federal Bureau of Investigation, Washington, D.C., July 14, 1966.

Quinlan, John to J. Edgar Hoover. "Memorandum," Federal Bureau of Investigation, Washington, D.C., July 17, 1966.

Quinlan, John P. to J. Edgar Hoover. "Memorandum: Richard Franklin Speck." Federal Bureau of Investigation, Washington, D.C., July 21, 1966.

Radojevic, Namanja, Bojana Radnic, Stojan Petkovic, et al, "Multiple stabbing in sex-related homicides." July 2013, *Journal of Forensic and Legal Medicine,* 20(5): 502-7. DOI: 10.1016/j.jflm.2013.03.005 pub med

Rice, Linze. "70 Years After 'Lipstick Murders,' Doubt Over Killer's Guilt Still Lingers." January 7, 2016, https://www.dnainfo.com/chicago/20160107/edgewater/70-years-after-lipstick-murders-doubt-over-kill

"Richard Speck," www.youtube.com/watch?v=slm_YDzx4vl

"Speck Says He Killed Accomplice." *Journal Gazette,* (Mattoon, Illinois), March 3, 1978.

---

2. http://www.youtube.com/watch?v-W9-FPFXPTTig&t=599s

"Speck Trial May Exceed $150,000." *Chicago Tribune,* April 7, 1967.

Statement of Frank C. Conahan, "Human Experimentation: An Overview of Cold War Era Programs," Testimony before the legislation and National Security Subcommittee, Committee on Government Operations, U.S. Government Accounting Office, Washington, D.C., September 28, 1994.

"Summer of Slaughter." *Murder Casebook 81, vol. 6,* Wiltshire, England, 1972.

U.S. Coast Guard, "Richard Speck," FOIA REF. 2022-CGFO-00688.

U.S. Federal Bureau of Investigation, "Richard Speck," FOIPA 1512360-000, RD 66646.

Wainwright, Loudon. "Who the Gentle Nurses Were." *Life,* vol 61, No. 5, July 29, 1966.

Wainwright, Loudon. "The Nine Nurses." *Life,* vol 61, No. 5, July 29, 1966.

"Walkout in NYC." *Chicago Tribune,* July 12, 1966.

"Warns 1,000 Nurses Set to Quit." *Chicago Tribune,* July 12, 1966.

Welsome, Eileen. *The Plutonium Files: America's Secret Medical Experiments in the Cold War.* (New York: Dell Publishing, 1999).

Wiedrich, Robert, and William Jones. "2 Witnesses Give Alibi On Death Night." *Chicago Tribune,* April 14, 1967.

Wiedrich, Robert, and William Jones. "Speck's Kin Take Stand in His Trial." *Chicago Tribune,* April 13, 1967.

Wiedrich, Robert, and William Jones. "Survivor Accuses Speck." *Chicago Tribune,* April 6, 1967.

APPENDIX A

FIRST POLICE STATEMENT

EXCERPT FROM SUPPLEMENTARY HOMICIDE REPORT OF DETECTIVES BYRON CARLILE AND JACK WALLENDA DATE JULY 14, 1966

ASS'D 6:10 HRS.

DATE & TIME INTERVIEWED 6:30 HRS. JULY 14, 1966

My comments are in italics.

This is Corazon Amurao's first statement to the police. Note the time of the interview, 6:30 AM. Many reports erroneously stated that when police arrived on the scene Corazon was in too severe a state of shock to be interviewed. Instead, she was walked two doors down to unit 2315 and immediately questioned with the help of nursing supervisor Josephine Chan, who spoke Tagalog, Corazon's native language.

First came a description of the assailant:

"One M/W, 25-26 yrs., 6'0" tall, slender build, wearing a black suit coat, black pants, black shoes. Had been drinking. Carried a small black revolver and knife. Offender's clothing possibly badly blood stained."

Note the mention of a revolver. Speck had stolen a black Röhm 22 caliber revolver from Ella Mae Hooper on the day of the murders. However, Corazon was never able to describe the gun other than that it was black. It is odd that police knew what type of gun it was so early in the investigation.

The prosecution referred to the gun as a pistol that housed live cartridges in its clip. However, a revolver does not have a clip; its cartridges are loaded into a rotating cylinder. Nevertheless, law enforcement continued to describe the gun incorrectly.

"Offender's clothing possibly badly blood stained." Richard Speck awoke the next morning wearing the same black clothing he had fallen asleep in, with no blood anywhere on his clothing or jacket. There was a blotch of blood on one hand that rinsed off under the faucet, but there was no wound on the hand. The other hand held the revolver.

"In the presence of [redacted] the witness was interrogated and she related the following: She and her [redacted] Merlita Gargullo had retired to the front east bedroom. In the west front bedroom at the time that they retired, was Nina Schmale, and in the rear bedroom were Victim #2 Patricia Matusek, Victim # Pamela Wilkening, and Victim #8, Valicentia (sic) Pasion.

"Sometime after going to bed, the witness was awakened by someone knocking on her bedroom door. She went to the door and on opening the door found an unknown white man standing there and he was pointing a small black revolver at her. He forced her back into her bedroom and then he awakened victim #2 Patricia Matusek.

"He forced both girls to walk to the rear bedroom during which time he took victim #6, Nina Schmale with them. On their entering the rear bedroom he awakened victims #2, Patricia Matusek, victim #3, Pamela Wilkening, and victim #8, Valentina Pasion (really victim #7).

"He then made all of the victims sit on the floor close to the south wall and he sat on the floor in front of them. He demanded money, stating that he needed the money to finance his going to New

Orleans. The victims gave him what money had and about this time victim #1, Gloria Davy came into the bedroom.

"She was forced to join the others on the floor and she also surrendered some money to this man. He then bound all their hands and feet, with strips of sheeting he tore from one of the beds. After tying up the victims, Victim #4, Suzanne Farris, and Victim #5, Mary Ann Jordan came up the stairs and he forced them into the bedroom with the others and he tied them up in the same manner as the others, their hands behind their backs and their feet bound at the ankles.

"This man then took the Davy girl out of the bedroom, leaving the others bound and on the floor. The witness at this time rolled under one of the beds, where she remained. After the man had taken the Davy girl out, he returned in a short time and took another of the girls out and he continued to take the girls out one by one until all had left the bedroom in question, with the exception of the witness.

"The witness then remained under the bed until she heard the alarm clocks sound off at 0500 hrs. She then got out from under the bed, managed to remove the cloth used to bind her hands and feet and left the bedroom and walked north down the upstairs hall to her room, the east front bedroom and there she saw the bodies of three of the victims, now identified as victims #3, Pamela Wilkening, victim #4 Suzanne Farris and victim #5, Mary Ann Jordan.

"The witness got out of the front window and stood on the ledge and began screaming. She then remembers, another student nurse, [redacted, but I believe this was Judy Dykton], who is living at 2315 E. 100th Street assisting her out of the house. The time elements as to when she first saw this unknown white man, the time that the Davy girl came in and the time that the Farris girl and Jordan girl came in, the witness was unable to tell. She described the assailant as previously described."

.... *Further down the report* ...

"The witness was again questioned in the presence of [redacted] for the hospital and also [redacted] for the South Chicago Community Hospital and the witness again related the same account as she had originally given with the exception that she made mention of the man having a knife, which he used in cutting the bed sheet up to use for the binding of the victims.

"Neither [redacted] nor [redacted] had received any complaints from any of the student nurses, and could not place anyone answering the description of the assailant. The witness at the time that she made mention of the knife, could give no description of the weapon."

Deconstructing the Initial Statement of Corazon Amurao (comments in italic)

First came the assailant's description. Only the physique and type and color of clothing were noted. No description was given of hair or eye color, style of hair, or distinguishing facial or physical features. The hair color and style, and Speck's distinctive acne scars, later became an issue in the identification process as they were not included in the composite sketch.

"In the west front bedroom at the time that they retired, was Nina Schmale, and in the rear bedroom were Victim #2 Patricia Matusek, Victim # Pamela Wilkening, and Victim #8, Valicentia (sic) Pasion .... He forced her back into her bedroom and then he awakened victim #2 Patricia Matusek."

Corazon has just stated that Patricia Matusek was in the south bedroom down the hall from Corazon; how could the intruder have forced Corazon back into her own room and then awakened Patricia? Note below that she then accounts for Patricia being in the south bedroom.

"He forced both girls to walk to the rear bedroom during which time he took victim #6, Nina Schmale with them. On their entering the rear bedroom he awakened victims #2, Patricia Matusek, Victim #3, Pamela Wilkening, and victim #8, Valentina Pasion (really victim #7)."

There is no mention of the flight into the closet, where Corazon allegedly encouraged Merlita and Valentina to fight the intruder. The heroic story issued shortly thereafter, but later underwent several changes.

"After tying up the victims, Victim #4, Suzanne Farris, and Victim #5, Mary Ann Jordan came up the stairs and he forced them into the bedroom with the others and he tied them up in the same manner as the others, their hands behind their backs and their feet bound at the ankles. This man then took the Davy girl out of the bedroom, leaving the others bound and on the floor."

There are many contradictions here. Suzanne and Mary Ann were not tied up. According to the official story, everyone else was taken from the room before Gloria, at which time she was then raped, carried downstairs, sodomized, and strangled. In this initial statement, there was no description of the sexual assault and Gloria was the first to be taken from the south bedroom. But, like the closet caper, the story changed.

"The witness then remained under the bed until she heard the alarm clocks sound off at 0500 hrs. She then got out from under the bed, managed to remove the cloth used to bind her hands and feet and left the bedroom and walked north down the upstairs hall to her room, the east front bedroom and there she saw the bodies of three of the victims, now identified as victims #3, Pamela Wilkening, victim #4 Suzanne Farris and victim #5, Mary Ann Jordan."

In order to pass from the south to the east bedroom she had to walk down the hall, where she would have seen the body of Patricia Matusek just outside the bathroom, but there was no mention of this.

"The time elements as to when she first saw this unknown white man, the time that the Davy girl came in and the time that the Farris girl and Jordan girl came in, the witness was unable to tell."

By the time Corazon testified some nine months later, she recollected every movement and sequence of the evening down to intervals of minutes – one to two minutes, five minutes, twenty minutes, twenty-five minutes, about forty minutes, and so on. She had undergone extensive coaching and preparation for the trial, even though much of what she described was either contradictory or plainly implausible.

"The witness was again questioned in the presence of [redacted] for the hospital and also [redacted] for the South Chicago Community Hospital and the witness again related the same account as she had originally given with the exception that she made mention of the man having a knife.... The witness at the time that she made mention of the knife, could give no description of the weapon."

In her first interview with police, Corazon described the incidents of the evening without any mention of a knife. It was only after her second questioning, later that morning, that she included the knife, which she estimated to be about three or four inches in length. The folding knife retrieved from the Calumet River and thought to be the murder weapon measured two and three quarters inches in length. It was not admitted into evidence.

In spite of her detailed account, it seems incongruous that she would not give a more complete description of the assailant or the weapons. She stated at trial that she looked him in the face for one to two minutes, and she sat in the south bedroom with him for a considerable length of time before hiding under the bed. If the FBI file is to be believed, she also engaged in a 30 minute conversation with him at 12:30 AM, which seriously jeopardized the entire narrative.

Maybe it was expecting too much for her to remember certain things, and maybe certain things understandably got confused. Given that scenario, though, then she was not nearly as reliable a witness as she was made out to be.

APPENDIX B

SPECK'S STAY IN MONMOUTH, APRIL 1966

On July 23, 1966, Detective John Boeger and others from Area 2 Homicide of the Chicago PD went to Monmouth to question various individuals about Speck's behavior and whereabouts during the months of March and April 1966. We know that Speck apprenticed as a carpenter for several weeks between March and April, staying at the home of a family friend before moving on to the Christy Hotel. He then left town for Chicago around April 19th. However, the hotel manager gave Boeger some startling information.

"... around the first part of April 1966 he (Speck) rented a room at the Christy Hotel. He stayed at this hotel until the latter part of May or the first part of June 1966 at which time he left Monmouth."

This is another strange inconsistency in the reports. Speck could not have stayed at the hotel from the first part of April until the latter part of May. Documents verify that he joined the Coast Guard in Chicago on April 25th and worked on board a freighter from April 30th until May 3rd, when he suffered an attack of appendicitis and was hospitalized in Michigan.

So either the manager was confused, or someone closely resembling Speck was staying at the Christy Hotel during the same time that Speck was in Monmouth. Could this mystery hotel guest have had anything to do with the crimes that were attributed to Speck? It's just another conundrum that went unnoticed.

APPENDIX C

SUICIDE OR ACCIDENT?

Speck's alleged suicide attempt at the Starr Hotel was a strong indication that he feared capture, and was therefore guilty of committing the eight murders. But there were contradictory reports of his suicide attempt: He was bleeding to death, but the injuries were superficial. One cut was a slice on the right wrist, while the other, on his left elbow, had jagged irregular edges.

A witness at the Starr Hotel, who was admittedly intoxicated, provided information to the effect that the injuries were the result of an accident and not intentional. The following information was taken from the "Supplementary Report" of Detectives J. Beirne and J. Downey, Chicago PD, Area 2 Homicide, July 17, 1966. The witness described how a disoriented Speck trudged down the hallway to the bathroom, where the incident occurred:

"... he observed the man leaving his room and at the time, he thought the man had been painting as his shirt was all red. The man staggered down the area of the bathroom where he was lost to sight for a moment and it was at this time he heard glass breaking near where the trash can is kept. The reporting officer viewed this trash can which was full of wine bottles and other miscellaneous trash and on top was a splintered bottle with blood on the broken pieces. This bottle was taken by the Crime Lab."

Speck had a red shirt, the same one that he wore the night of the murders, which may explain how the witness thought he saw blood on Speck's shirt. Also, he heard the glass break after Speck entered the bathroom, so how could his shirt appear bloodstained before he broke the bottle and slashed himself? The nature of the wounds was also questionable – why cut one wrist with a razor, but then use the jagged edge of a broken bottle to cut the other? Why not just cut both wrists?

I believe the elbow wound was the result of an accident at the bathroom sink, where he dropped a bottle and reflexively tried to trap it in his elbow as it shattered. This would have produced the irregular jagged injury on his left elbow.

If suicide was on his mind, Speck could have smashed the bottle in his cubicle without having to travel 50 feet down the hall into the bathroom. It doesn't stand to reason that he would use a razor to inflict a small slice on the right wrist and then break a bottle in order to cut his left elbow with broken glass.

In any case, he was far from bleeding to death, as Jack Wallenda noted. The doctors in the emergency room indicated that the cuts to his arms were superficial.

The suicide story played into the appearance of guilt. Had he really wanted to kill himself he could have done a better job of it at the Starr. And later on he had the perfect accessories in the Bridewell jail. The warden had given him a razor blade, and there were water pipes overhead from which to hang himself with his bedsheet if he chose to end his life.

A final note on the suicide attempt at the Starr: The attending police officers, Krause and Burns, carried their feverish, bloody suspect down from Room 584 on his mattress. They then placed him on a gurney for transport to the hospital. Unbelievably, management at the Starr then returned the mattress to Room 584 for immediate use by the next occupant. Would they have done so if the mattress was saturated with blood? I hope not!

APPENDIX D

MY RESOURCES

In addition to the police reports, FBI and Coast Guard files, autopsy reports, and newspaper articles, I searched high and low for a copy of the trial transcript for *Illinois v. Richard Speck*. In response to a FOIA request made with the County of Peoria, I learned that the 10,000 page trial transcript is stored at the office of the Cook County Clerk, along with other documentation. A staff member there informed me that I would need to visit their office in person to view and make copies of the materials.

Unfortunately, my budget would not allow for an extended stay in Chicago, but I was fortunate to discover a substantial excerpt from the trial testimony of Corazon Amurao in the *Chicago Tribune*. This testimony was a treasure trove of information which, when compared against my other research materials, helped provide the basis for my claim that the crime did not happen as we were told.

Although I am not an experienced investigator, I drew on my diverse professional experience as a personal resource. For many years I was a paralegal, which required strict attention to detail and a fearless attitude when it came to sorting through, making sense of, and explaining the contents of huge stacks of documents and other organizational nightmares.

For some years I also practiced medical massage therapy and acupuncture, in which I was licensed and board certified. These disciplines required auxiliary study in anatomy, physiology, and human pathology. This background enabled me to read and make sense of the terminology in the autopsy reports and related research.

Two best-selling references were essential to this endeavor: *The Crime of the Century: Richard Speck and the Murders That Shocked the Nation,* co-authored by Assistant State's Attorney William J. Martin, and *Born to Raise Hell: The Untold Story of Richard Speck,* co-authored by his prison psychiatrist, Dr. Marvin Ziporyn.

While providing invaluable information, the two works were a study in contrast. Predictably, the Martin book was heavily biased against Speck, while Ziporyn's work portrayed Speck in a more sympathetic, humane light. While both challenging and annoying at times, both books provided a welcome counterbalance to the subject matter.

Don't miss out!

Visit the website below and you can sign up to receive emails whenever B D SALERNO publishes a new book. There's no charge and no obligation.

https://books2read.com/r/B-A-WFDW-MOTJC

BOOKS 2 READ

Connecting independent readers to independent writers.

About the Author

BD Salerno attended Rutgers University in New Jersey and also obtained professional secondary education in New York City. Her eclectic interests include alternative healing, true crime, music, and astrology.

www.ingramcontent.com/pod-product-compliance
Lightning Source LLC
Chambersburg PA
CBHW020730160426
43192CB00006B/173